D1607105

FIXING SOCIAL SECURITY

Fixing Social Security

THE POLITICS OF REFORM
IN A POLARIZED AGE

R. DOUGLAS ARNOLD

PRINCETON UNIVERSITY PRESS
PRINCETON & OXFORD

Published by Princeton University Press
41 William Street, Princeton, New Jersey 08540
99 Banbury Road, Oxford OX2 6JX

press.princeton.edu

All Rights Reserved
ISBN 978-0-691-22443-5
ISBN (e-book) 978-0-691-22444-2

British Library Cataloging-in-Publication Data is available

Editorial: Bridget Flannery-McCoy and Alena Chekanov
Production Editorial: Jenny Wolkowicki
Jacket design: Chris Ferrante
Production: Erin Suydam
Publicity: James Schneider and Kathryn Stevens
Copyeditor: Maia Vaswani

Jacket image: DNY59 / iStock

This book has been composed in Arno Pro

Printed on acid-free paper. ∞

Printed in the United States of America

10 9 8 7 6 5 4 3 2 1

For my mentors,
Gerald Kramer
David Mayhew
Charles Tidmarch

CONTENTS

ACKNOWLEDGMENTS

MY EXPERTISE on Social Security is largely accidental. I had the good fortune to spend a year at the Brookings Institution, three doors from the political scientist Martha Derthick, who was finishing her magisterial book *Policymaking for Social Security*. Two decades later, the economist Peter Diamond asked me to join a national study panel sponsored by the National Academy of Social Insurance, examining Social Security privatization, where I learned far more than I contributed. Next, I taught a graduate workshop on Social Security reform with Josh Goldstein, a demographer. And that is how I learned from world-class experts about the politics, economics, and demography of Social Security. I am grateful to them all.

More recently, Nick Carnes, Pat Egan, Markus Prior, Alex Quinn, and Larry Whitney offered superb critiques of the first draft of this manuscript, as did several anonymous reviewers of the second. I am also grateful for help and advice along the way from Chuck Cameron, Tom Clark, Jesse Crosson, Sandy Gordon, Virginia Reno, and Helene Wood.

The book is dedicated to three mentors who shaped me. Charles Tidmarch, in his first semester teaching at Union College, found a political scientist lurking within me and pointed me toward graduate school. Gerald Kramer taught me how to think theoretically and how to weigh evidentiary claims. David Mayhew helped me apply those lessons to American politics, and through his exemplary scholarship, set standards for clear thinking and precise writing.

1

The Solvency Problem

SOCIAL SECURITY—the centerpiece of retirement security for most Americans—will soon be insolvent. Government actuaries forecast the program can pay all promised benefits until 2034. At that point, the $2.9 trillion trust fund will be empty and dedicated Social Security taxes will be the only source of revenue. Since the program will have enough annual revenue to pay only 79 percent of annual benefits, every retiree will face an immediate benefit cut of 21 percent. Similar cuts will be imposed on disabled workers, spouses, survivors, and new applicants. In all, 83 million beneficiaries will lose more than one-fifth of their expected benefits.[1]

All this is old news. In 1994, the actuaries forecast trust fund depletion in 2029. Fifteen years later, they forecast 2037.[2] Although the exact year bounces around a bit, largely because of short-term economic fluctuations, the central message does not change: Social Security is racing toward insolvency. If Congress continues to do nothing, the program will be unable to pay all promised benefits. Moreover, the date of insolvency is getting closer. Once 35 years distant, trust fund depletion is now a dozen years away.

This book explores why Congress has done nothing to fix Social Security over the last three decades. Polls show the program remains popular among virtually all groups: Democrats and Republicans, workers and retirees, the young and the old, the poor and the affluent. Polls also show that many people place Social Security near the top of the list of problems they want Congress to fix. Still, Congress does nothing. Legislators have not voted on a single solvency plan since 1983, not in the House, not in the Senate, not in committee, not on the floor.

This book also explores what legislators are likely to do as insolvency nears. Although legislators are unlikely to allow Social Security to slide over the fiscal cliff, thus imposing deep cuts on beneficiaries, it is less clear how they will fix the program. Will they raise taxes as they did to restore solvency in 1977? Will they cut benefits as they did in 1983? Will they reinvent Social Security as President Bush proposed in 2005?

Roots of Insolvency

Why is Social Security headed toward insolvency? One reason is the long and steady decline in *mortality*. Retired people live longer today than they did when Congress created the program. Life expectancy for 65-year-olds has increased from 13.7 years, when Social Security began paying benefits in 1940, to 20.3 years today. Demographers predict it will continue to increase, reaching 24.3 years in 2095.[3] Although there is much to celebrate in this extraordinary increase in life span, it presents enormous problems for Social Security. A system designed to support retirees for 14 years cannot easily support them for 24.[4]

A second reason is the long but unsteady decline in *fertility*. The long-term trend is clearly downward, from 3.3 children per woman in 1918 to 1.8 in 2017.[5] Fewer children today mean fewer taxpayers tomorrow. But fluctuations in fertility also create troubles for Social Security. Fertility averaged 2.4 children per woman during the Great Depression and World War II (1933–45), increased to 3.3 during the postwar baby boom (1946–64), and then dropped to 2.1 during the equally long baby bust (1965–83).[6] The baby boom generation is larger than its immediate predecessor, which makes paying for the earlier generation's retirement relatively easy. The baby boom generation is then followed by a smaller generation, which makes paying for the boomers' retirement more difficult. Indeed, the retirement of the baby boom generation, which occurs gradually between 2008 and 2034, is the proximate cause of Social Security's insolvency.

For Social Security, demography is destiny. Increasing longevity means retirees, spouses, and survivors collect benefits longer than ever before. Decreasing fertility means fewer workers to support each beneficiary. The resulting decline in the ratio of taxpayers to benefit collectors—from 3.4 workers per beneficiary in 2000 to 2.8 in 2020, 2.3 in 2035, and 2.1 in 2070—underscores the magnitude of the problem.[7]

Financing Social Security

The most important thing to know is that Social Security is largely a pay-as-you-go program. Some pension systems are *advance funded*. They extract money from current workers, invest those funds in stocks and bonds, and use investment returns to support those workers when they retire. In contrast, *pay-as-you-go* systems extract money from current workers and immediately redistribute those funds to current retirees. It is also relevant that Social Security is *self-supporting*. Social Security taxes cannot be used to fund other programs. Other revenues cannot be used to support Social Security.

The top half of figure 1.1 shows how Social Security's revenues and benefits increased from 1970 to 2019, and how they are expected to change through 2034. Most of the increases are the result of wage growth and population growth. They do not reflect inflation, since all values are expressed in 2020 dollars. The increases also reflect several policy changes that Congress enacted in 1983. Three distinct periods stand out. From 1970 to 1983, annual revenues approximated annual benefits. From 1984 to 2020, annual revenues exceeded annual benefits, with the surpluses added to the trust fund. From 2021 to 2034, annual revenues will be less than annual benefits, with trust fund redemptions covering the shortfall.

The bottom half of figure 1.1 shows how the value of Social Security's trust fund has varied, or is projected to vary, throughout this period. Historically, the trust fund was just a small buffer, accumulating occasional surpluses, funding occasional deficits, but never totaling more than a few months of benefits. It functioned like a rainy-day fund, insuring that short-term revenue declines during a recession did not threaten monthly benefits. In 1983, however, Congress created a much larger reserve, both by moderating the growth of benefits and by increasing the growth of revenues. Those decisions are shown in the top half of the figure, where revenues suddenly exceed benefits, and in the lower half, where the trust fund begins its rapid ascent. By 2008, the trust fund was nearly $3 trillion (in 2020 dollars), enough to fund 46 months of benefits. The trust fund peaked in 2020, before beginning to decline in 2021. Absent congressional action, it will hit zero in 2034. At that point, annual benefits will plummet by 21 percent in order to equal the program's actual revenues.

Legislators' actions in 1983 reflected the fact that strictly pay-as-you-go systems are ill suited to handle demographic booms and busts. The solution was to move toward a *modified pay-as-you-go system*, where some revenues would be salted away to support the retirement of unusually large cohorts. Congress took actions that enlarged the trust fund by postponing cost-of-living adjustments for beneficiaries, accelerating already scheduled tax increases for employed workers, and increasing the tax rate for self-employed workers. It also reduced benefits for future retirees by gradually raising the full retirement age from 65 to 67 over 39 years.

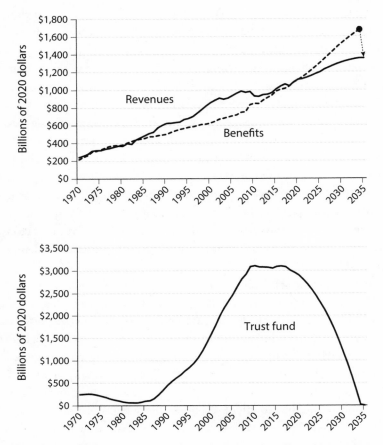

FIGURE 1.1. Revenues, benefits, and trust fund balances in 2020 dollars, 1970–2034. Revenues include payroll taxes, income taxes on Social Security benefits, and interest from the trust fund. Revenues, benefits, and trust fund balances, which are for the combined old-age, survivors, and disability programs, are indexed to the consumer price index. Historical results to 2019, then actuarial projections.

Source: Social Security Administration 2020d, table VI.G7.

The 1983 reforms worked. Congress not only solved the 1983 solvency crisis, it made Social Security financially healthy for more than a half century. But Congress did not solve all the problems associated with declining fertility and mortality. Raising the retirement age by 2 years is not a long-term fix when life expectancy is increasing by 10. Raising the tax rate just for self-employed workers—then about 8 percent of the workforce—is not a long-term solution when the total number of workers per beneficiary is declining by one-third.[8]

Revenues and Benefits

Social Security has five revenue sources. *Employed workers* pay 6.2 percent of their wages up to the maximum taxable wage base ($142,800 in 2021). *Employers* pay an equal amount from their own coffers. These two sources account for 84 percent of system revenues. *Self-employed workers* pay both sums— 12.4 percent in all—subject to the same wage limit, accounting for 5 percent of system revenues. Many *beneficiaries* pay income taxes on a portion of their Social Security benefits. Collected by the Internal Revenue Service, these assessments are redirected to the Social Security Administration, where they make up 3 percent of total revenues. Social Security currently earns *interest* from the trust fund, accounting for 8 percent of system revenues. This source will vanish once the trust fund runs dry.[9] When revenues are insufficient to pay promised benefits, Social Security withdraws money from the trust fund. Redemptions began in 2021 and will continue until 2034.

Social Security is called a *defined benefit program* because monthly benefits are established by law as a fraction of what individual workers contributed to the system over their careers. Although the formulas for distributing benefits are complex, they are based on simple principles. Workers are entitled to retirement benefits after contributing to the program for 10 years. The amount they collect depends on their past taxed wages, and specifically on their 35 highest-earning years. Consequently, those with short careers collect less than full-career people. Similarly, those with low average wages collect less than people with high average wages. The benefit formula, however, is highly progressive, so that lower-wage people realize a much greater return on their contributions than higher-wage people do. As chapter 8 shows, a hypothetical worker who earned Social Security's maximum taxable wage for an entire career would have contributed 8.5 times as much as a person who earned the federal minimum wage during the same period, yet would collect only 2.8 times as much during each retirement year.

Benefits are first calculated for an individual's so-called *full retirement age* (FRA), currently age 67 for those born after 1959. Those who choose to collect benefits earlier than 67 receive reduced benefits. For example, people who file at age 62 receive 70 percent of the FRA benefit. Those who choose to collect benefits later receive augmented benefits—124 percent of the FRA benefit for people filing at age 70. These age-related adjustments are designed to be actuarially fair: Retirees receive, on average, the same lifetime benefits no matter when they start collecting benefits. All benefits are adjusted annually for price inflation.

Workers are entitled to disability benefits if they are unable to perform gainful employment. The amount they collect also depends on their past taxed wages. Spouses of retired, disabled, or deceased workers are eligible for spousal benefits based on workers' past wages. Other beneficiaries include divorced spouses and the minor children of retired, disabled, or deceased workers.

The cost of administering the entire Social Security system is remarkably low, just 0.6 percent of annual benefits. Operating the retirement program is less costly (0.4 percent) because verifying age-based eligibility and delivering benefits electronically are simple tasks. Operating the disability program is more costly (1.8 percent) because disabilities are difficult to verify and monitor.[10]

Fixing Social Security

Policymakers have two fundamentally different routes for making Social Security fiscally solvent. One approach is to adjust the various revenue and benefit streams until they are in balance. These *incremental solutions* resemble what Congress adopted to solve the 1977 and 1983 solvency crises. For the first shortfall, Congress simply raised the payroll tax. For the second, legislators postponed cost-of-living adjustments, reduced benefits for current beneficiaries by taxing some of their benefits, reduced benefits for future beneficiaries by raising the retirement age, and raised taxes for self-employed workers. The benefit cuts were seven times greater than the tax increases.

Over the past quarter century, experts and policymakers have developed hundreds of provisions that would modify the revenue and benefit streams to restore solvency. Government actuaries have appraised most of them, estimating how much each provision would affect annual revenues and benefits. Congress has yet to act on any of these incremental solutions. In fact, neither the House nor the Senate has held a single roll call vote on Social Security solvency since 1983.

Another way to fix Social Security is to reinvent it. Some policymakers propose transforming the current pay-as-you-go defined benefit program into an advance-funded system. Their model is the employer-sponsored *defined contribution plan*, widely known as 401(k) and 403(b) plans, where workers and employers contribute money to individually controlled retirement accounts that are invested to fund each worker's retirement.

Over the past quarter century, experts and policymakers have developed many proposals of this type. They are often called *privatization plans* because they would direct workers' contributions to individually owned private accounts. Retirement benefits would depend on how much workers contribute over their lifetimes and how well their individual portfolios perform. The various plans differ from one another in how they would pay the transition costs of moving to an advance-funded system and on whether they would replace all or part of traditional Social Security. Government actuaries have reviewed many of these plans, estimating how well various cohorts of workers and retirees would do and how much each plan would contribute to solvency. Congress has yet to act on any of these privatization plans.

Retirement Income

Why has Congress done nothing to fix an increasingly urgent problem? Perhaps legislators do not believe that cutting benefits by 21 percent is a big deal. After all, don't most retirees have alternative sources of income? Given the existence of employer-sponsored defined benefit plans, employer-sponsored defined contribution plans, individual retirement accounts, and private savings, won't most retirees be able to cope with a reduction in just one income stream? Unfortunately, the image of Social Security as a small element in retirement security applies to only a fraction of current and future retirees.

One careful study of 2016 retirees found that households in the bottom fifth of the income distribution received, on average, $10,800 in annual retirement income, with 95 percent coming from Social Security (see chapter 8 for details). Those in the next fifth received, on average, $22,700 in retirement income, with 84 percent from Social Security. For people in these two groups, already struggling to support themselves, a 21 percent cut in benefits would be devastating. Those in the middle fifth, who received, on average, $35,500 (66 percent from Social Security), and in the next fifth ($50,200 and 49 percent), would be in better shape to cope with a 21 percent benefit cut. But losing 10 to 14 percent of total income would still cut deeply into their ability to pay medical, food, and household expenses. Only retiree households in the top fifth, who received, on average, $87,000 in retirement income (28 percent from Social Security), would be reasonably well insulated from the effects of insolvency.[11]

What about current workers? Will they be better prepared to fund their retirement than current retirees? So far, it does not look promising. Traditional employer-sponsored pension plans, which guarantee retirement benefits for as long as people live, are disappearing. Only 20 percent of current workers participate in these defined benefit plans. Although these plans are still common in state and local governments, where 76 percent participate, and still common among unionized private sector employers, where 54 percent participate, only 8 percent of nonunionized private sector workers are active participants.[12] Most people participate in exactly one defined benefit plan: Social Security.

Most employers today offer only defined contribution plans. These plans are riskier than defined benefit plans for both workers and retirees. First, they shift to workers the burden of saving. Some workers do not save enough. Second, they shift to retirees the risks of investment losses and outliving their assets. Although 64 percent of private sector workers have access to defined contribution plans, only 47 percent actually contribute.

The most ominous finding is that *half* of all private sector workers do not participate in any employer-sponsored retirement plan, whether defined benefit or defined contribution. Nonparticipation is directly related to income, with 78 percent of workers in the bottom quarter of the wage distribution not participating in any employer-sponsored plan, compared with 52 percent, 36 percent, and 22 percent in the other quartiles.[13] In short, most future retirees cannot rely on employer-sponsored retirement plans to protect them from Social Security's insolvency.

The Cost of Reform

How much would it cost to save Social Security in its current form? The appropriate benchmark for comparison is the nation's gross domestic product, the value of all goods and services produced annually. GDP is the total pot available for public and private spending.

Current payments to Social Security beneficiaries—retirees, disabled workers, spouses, dependents, and survivors—constitute 5 percent of GDP. As figure 1.2 shows, Social Security's share of GDP will increase steadily to 5.9 percent in 2034, when the last boomers retire. What happens next depends on what Congress does. If legislators do nothing, the Social Security share of GDP would drop immediately to 4.7 percent, as benefits contract to equal that year's projected revenues. If legislators raise taxes to fund all promised

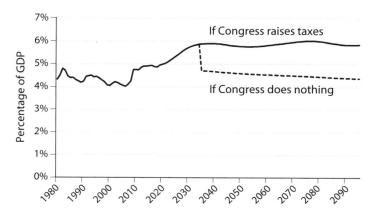

FIGURE 1.2. Social Security benefits as a percentage of GDP, 1980–2095. Historical results to 2019, then actuarial projections.
Source: Social Security Administration 2020d, table VI.G4.

benefits, they would need to allocate an additional 1.2 percent of GDP annually to Social Security beginning in 2034, with an additional 0.3 percent annually between then and 2095. In short, it would cost between 1.2 and 1.5 percent of annual GDP to preserve Social Security in its current form.

Why do actuaries project that benefits as a share of GDP will increase so modestly after 2035, especially given the share's rapid growth between 2008 and 2034? The answer is that a rough balance will emerge between two countervailing forces. Increasing longevity will drive up lifetime benefits, as Social Security pays beneficiaries for additional years. Meanwhile, the boomers' gradual demise will drive down total benefits, as a smaller successor generation of retirees replaces the baby boom generation. The latter is a one-time bonus. The former will continue until longevity plateaus or reverses, or until policymakers do something to compensate for increased longevity.

How does the cost of saving Social Security compare with what Congress has done to address other problems? Consider congressional action during George W. Bush's first presidential term. In 2001, Congress passed his sweeping tax cut, which legislators expected would cost $1.4 trillion over a decade. In 2003 and 2004, Congress enacted additional tax cuts, first for individuals and then for corporations, with an estimated decade-long cost of $476 billion. In 2004, Congress enacted prescription drug coverage for seniors, an action expected to cost $400 billion over the first decade. These three actions cost 1.0 percent, 0.4 percent, and 0.3 percent of GDP per year, or 1.7 percent in all.[14]

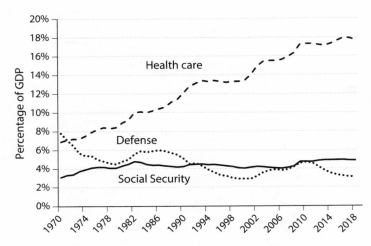

FIGURE 1.3. Spending on Social Security, defense, and health care as a percentage of GDP, 1970–2018. Social Security and defense are exclusively federal programs. Health care includes spending from all governmental and nongovernmental sources.
Sources: Social Security Administration 2020d, table VI.G4; Office of Management and Budget 2020, table 6.1; Centers for Medicare and Medicaid Services 2020, table 1.

Congress also authorized military action in Afghanistan and Iraq. Although legislators approved these military actions without cost estimates, one expert later estimated those wars cost $4.4 trillion over 14 years—averaging about 2.2 percent of GDP annually.[15] The point is *not* that allocating an additional 1.2 percent of GDP to Social Security annually would be easy. The point is that such allocations are common.

Society is endlessly reconfiguring the sectoral allocation of GDP. Figure 1.3 captures how three large sectors of the economy changed between 1970 and 2018. Notice the huge increase in the health sector, from 7 percent to 18 percent of GDP, and the huge decline in national defense, from 8 percent to 3 percent of GDP. The sector that changed the least was Social Security, which increased from 3 percent to 5 percent of GDP. Allocating an additional 1.2 percent of GDP to preserving Social Security is a relatively small adjustment compared with the huge sectoral shifts that legislators have created or tolerated in health care and defense. Of course, some of these sectoral shifts were unplanned. No one set out to double the share of the economy devoted to health care.[16] In contrast, preserving Social Security in its current form requires that legislators explicitly choose to devote an additional 1.2 percent of GDP to a single program.

No one can doubt that 1.2 percent of GDP is a great deal of money. It would be $255 billion in today's economy. Whether this is a reasonable sum to pay, year after year, to protect Social Security beneficiaries from a 21 percent benefit cut is a question that citizens and their elected leaders need to address. It is fundamentally a question about values and preferences. How citizens and legislators resolve this question between now and 2034 is the central subject of this book.

The Urgency of Reform

Does it matter when Congress fixes Social Security? Perhaps Congress does not address Social Security's insolvency because there is nothing urgent about fixing a program that actuaries expect will remain solvent for 12 years. After all, most individuals, organizations, and governments are not devoting 2022 to fixing 2034 problems.

The reasons for procrastination are many. First, it is human nature. Students pull all-nighters to finish course papers; labor negotiators reach settlements just before midnight; legislators pass budgets just as funding runs out. Why fight human nature? Second, waiting clarifies the choices. The forecast that Social Security will become insolvent in 2034 is just a prediction: it could be earlier; it could be later. Why not wait until everyone agrees on exactly what will happen and when? Third, compromise is easier when the consequences of stalemate are disastrous for both sides. Fourth, the last two times legislators faced solvency crises in Social Security—1977 and 1983—they did fine waiting until the last minute. Why does this solvency crisis warrant an earlier intervention?

Actually, there is little uncertainty about when Social Security's trust fund will run dry. Social Security is one of the most predictable spending programs in the federal budget. It would be folly to forecast the Pentagon's budget two decades in advance. Will we be at war or peace? What long-term conflicts will fade and what new conflicts will surface? What new weapons technologies will emerge and will they cost more or less than current technologies? Social Security is different because statutory formulas—not revised since 1983—largely determine the flow of revenues and expenditures. Of course, births and deaths matter too, but it takes two decades for infants to become workers, and six decades for infants to become retirees, so demographic uncertainty is not a problem during the next two decades. Although experts disagree about the best way to restore solvency, they do not disagree about the inevitability of insolvency or about its approximate date.[17]

The principal reason for fixing Social Security soon is to spread the costs of reform more widely. If Congress had dealt more thoroughly with the long-term solvency problem in 1983, the baby boom generation would have con-tributed more to the solution. The youngest boomers were then 19, the oldest 37. They had most of their careers ahead of them, during which they could have paid higher taxes or prepared for shorter or less lucrative retirements. The longer legislators wait, the less baby boomers can be part of the solution. If Congress waits until 2034, the youngest boomers will be 70, the oldest 88. At that point, the only way to make boomers part of the solution will be to cut benefits for everyone.

Another reason for fixing Social Security soon is that the repair options narrow as insolvency approaches. Many options that legislators could choose today, such as gradually increasing the retirement age or gradually increasing the tax rate, disappear in 2034. Once the trust fund is empty, gradualism is not an option. The remaining options will be to impose large and immediate tax increases, impose large and immediate benefit cuts, or borrow heavily to tran-sition to a new system.

Delay may also be a strategic choice. Some policymakers believe that if Congress waits until the trust fund empties, the chances will increase that Congress will enact their favorite reforms. For example, some people who seek to raise taxes accept that legislators are less likely to do so while benefits are flowing freely. But once the trust fund empties and benefits are about to de-cline, legislators will finally accept the inevitable and raise taxes. Similarly, some people who seek to reinvent Social Security by transitioning to a system of private accounts believe that reinvention will be easier once the 2034 preci-pice nears. Both groups are correct that legislators are more likely to act on the eve of automatic benefit cuts. But delay cannot possibly favor all sides.

Politics

Creating a large trust fund fundamentally changed the politics of Social Secu-rity.[18] When the trust fund was small, typically containing a few months' worth of benefits, the program could easily slip into insolvency, as it did in 1977 and 1983. Since inaction would lead to immediate benefit cuts, legislators had little choice but to fix the program immediately, whether by raising taxes or adjusting benefits. Once the trust fund became enormous—all courtesy of the 1983 reform—legislators could delay action for decades, drawing down the trust fund rather than working to preserve or enhance it. Delay has been legislators' collective choice for more than a quarter century.

After passing the 1983 reform plan, legislators transitioned from being active policymakers, who worked to maintain and improve Social Security, into being passive position takers. Between 1950 and 1983, legislators on the relevant House and Senate committees had become experts at negotiating complex bills as they drafted and enacted 16 major bills affecting the program's revenue and benefit streams. Since then, Congress has enacted only minor housekeeping bills, while leaving the tax and benefit formulas unchanged.[19] Today's Congress is bereft of legislators with experience bargaining about Social Security.

Freed of the need to hammer out compromises about taxes and benefits, today's legislators stake out increasingly extreme positions. Some Republicans talk about reinventing Social Security, harnessing the power of markets, and replacing the current pay-as-you-go defined benefit program with an advance-funded defined contribution program. Meanwhile, some Democrats talk about expanding traditional Social Security, making it more generous for low-wage workers, or using a more generous formula for cost-of-living adjustments—all this on top of making the program solvent. Democratic and Republican legislators also diverge on whether raising Social Security taxes is a good idea. Democrats seem willing; Republicans insist on tax-free solutions.

When partisan elites polarize, the mass public often follows. For example, when elected officials divided on health care, climate change, and defense policy, many citizens split along the same partisan fault lines. Social Security has not followed this script. We see some evidence of polarization in the early 1980s, when President Reagan sought to cut Social Security, and in 2005, when President Bush sought to privatize the program. But these episodes of polarization were mild and short-lived. What is striking about Social Security is that the program enjoys widespread public support, not only among Democrats and Republicans but also among workers and retirees, the young and the old, the poor and the better-off.

Elite polarization is real, however, and it makes fixing Social Security's solvency problem vastly more difficult. Ordinarily, simple majorities in Congress suffice for modifying tax and expenditure programs because simple majorities can enact the annual budget resolution. But the Congressional Budget Act explicitly prohibits using budget resolutions to modify Social Security. Fixing Social Security requires that Congress enact an authorization bill, something that requires a supermajority in the Senate—60 percent. In short, fixing Social Security is necessarily a bipartisan affair, requiring the support of a House majority, a Senate supermajority, and the president.[20] With Republican and Democratic legislators so deeply divided on how to fix Social Security, the incentives for compromise are minimal, especially with insolvency more than a decade away.

Social Security has survived unchanged since 1983 because it rests on three pillars. First, it enjoys broad public support. Second, it requires supermajorities in Congress to modify or replace it. Third, the trust fund has protected beneficiaries from the consequences of legislative stalemate. But this third protection is a pillar of sand, one that has already started to dissolve. Absent congressional action, the trust fund disappears in 2034.

The 2034 fiscal cliff towers over the revenue shortages of 1977 and 1983 because the $2.9 trillion trust fund has been protecting everyone from the reality that tax revenues have been insufficient to support Social Security benefits since 2010. For a while, interest on the trust fund papered over the gap. But each year, as more baby boomers retired, the gap grew larger. In 2021, administrators began liquidating the trust fund. Each successive year will require larger and larger redemptions. Finally—poof!—the trust fund will disappear. When it does, annual revenues will cover only 79 percent of benefits.

The trust fund's disappearance will make fixing Social Security an urgent issue, not just for beneficiaries, who will face enormous benefit cuts, but also for legislators who fear being blamed for the cuts and blamed for the fixes. Most legislators will feel cross-pressured when they vote on actual reform proposals. On the one hand, few legislators will want to enrage Social Security beneficiaries by allowing 21 percent automatic benefit cuts. After all, most congressional districts are brimming with retirees, and retirees vote more regularly than younger people do. On the other hand, most remedies are quite expensive. Extracting 1.2 percent of GDP from workers and their employers could infuriate them, too. Although workers may not vote as regularly as retirees do, they outnumber them. The dilemma is particularly difficult for Republican legislators, since most have signed pledges never to raise taxes.

For most budgetary decisions, members of Congress do not have to worry about keeping revenues and expenditures in balance. If they want to spend more without taxing more, they run deficits. If they choose to cut taxes without cutting spending, they run more deficits. Deficit spending, however, is not an option for Social Security. "No deficits" is not a norm. It is not a quaint custom. It is the law. The trust fund is the only legal source for paying benefits. Social Security taxes are the only legal source for filling the trust fund. It has been that way since 1935. When the trust fund runs dry, program administrators have no choice but to reduce benefits until they equal incoming revenues. Only Congress can prevent those cuts by passing legislation that restores the balance between taxes and spending.

The Plan

This book explores the politics of fixing Social Security. I investigate two important questions, one about agenda setting, the other about decision making. *Agenda setting* refers to the process by which an issue becomes the focus of legislators' attention. I explore why Social Security became a central issue on legislative agendas in 1935, 1939, 1950, 1972, 1977, and 1983—the major turning points in the program's history—and why legislators have largely ignored Social Security since 1983, despite the program's known and serious solvency problem. *Decision making* refers to the process by which legislators enact new policies once an issue appears on the agenda. I explore why they selected some options rather than others. Why, for example, did legislators fix the 1977 solvency problem exclusively by raising taxes, and then fix the 1983 solvency problem largely by cutting benefits?

My discussion of agenda setting is structured by John Kingdon's model, where political leaders join three otherwise separate streams, consisting of problems, policies, and politics.[21] For Social Security, the original problem was that workers were unable to provide for their own retirement. Alternative policies for addressing the problem included need-based old-age assistance and contributory-based old-age insurance. Politics includes the range of pressures on elected officials, including elections, public opinion, mass movements, and interest groups. President Roosevelt's signal contribution was to join those three streams and persuade Congress to enact the Social Security Act of 1935. Subsequent problems emerged, including the adequacy of benefits, the scourge of inflation, and the mismatch between revenues and expenditures. Sometimes legislators found solutions for these problems. Sometimes legislators ignored them.

My discussion of legislative decision making is guided by the notion that legislators care intensely about reelection. They regularly calculate whether particular actions—even particular votes—would enhance or diminish their electoral prospects. For half of Social Security's history, roll call voting was a breeze for legislators because they were repeatedly conferring new benefits on their constituents. Since 1977, voting has been more of a nightmare. Social Security is now on its third solvency crisis. Each time legislators have had to choose between raising their constituents' taxes and cutting their constituents' benefits. Imposing costs is the toughest part of a legislator's job.

My investigation is part chronological and part thematic. Chapter 2 examines how Congress created Social Security in 1935, expanded it from 1939 to 1974, and handled the solvency crises of 1977 and 1983. This historical account helps explain why legislators designed the system as they did and how they allocated—and reallocated—costs and benefits among workers, employers, and retirees. It also shows how early decisions shaped later decisions. Chapter 11 picks up the historical account in 2005 and examines President Bush's attempt to reinvent Social Security with voluntary personal accounts. Legislators never acted on his ambitious plan.

A second theme focuses on the policy options themselves. Chapter 4, for example, explores alternative retirement systems, examining the advantages and disadvantages of advance-funded versus pay-as-you-go systems. This provides the foundation for discussing proposals to reinvent Social Security. Chapter 5 explores incremental options for fixing Social Security. What are the arguments for and against proposals such as raising the retirement age, increasing the tax rate, or modifying the benefit formula?

My central theme is politics itself, as I explore why legislators make the choices they do. Explaining legislators' decisions would be relatively easy if I cared only about the past. Any congressional scholar—and that, by the way, is what I am—can do that with ease. My larger ambition, however, is to help readers think about the future, to think about how legislators will, or will not, fix Social Security between 2022 and 2034. And for that task, I need to theorize about what makes legislators tick, not just in 1977 or 1983, but in general. Chapter 9 sets out a framework for accomplishing that task based on my previous work on legislative decision making. Because legislators are politicians who care intensely about reelection, chapters 6, 7, and 8 first examine the interests and actions of various players who affect legislators' decisions, including voters, donors, and interest groups.

The final chapters employ these tools to analyze future policymaking. Chapter 10 explores the politics of adjusting the revenue and benefit streams to restore solvency. Chapter 11 explores the politics of reinventing Social Security, using a 2005 case study to think more generally about options to alter the program's basic structure. Chapter 12 analyzes politics at the precipice. What happens in 2034 when the trust fund runs dry and every beneficiary faces a 21 percent benefit cut? And who would be advantaged by decades of procrastination? Would it be those who sought to preserve traditional Social Security or those who sought to reinvent it? Chapter 13 concludes by examining what might stimulate legislators to act more responsibly and fix Social Security now.

PART I

The Evolution of
Social Security

2

Creation, Expansion, and Solvency

WHY, IN THE MIDDLE OF THE GREAT DEPRESSION, did Congress create an advance-funded retirement program that would collect substantial payroll taxes for five years before delivering retirement benefits to anyone? Although later transformed into a pay-as-you-go system, where current workers support current retirees, Social Security began as an advance-funded program, where workers' contributions were socked away for the future.

Congress has made and remade Social Security several times, sometimes favoring advance funding, sometimes not. The first system, created in 1935, was advance funded. Workers began contributing to the system in 1937; their contributions were invested in a collective trust fund; workers aged 65 or older could retire and receive benefits from the trust fund beginning in 1942. The second system, created between 1939 and 1947 and lasting until 1983, was a pay-as-you-go system. Workers' contributions were still sent to a collective trust fund, but the funds were almost immediately disbursed to current retirees. This trust fund was more like a checking account than an investment account. This new system allowed Congress to deliver increasingly generous retirement benefits in the early years because workers vastly outnumbered retirees.

The third system, created in 1983 and still operating today, is a modified pay-as-you-go system. It operates much like the second system, except that legislators first adjusted the tax and benefit formulas so that enormous sums would accumulate in the trust fund while the oversized baby boom generation was still working, with those sums later disbursed to help fund the boomers' retirement. This trust fund is more like a savings account, with money first stockpiled for a particular purpose and later spent for that purpose. Unless Congress does something soon to readjust the tax and benefit formulas, this trust fund will disappear in 2034, just as the youngest boomers retire. At that point, Social Security will become a pure pay-as-you-go program, but with monthly revenues sufficient to pay only 79 percent of benefits.

The central puzzle for this chapter is to explain why Congress has made such disparate choices about the financing of Social Security. My basic argument is that advance-funded, government-administered retirement systems are inherently unstable. Although politicians had good reasons for creating advance funding in 1935, and again in 1983, they were unable to devise self-maintaining systems.[1] Their successors were under no obligation to maintain advance funding, just as they are under no obligation to retain any other laws or programs. Soon after the advent of Social Security, the political pressures were for more benefits, not more taxes, so legislators quickly dismantled the original funding scheme. Legislators did better when they reintroduced advance funding in 1983. That is, their successors have not raided the reserve set aside for the boomers' retirement. But neither have their successors augmented this reserve, despite the actuaries' decades-ago forecast that the trust fund was inadequate to fund the extra costs of the boomers' retirement.

My overall argument is that legislators are more concerned with the near-term distribution of costs and benefits than they are with any long-term consequences.[2] In the late 1930s and early 1940s, they opposed scheduled tax increases that would have filled the trust fund because those increased taxes were not needed to fund current benefits. Instead, they preferred increasing current benefits. In recent decades, legislators have opposed raising taxes to augment the reserve designed to support the boomers' retirement. Instead, they have left the solvency problem to their successors.

Despite the instability of its financing scheme, Social Security has survived for nearly a century. The secret of its survival is that it is self-supporting. Once workers contribute to the system throughout their working lives, they expect the program to deliver all promised benefits.[3] What is not yet clear, however, is how legislators might fix the system in 2034. Will they dare increase taxes by 21 percent in order to forestall 21 percent benefit cuts? Or will they once again reinvent the system?

The Politics of Advance Funding

Establishing an advance-funded system in the middle of the Great Depression is puzzling because it did nothing to address the urgent problem. The economic condition of older people in the mid-1930s was dire. Work was difficult to find for everyone, but especially for seniors. The unemployment rate for men in their late sixties was 19 points higher than for men in their late twenties.[4] Older workers who were laid off were less likely to be recalled than younger workers.[5] Formal retirement plans were scarce. Among people aged 65 and older, fewer than 230,000 out of 7.8 million individuals—about 3 percent—collected pensions.[6] Personal savings were often decimated by bank failures, property market declines, and the stock market crash.[7] Twenty-eight states provided relief for destitute retirees, but this relief covered only 3 percent of seniors and averaged less than $15 per month.[8]

Establishing an advance-funded system is also puzzling because legislators' natural inclination is to spend now, tax later, not tax now, spend later. For politicians, the rewards are for delivering benefits, not imposing costs. But the law, officially known as the Social Security Act of 1935, offered zero retirement benefits until 1942. Moreover, raising taxes during the Depression and adding those funds to national savings was an odd choice when Keynes and others advocated spending, not saving, as the proper macroeconomic choice.

Political pressures in the 1930s forced retirement policy on the national agenda. Francis Townsend, a retired doctor, proposed a program of generous pensions for everyone aged 60 or older. His plan took the country by storm. Millions of people signed petitions urging Congress to create such a program. Before long, there were Townsend Clubs everywhere, claiming two million members, and pressuring legislators to address the urgent needs of older people.[9] Legislators had to do something. The only question was what route they would take.

One reason Congress created an advance-funded system was that Franklin D. Roosevelt insisted. The president sought to build a retirement system based on insurance principles. Having spent eight years working in the insurance industry, he thought in terms of premiums, reserves, actuarial assumptions, and benefits.[10] Moreover, the two principal staff members assisting the Committee on Economic Security, the cabinet-level committee tasked with designing Social Security, were insurance experts.[11] An insurance program is by definition advance funded.

President Roosevelt also demanded that Social Security be *self-supporting*— that is, funded exclusively by workers and their employers.[12] Although some experts, including the cabinet-level committee, advocated using some general revenues to support retirement security, the president was adamant that a dedicated payroll tax would secure Social Security against future political harm.[13] Years later, when a visiting political scientist questioned the wisdom of creating a new tax in difficult economic times, Roosevelt responded:

We put those payroll contributions there so as to give the contributors a legal, moral, and political right to collect their pensions and their unemployment benefits. With those taxes in there, no damn politician can ever scrap my social security program. Those taxes aren't a matter of economics, they're straight politics.[14]

In short, a self-supporting, advance-funded scheme was the best protection against future political harm. Roosevelt also viewed a self-supporting system as a protection against unreasonable expansion. Legislators would need to vote for tax increases in order to expand benefits.[15]

Although it is easy to see why President Roosevelt championed an advance-funded system, why would legislators approve a plan that would not deliver any near-term benefits? The answer is that the Social Security Act of 1935 created two programs for seniors. First, it established a program of *old-age assistance* for needy retirees. This program, funded with general revenues, would provide matching grants for state-administered programs that offered financial assistance to needy individuals aged 65 or over. Old-age assistance was designed to deal with the immediate problem. Second, the Act created a program of *old-age insurance* for private sector workers. This program, now known as Social Security, would deal with the long-term problem of preventing poverty among the aged. Moreover, the administration's bill was full of other enticements, including assistance programs for expectant mothers, newborns, needy children, and the blind, and federal funding for state-administered unemployment insurance.

Old-age assistance, not old-age insurance, attracted legislators' attention and support.[16] Bill drafters knew this, so they placed old-age assistance first in the bill. Most legislators expressed little enthusiasm for the president's insurance program. Indeed, the House Ways and Means Committee nearly stripped it from the omnibus bill.[17] But President Roosevelt was adamant that legislators needed to support his signature Social Security program in order to obtain immediate assistance for their constituents.[18]

The program for old-age assistance was colossal. The year before Congress created the program, 28 states provided $32 million for 206,000 needy seniors. Three years later, federal and state governments together provided 10 times as much for 1.6 million seniors. By 1940, they were providing 15 times as much for 2.1 million seniors.[19] Even after Social Security began delivering retirement benefits, the old-age assistance program was the behemoth. It was not until

1951 that total Social Security benefits exceeded total old-age assistance benefits,[20] and that milestone was a consequence of Congress raising Social Security benefits that year by 77 percent.[21] Moreover, old-age assistance was just one of several large programs in the omnibus bill. Programs for the unemployed, the blind, and families with dependent children delivered even more benefits than old-age assistance did.[22]

The Social Security Act contained something for everyone. The president obtained Social Security, a self-supporting, advance-funded system that held few attractions for legislators. It would be his lasting legacy. Members of Congress obtained immediate relief for the aged, the unemployed, needy children, and the blind. By 1938, these four assistance programs totaled 13 percent of federal expenditures and 1 percent of the nation's GDP.[23] No wonder politicians found the Social Security Act so appealing. How often do legislators distribute 1 percent of GDP with a single vote?

Legislators supported the overall bill enthusiastically, with 95 percent of House Democrats and 84 percent of House Republicans voting for final passage, as did 98 percent of Senate Democrats and 76 percent of Senate Republicans.[24] Although Republicans had worked to derail the bill at earlier stages, their opposition faded once passage was certain, for they, too, wanted credit for delivering immediate benefits to their constituents.

Taxes and Benefits

Program designers were careful in how they allocated the costs of this advance-funded retirement system. Although actuaries calculated that a 6 percent payroll tax was necessary to fund the recommended level of Social Security benefits, program designers did two things to soften the blow. First, they split the tax in two, imposing identical payroll taxes on workers and their employers. Although economists insist that workers, in effect, pay the employers' share with forgone wages, politicians believe that workers notice only taxes withheld from their wages, not their employers' hidden share or something as nebulous as forgone wages. Second, program designers imposed the two payroll taxes gradually, beginning with initial rates of 1.0 percent each on workers and employers in 1937, and then raising the two rates 0.5 percentage points every three years until reaching the final rates of 3.0 percent in 1949.[25] Workers and their employers would not pay the full tax until 14 years after Congress first approved it. In short, policymakers increased costs as slowly and imperceptibly as possible, thus blunting the political risks of supporting a tax that would eventually equal 6 percent of taxable payroll.

Gradualism was an option for imposing costs because there was no immediate need for revenue in an advanced-funded system. No workers were eligible for retiree benefits until 1942, and even then, the cohort of workers turning 65 would be a tiny fraction of all tax-paying workers. The committee's actuaries projected that Social Security would quickly accumulate a large reserve fund. By 1950, the reserve fund would be 9 times annual contributions; a decade later, it would be 15 times annual contributions.[26] Interest on the reserve fund would not only help support future benefit payments, it would insulate Social Security from economic shocks. The system could pay full benefits even if a recession temporarily reduced revenues.

Social Security was never a pure advance-funded system. The contributions of workers and their employers were never segregated in individual investment accounts. Instead, all contributions were placed in a collective reserve fund. Although the actuaries projected that interest on the reserve would support a large fraction of future benefit payments, the reserve fund was never meant to be the sole source for retirement payments. Current revenues from the payroll tax were always part of the support structure. The reliance on current revenues was partly because policymakers sought to give early cohorts of retirees more retirement benefits than they could possibly earn from just a few years of contributions. Moreover, policymakers built redistribution into the system, offering low-wage workers larger benefits than their own contributions could otherwise justify.[27] Still, the role of the trust fund was critical. The actuaries projected that, given the tax and benefit rates in the enacted plan, the reserve fund would still be growing when the youngest workers reached retirement age in the early 1980s.[28]

Social Security was never a universal plan. The original design excluded government workers because taxing state and local governments could invite constitutional challenges. It excluded railroad workers because the Railroad Retirement Act already covered them. Although the original proposal included workers in educational, religious, and charitable institutions, and allowed voluntary participation by self-employed workers, legislators removed both provisions.[29] The original proposal also included agricultural and domestic workers, but the Treasury Department objected, arguing that it would be administratively impossible to collect payroll taxes from dispersed, seasonal, and often part-time workers.[30] As passed, the Social Security Act included workers in industry and commerce, about half the workforce.[31]

Political Equilibrium

By all accounts, the Social Security Act of 1935 created a retirement system that would be in *financial equilibrium* for many decades. Left untouched by political hands, the revenue stream would fully support the benefit stream. Since individual benefits were based on individual wage histories, initial retirement benefits would not grow faster than wages. Since the reserve fund was projected to grow every year, there was ample protection against recessions that might temporarily reduce revenues.

Notice that Social Security would be in financial equilibrium if left untouched by political hands. But would elected officials keep their hands off? If legislators decided to modify Social Security, would they do so without dismantling the self-supporting, advance-funded features that ensured financial equilibrium? Put differently, was Social Security in *political equilibrium*? Was the program designed so that elected officials would preserve its basic structure? Or were there incentives for legislators to unravel the program's core features?[32]

President Roosevelt had clearly thought about political equilibrium. When he insisted on using payroll taxes rather than general revenues to fund the system, because payroll taxes would give contributors "a legal, moral, and political right to collect their pensions," he was speaking the language of political equilibrium. As he said, "those taxes aren't a matter of economics, they're straight politics."[33] But was Social Security protected against other political threats? Most importantly, what would keep legislators from abandoning the insurance model, where contributions are invested for the future, and moving toward a pay-as-you go model, where current workers completely fund current beneficiaries? In short, what would keep legislators from doing what they do best: Spend now, tax later?

The first challenge appeared in 1936, when Governor Alf Landon (R-KS), the Republican nominee for president, denounced Social Security and promised to repeal it if elected.[34] The question of repeal was settled decisively when Landon lost in a landslide. That was the last serious challenge to Social Security's existence.[35]

The second challenge appeared in 1937, when Senator Arthur Vandenberg (R-MI) objected to accumulating a huge financial reserve for Social Security. An influential member of the Senate Finance Committee, Vandenberg argued that the planned accumulation of a trust fund of $47 billion by 1980 would be "the most fantastic and the most indefensible objective imaginable. It is scarcely conceivable that rational men should propose such an unmanageable accumulation of funds in one place in a democracy."[36] Vandenberg was not challenging

Social Security's existence, for he had voted in favor of it two years before. He objected to the government assembling and controlling a huge financial reserve. He proposed altering the financing scheme, replacing a large, income-generating reserve with a smaller contingency reserve. Of course, eliminating the large reserve would undermine the insurance-based principle of advance funding.

The third challenge appeared in 1938, when some legislators, including Senator Vandenberg, questioned the wisdom of increasing the payroll tax by 50 percent in 1940, as the Social Security Act specified. Here the objections were macroeconomic. Although unemployment was declining in 1935 when Congress enacted Social Security, three years later it was increasing. Many policymakers feared that an automatic tax increase, especially one that would be saved, not spent, would only deepen the recession.

The fourth challenge also appeared in 1938, when program leaders advocated accelerating the payment of benefits. The Advisory Council on Social Security was especially forceful in making two cases: eligible workers should not have to wait until 1942 to collect much-needed benefits and initial retirement benefits should be higher.[37]

Legislators addressed the last three problems by enacting the Social Security Amendments of 1939. This legislation postponed for three years the scheduled 1940 increase in the payroll tax, accelerated by two years the scheduled 1942 payment of retirement benefits, increased initial benefit payments for early cohorts, and extended Social Security benefits to spouses, dependents, and survivors of retired workers. By postponing revenue increases and expanding benefit payments, the bill slowed the trust fund's growth. Although policymakers agreed on the final package, they disagreed on whether they were fundamentally changing Social Security. President Roosevelt believed that postponing the scheduled tax increase was a one-time deviation from his advance-funding principle, justified by the precarious economy and the need to appease conservative critics, but setting no precedent for the future.[38] Many conservatives believed they were charting a new course, namely that current revenues need only be sufficient to pay current benefits and that a small contingency reserve was adequate.

The Transition to Pay as You Go

The question whether Social Security would be advance funded, with a large income-earning reserve, or pay as you go, with a small contingency reserve, was settled decisively in seven laws enacted between 1942 and 1947.[39] In each bill, Congress voted to postpone scheduled tax increases, so that by 1949, when the payroll tax was scheduled to reach 3 percent each on workers and employers, the actual rate was unchanged from the original rate of 1 percent each.[40] President Roosevelt objected from the start. Before the first attempt, he wrote, "In 1939, in a period of underemployment, we departed temporarily from the original schedule of contributions. . . . There is certainly no sound reason for departing again under present circumstances."[41] Legislators saw things differently and voted overwhelmingly to postpone the increase. Two years later, when legislators again tried to postpone a scheduled rate increase, the president vetoed the bill. Both houses of Congress overrode his veto. It was the first time in American history that Congress enacted a tax bill over the president's veto.[42]

In retrospect, President Roosevelt's advance-funded retirement system was never in political equilibrium. Legislators were never enamored by Social Security's philosophy of tax now, spend later. Violating the principle of advance funding was easy in 1939, with the economy sputtering and the president open to deal making. But if legislators had not succumbed to temptation then, they would have done so eventually because few legislators favor extracting revenue from taxpayers sooner than necessary. Although legislators never proclaimed that they were replacing an advance-funded system with a pay-as-you-go system, that was the inevitable result of the eight Social Security bills they enacted between 1939 and 1947.

President Roosevelt got the politics right on one thing. By creating a self-supporting retirement system, "no damn politician" has ever devised an effective strategy for eliminating his signature program. Before long, nearly everyone had a stake in Social Security's survival. Current retirees expected their benefits to continue undiminished. Near retirees expected to do at least as well as those who had already retired. Workers who paid into Social Security expected to collect what they had been promised. Moreover, people kept moving through the system. Those with the least at stake—the youngest workers— soon became middle-aged stakeholders, reacting just as their parents had to previous proposals to reduce or eliminate Social Security. When Roosevelt argued that payroll taxes gave contributors "a legal, moral, and political right to collect their pensions," he knew both politics and human nature. The key program feature, however, was that it was self-supporting, not advance funded.

Expansion

Once Social Security became pay as you go, the political constraints on expanding the program diminished. Before long, policymakers transformed a program that originally covered half the workforce and paid modest retirement benefits into a program that covered most workers and paid substantial benefits to retirees, spouses, dependents, and survivors. Legislators even grafted on to the original retirement plan a program for disability insurance, first for disabled workers over 50, and eventually for all disabled workers and their dependents.

Legislators increased Social Security benefits eleven times between 1950 and 1974. They increased nominal benefits by 77, 13, 13, and 7 percent in the 1950s, and then by 7, 13, 15, 10, 20, 7, and 4 percent.[43] Although a portion of these increases merely restored what inflation had eroded, inflation-adjusted benefits increased by 141 percent between the first year that Social Security paid benefits and 1974.[44]

This expansionary period was delightful for legislators. They regularly and enthusiastically voted for whatever benefit hikes the House Ways and Means Committee recommended. Legislators deployed newsletters, press releases, and constituency visits to ensure that retirees noticed and appreciated their support. Roll call votes on Social Security were especially attractive to legislators because seniors began to vote in congressional elections at much higher rates than younger people.[45] Expansion was a bipartisan affair, with Republican and Democratic legislators equally supportive.[46] Indeed, some of the largest benefit increases happened under divided government, as Republican presidents and Democratic congresses competed to claim credit for their generosity.[47]

In order to fund this benefit growth, legislators increased the initial payroll tax from 1.0 percent each on workers and employers to 4.95 percent each in 1974. Although enacting such large increases might seem politically perilous, it was remarkably easy. First, legislators relied on automatic statutory increases. Recall that the original Social Security Act scheduled four rate increases to bring the tax from 1.0 percent in 1937 to 3.0 percent in 1949. Since Congress had postponed but never repealed those increases, legislators simply allowed them to go into effect as needed, first to 1.5 percent in 1950, and eventually to 3.0 percent in 1960.[48] Second, when legislators created the new disability insurance program, they established a dedicated tax of 0.25 percent each on workers and employers to fund the program. No one questioned the need for a new tax to support an attractive new benefit. Third, gradualism remained legislators' best friend.[49] Legislators increased the retirement and disability tax rates in 12 barely noticeable steps, averaging 0.16 percentage points per step.[50] Unlike the benefit increases, which took effect immediately, Congress often approved tax changes years before their effective dates.[51] In short, legislators made the benefit increases as large, visible, and traceable as possible, while making the necessary tax increases as small, invisible, and untraceable as possible.[52]

Perhaps no subterfuge was necessary for increasing the payroll tax. This was a prosperous time in the United States. Real GDP increased by 41 percent in the 1950s and 51 percent in the 1960s, so the payroll tax diverted only a tiny fraction of income growth toward Social Security.[53] Moreover, when Congress created disability insurance in 1956 and Medicare in 1965, each with dedicated payroll taxes, legislators experienced no political backlash. This was not a time when voters and politicians reacted instinctively against taxes. Taxation had not yet become the partisan issue that it is today. It also helped that Social Security was now delivering cash benefits to millions of retirees. Most workers had parents or grandparents collecting benefits, so small tax increases for workers to fund large benefit increases for their parents and grandparents did not seem unreasonable.

Legislators also expanded the scope of Social Security. The original legislation covered workers in commerce and industry—about half the workforce. In 1950, legislators added compulsory coverage for domestic, farm, and most self-employed workers, and optional coverage for employees of nonprofit organizations and state and local governments. They added compulsory coverage for architects, accountants, and farm owners in 1954, lawyers and dentists in 1956, and doctors in 1965. By then, Social Security excluded only some government workers.[54] Whereas in 1935 many people agitated to stay out of Social Security, by the 1950s many workers were clamoring to join.

Despite the increasingly broad support for Social Security, legislators remained vigilant about managing tax rates, especially the visible tax that workers—also known as voters—paid directly. Nowhere was that vigilance more obvious than in legislators' treatment of self-employed workers. By definition, a self-employed person is both employer and employee, so one should expect such a worker would pay both halves of the payroll tax. Unfortunately, that would make the tax doubly painful for self-employed workers compared with company-employed workers. Legislators split the difference, allowing self-employed workers to pay 75 percent of the combined tax and still receive 100 percent of Social Security benefits. Legislators actually increased the subsidies for self-employed workers in the 1970s, at one point allowing them to pay only 69 percent of the combined tax rate.[55]

What kept legislators from currying favor with retirees by increasing their benefits even more? The principal constraint was that Social Security was a self-supporting program. Dedicated payroll taxes not only prevented politicians from eliminating benefits, they also deterred politicians from expanding retirement benefits beyond what they believed workers and employers would support.[56] In the early years of pay-as-you-go Social Security, when workers vastly outnumbered beneficiaries, the constraints on expansion were small.[57] Modest tax increases funded generous benefit increases. As the program matured, however, the constraints became more powerful.

The expansionary era ended in 1972, when legislators voted to place Social Security on autopilot. Beginning in 1975, program administrators would use a cost-of-living formula to adjust benefits for price inflation. The stimulus for this decision was accelerating inflation. The consumer price index, which increased an average of 1.5 percent annually in the six years beginning in 1961, increased an average of 4.4 percent annually in the next six years.

One reason for choosing automatic adjustments was that policymakers believed retirees should not suffer from inflation while waiting for legislators to act. A second reason was that legislators often overcompensated retirees for inflation, a stance that was increasingly unaffordable. In a sense, automatic adjustments were designed to protect retirees from inflation and legislators from themselves.[58] To prove the latter point, legislators increased Social Security benefits by 34 percent in the three years before automatic adjustments took effect, a period during which actual prices increased only 22 percent.[59]

Deficits

When Congress enacted these last benefit increases, generous though they were, Social Security's actuaries believed the program would remain in financial equilibrium for decades to come. The actuaries were wrong. No one had envisioned the emerging economic scourge—stagflation—where high unemployment and high inflation occurred simultaneously. No one had imagined that prices would increase faster than wages.[60] Soaring inflation triggered automatic benefit increases totaling 22 percent between 1975 and 1977.[61] Sluggish wage growth and elevated unemployment delivered unexpectedly low revenues.[62] As a result, total expenditures for Social Security exceeded total revenues in 1975, 1976, and 1977.[63] With a contingency reserve that could pay benefits for only a few months, legislators were forced to act quickly.

The debate about how Congress should address this financial shortfall is revealing because it was the first time that legislators had to fix Social Security.[64] The need for revenue was immediate. Legislators could not dawdle without imperiling the regular delivery of Social Security checks. Worst of all, legislators had to impose substantial costs on their constituents without opportunities to deliver new benefits to anyone.

Most legislators defended Social Security against challenges to its basic structure.[65] Although President Carter recommended using general revenues to shore up Social Security during recessions, and recommended applying this change retroactively to 1975, legislators rejected his proposal. They retained Roosevelt's self-supporting system. Carter also recommended making the employers' share of the payroll tax larger than the workers' share. Congress rejected this proposal too, retaining parity between workers and their employers.

Most notably, legislators rejected any notion that current retirees should suffer diminution of benefits. Inflation was raging, imposing huge costs on most segments of society. But Congress was clear: retirees would remain fully shielded from inflation's nasty effects. With retirees' benefits protected, legislators' only option was to raise taxes. Not surprisingly, they raised the tax rate as slowly as possible. Legislators increased the tax rate from 4.95 percent each on workers and employers in 1977 to 6.20 percent each in 1990, with six small steps averaging 0.21 percentage points per step.[66]

Legislators also raised the *maximum taxable wage base*—the ceiling on wages subject to the Social Security tax—taking it from $17,700 in 1978 to $29,700 in 1981. Here the surprise is that legislators raised the wage base so rapidly, a 68 percent increase spread over three years. The origin of the maximum taxable wage base is murky. The original 1935 proposal offered no coverage to workers earning more than $3,000 annually, then about 3 percent of the workforce. Apparently no one was worried about whether affluent workers could afford retirement, so program designers simply excluded them from the program—no taxes, no benefits. Several weeks later, however, the House Ways and Means Committee decided to eliminate this exclusion, in part because it would be administratively cumbersome when affluent workers' wages drifted above or below the threshold. The committee simply transformed the $3,000 threshold for coverage into a ceiling on taxed wages, and thus on earned benefits.[67] Although Congress raised the maximum taxable wage base eight times between 1950 and 1974—always gradually—the increases did not keep up with inflation. What changed in 1977 was that legislators were now desperate to find new revenues. Increasing the wage base became an attractive option because it would affect only one in seven workers. Moreover, by raising the wage base rapidly, legislators could moderate the rate increases, which affected all workers.[68]

Legislators displayed extraordinary support for the Social Security system when they enacted the Social Security Amendments of 1977. This time it was the president recommending fundamental changes in the revenue structure while legislators stood firmly against such alterations. Legislators worked diligently to preserve a self-supporting, pay-as-you-go system where workers and employers shared all costs equally. It was no longer Roosevelt's retirement program. It was theirs.

Legislators also revealed strong preferences for protecting current retirees over current workers. They could have fiddled with the automatic adjustment mechanism to moderate the growth of benefits. Perhaps when inflation exceeded wage growth, retiree benefits could be indexed to wage growth. Such a modification would help synchronize Social Security's revenue and expenditure streams. Instead, legislators raised the tax rate by 25 percent and the wage base by 68 percent. Legislators were also willing to differentiate among taxpayers. By raising the maximum taxable wage base substantially, they ensured that the richest workers would pay more than others to rescue Social Security. Clearly, legislators feared the electoral wrath of retirees more than that of workers, and the wrath of ordinary workers more than that of affluent workers.

Legislators did what was necessary to keep Social Security solvent, but they did so with little enthusiasm and great difficulty. A quarter century of expanding Social Security benefits had been a bipartisan romp. Imposing large costs on workers and their employers was dreadful. Conflict within the House Ways and Means Committee and the Senate Finance Committee over how to allocate costs spilled onto the House and Senate floors, where legislators proposed, and sometimes approved, revisions to the committees' recommendations. The House held 12 roll call votes, some of them close.[69] The Senate held 21 roll call votes, including one where Vice President Mondale had to break a tie.[70] Moreover, the votes were increasingly partisan as legislators indulged their core supporters. Republican senators proposed reducing the pain for well-off workers by scaling back the proposed increases in the maximum taxable wage base and raising the proposed increases in the tax rate. They lost by a single vote. Legislators showed little appetite for the perilous politics of fixing Social Security.

Contraction

When they enacted the Social Security Amendments of 1977, legislators thought they had fixed Social Security for many decades. In fact, the fix lasted three years. The actuaries soon forecast both near-term deficits, again a consequence of soaring inflation and elevated unemployment, and long-term deficits, largely the consequence of demographic changes.[71] The economic problems were unprecedented. The actuaries forecast 28 percent inflation from 1978 to 1982. Actual inflation was 60 percent. The actuaries forecast 13 percent real-wage growth for the same period. In fact, real wages *declined* by 7 percent.[72] Declining real wages could not possibly support benefits that were now increasing automatically with inflation.

The near-term deficits were the action-forcing problem. Once the tiny contingency reserve hit zero, program administrators would have no choice but to cut retirees' monthly benefits. But the long-term demographic problems— declining fertility and declining mortality—were also serious. The baby boomers, the huge generation born between 1946 and 1964, who were providing a huge boost to revenues during their working years, were producing fewer children than their parents did. Once the baby boomers retired, fewer workers would be available to support them. Moreover, life expectancy continued to increase. So far, the cost of paying benefits for a few extra years had been obscured by the influx of revenues as larger cohorts joined the workforce. But what would happen when the boomers retired and then lived even longer than their parents and grandparents?

Four months after taking office, President Reagan addressed both the near-term deficits and the long-term demographic problems. He proposed massive benefit reductions for both current and future retirees. Among other things, he advocated reducing benefits for those choosing to retire at age 62 by nearly a third, from 80 percent of full benefits to 55 percent. This immense cut would be effective immediately—no phase-in, no gradualism, no time for seniors to prepare. In addition, current beneficiaries would lose a quarter of the 11.2 percent cost-of-living adjustment scheduled for 1981. Future beneficiaries would face a much less generous benefit formula than current beneficiaries enjoyed. The benefit reductions were so enormous that the president proposed reducing some of the 1977 tax increases scheduled for 1985 and 1990.[73]

Democrats in Congress were ecstatic. Having just lost control of both the presidency and the Senate to the Republicans, and fearful of losing control of the House in 1982, Democrats desperately needed an issue to use against the president. It would be hard to imagine a better one than Social Security. The program was not only crucial to the financial health of 36 million beneficiaries, it remained popular among all age cohorts. Republicans in Congress were appalled. They knew any association with such brutal benefit cuts would be dangerous to their electoral well-being.

The ensuing rhetoric was memorable. The next day, Speaker Thomas O'Neil (D-MA) charged that Republicans were "willing to balance the budget on the backs of the elderly." The House Democratic caucus unanimously approved a resolution that called the proposal to reduce early retirement benefits "an unconscionable breach of faith with the first generation of workers that has contributed to Social Security for their whole lives." When Senator Robert Dole (R-KS), chair of the Senate Finance Committee, sponsored a resolution stating that Congress should not "precipitously and unfairly penalize early retirees," the Senate adopted it unanimously.[74] Nine days after proposing his solvency plan, the president abandoned it.

The atmosphere for problem solving quickly became poisonous. Before the president unveiled his plan, the House Ways and Means Committee had been quietly drafting a bipartisan bill that would have shared the unavoidable pain among current workers, near retirees, and future retirees.[75] Once Reagan forced the issue on the public agenda, however, legislators stopped negotiating. No one wished to be called an "enemy of Social Security" by advocating painful fixes. Yet all the fixes were painful. What legislators needed was a procedure to negotiate a rescue package outside the partisan halls of Congress.

Eventually, Congress and the president delegated the task of drafting a solvency plan to a bipartisan commission.[76] The president, the House Speaker, and the Senate majority leader each appointed five members. Known as the Greenspan Commission—after its chair, Alan Greenspan—it included four senators, three representatives, two former representatives, and six people from the worlds of business, labor, and social insurance. Eight were Republicans; seven were Democrats. To give the commission time to act, Congress authorized the Social Security Administration to borrow funds from the Medicare and disability trust funds to shore up the retirement trust fund. If Congress did not act by June 1983, however, the borrowing authority would expire and the government would be unable to pay full retirement benefits in July.

The commission drafted a plan that carefully allocated the rescue costs. On the revenue side, tax rates that were already scheduled to increase in 1985 and 1990 would increase sooner. Self-employed workers would lose their preferential tax rate. On the benefit side, all current and future cost-of-living adjustments would be postponed for six months, and upper-income retirees would have their benefits effectively reduced by paying income taxes on a portion of those benefits.[77] Coverage would become mandatory for employees of nonprofit organizations, all elected and appointed federal officials, and all new employees of the federal government. These coverage extensions would contribute to solvency because government workers earn more, on average, than nongovernmental workers, and because new participants pay taxes long before they claim benefits.

Although the commission's recommendations would fix the short-term solvency problem, members were unable to solve the long-term problem. Most Democratic members of the commission favored increasing the payroll tax. Most Republicans preferred cutting benefits—for example, by raising the retirement age. Eventually, the House of Representatives, before approving the commission's plan, addressed the long-term problem. Representatives rejected a floor amendment that would have raised the tax rate from 6.20 percent to 6.73 percent in 2010, and approved an amendment that would raise the full retirement age from 65 to 67. Enough Democrats sided with the minority Republicans to choose future benefit cuts over future tax increases.[78] When possible, policymakers imposed costs gradually. It would take 7 years before self-employed workers would pay their full share, and 39 years before the full retirement age would reach 67. The only immediacy was that legislators no longer exempted themselves from Social Security. They could no longer justify imposing costs on everyone but themselves.

The 1983 solvency plan was a stark departure for Congress. Legislators had spent decades expanding Social Security, never once cutting benefits. The 1977 solvency plan continued down the same path, imposing costs on workers and employers, while completely protecting beneficiaries—both current and future—from any benefit cuts. Finally, benefit reductions took the lead. Net benefit cuts closed 70 percent of the 75-year actuarial shortfall. By comparison, total tax increases closed 10 percent of the shortfall and coverage extensions 20 percent (see table 2.1, right column).[79]

Before turning to the question of why legislators approved a solvency plan that relied so heavily on benefit cuts, we need to examine how the various revenue and benefit provisions affected both short-term solvency (the first 7 years) and long-term solvency (the full 75 years). The reason for separating the short- and long-term effects is that legislators think differently about what happens in the first few years after enactment compared with what happens in the distant future.

As table 2.1 shows, tax increases were 35 percent of the short-term solution, but only 10 percent of the long-term solution. The reason for the sharp drop is that the largest short-term revenue enhancer—accelerating rate increases that were already scheduled for implementation in 1985 and 1990—provided no extra revenue after 1990. Only two measures raised additional revenue

TABLE 2.1. Projected Impact of 1983 Bill on Short-Term and Long-Term Solvency, 1983–2058

	Share of Solution	
Policy Provision	1983–89 (%)	1983–2058 (%)
Higher Taxes for Contributors		
Increase tax rate for self-employed workers	11	8
Accelerate already-scheduled tax rate increases	24	1
Income tax on contributions to 401(k) plans		1
Total tax increases	35	10
Lower Benefits for Beneficiaries		
Raise full retirement age from 65 to 67		34
Tax upper-income beneficiaries on part of benefits	16	29
Delay COLA by six months (forever)	24	14
Eliminate windfall benefits for government workers		2
Total benefit cuts	40	79
(Increase benefits for several groups)	(1)	(9)
Net benefit cuts	39	70
Coverage Extensions		
Extend coverage to currently uncovered workers	16	20
Other		
Accelerate federal payments for military service credits	10	
Total	100	100

Sources: Svahn and Ross 1983, tables 1 and 4; Gregory et al. 2010.

COLA, cost-of-living adjustment.

beyond that year. Raising the tax rate for self-employed workers covered 8 percent of long-term solvency costs; taxing employee contributions to retirement plans covered 1 percent. The various coverage extensions had similar short- and long-term impacts (16 and 20 percent). Accelerating transfers from the regular budget to the Social Security trust fund to cover earned but not yet disbursed benefits for military personnel was an important short-term infusion—the entire transfer took place in 1983—but it had no long-term impact.

Net benefit cuts covered 39 percent of short-term solvency costs and 70 percent of long-term costs. Raising the retirement age, which had no short-term impact, covered 34 percent of long-term costs. Taxing upper-income retirees on a portion of their benefits covered 16 percent of short-term costs but 29 percent of long-term costs. The reason for the increased impact is that policymakers did not index the income threshold for inflation, so the tax eventually ensnared middle-income retirees. Delaying cost-of-living adjustments covered 24 percent of the short-term costs and 14 percent of the long-term costs. Although these long-term benefit cuts totaled 79 percent of solvency costs, the overall plan also increased benefits for several groups, so net benefit cuts were 70 percent.[80]

It is a mystery why many observers call the 1983 reform a grand compromise, a share-the-pain reform requiring sacrifices by all participants. A plan where benefit cuts are seven times greater than tax increases does not sound like a compromise. A plan where Congress raised neither the tax rate nor the maximum taxable wage base does not seem like it shared the pain very widely. The reason for people's confusion—including my own in previous work—is that *short-term* benefit cuts were roughly equal to short-term tax increases.[81] Only in the long term did beneficiaries bear most costs.

One explanation for why legislators approved so much benefit cutting is that Democrats no longer controlled the agenda. In 1977, they held the House, Senate, and presidency. In 1983, they held only the House. Shared control allowed a wider range of alternatives to reach the decision agenda. Second, President Reagan simply ruled out raising the tax rate. He was a tax cutter, not a tax raiser, and that was his bottom line. Third, many legislators had been hearing from constituents about how unhappy they were with the huge 1977 tax increases. Indeed, the outcry was so great that in 1978 the Democratic caucus voted 150 to 57 to instruct the Ways and Means Committee to find a way to roll back increases in the payroll tax.[82] Fourth, there was a rightward drift in views about taxes, not just among Republicans, but also among some Democrats. Given these changes, many legislators feared giving future challengers a "voted-for-higher-taxes" bludgeon to use against them.

Both sides worried about the short-term solvency problem. No one wanted to be blamed for reducing the July benefit checks. For the short term, therefore, policymakers did agree to share the political pain as equally as possible. During the serious negotiations within the Gang of Nine—the subset of the commission that drafted the solvency plan—members first decided on a 50–50 split between tax increases and benefit cuts before then selecting an acceptable mix. Republicans' big concession was to raise the tax rate for self-employed workers and accelerate already-scheduled rate increases for everyone else. Democrats' big concession was to postpone cost-of-living increases. Then, a gift from the gods arrived. On a proposal to tax the Social Security benefits of upper-income retirees, Democrats considered the provision a tax increase, while Republicans considered it a benefit cut. Those differing perspectives allowed for the Gang's final compromise.[83] In reality, of course, it was a benefit cut. It made no difference whether the Social Security Administration applied the cuts before mailing out the checks or the Internal Revenue Service clawed back some of the benefits after the checks cleared. Either way, upper-income folks lost a portion of their retirement benefits.

Elected officials had much less to fear from making long-term changes because the changes would not occur while they were in office. Once short-term insolvency was off the table, they could refuse to compromise and nothing horrible would happen. President Reagan could stand firm against raising the tax rate beyond its 1990 level. What mattered to him was reducing the scale of government. If it took a few years longer, so be it. Representative Claude Pepper (D-FL), the octogenarian champion of Social Security, a member of the Greenspan Committee, and chair of the gatekeeping House Rules Committee, could insist on future tax increases to protect future beneficiaries. In such an environment, the commission was unable to close the long-term solvency gap.

Two surprises occurred on the House floor. One was that legislators closed the entire 75-year actuarial gap, something that had eluded the Greenspan Commission. Another was that in a chamber dominated by Democrats—the same Democrats who approved the tax-only solvency plan in 1977—legislators chose to raise the full retirement age from 65 to 67 beginning in 2000 rather than raise the tax rate beginning in 2010. The decision tree, engineered by Claude Pepper himself, involved first voting on an amendment, sponsored by Representative Jake Pickle (D-TX), chair of the House subcommittee on Social Security, to raise the retirement age, and then voting on Pepper's substitute amendment that, if approved, would raise the tax rate, not the retirement age. Dubbed "the battle of the condiments" in the press, Pepper lost badly.[84] House members first approved the Pickle amendment 228 to 202, with 76 Democrats joining 152 Republicans. Then the Democrats split evenly 131–131 to join a nearly unanimous Republican caucus in rejecting the tax increase, 296 to 132.

Why would legislators choose future benefit cuts over future tax increases? In retrospect, the political risks of raising the retirement age were small. Labor unions were the principal opponents. Although that mattered in some northern districts, it did not matter for Republicans or Southern Democrats. Moreover, the proposal would not affect anyone over 45. Younger folks were much less attentive to the Social Security debate than their elders. But mostly it reflected an unhappiness with another vote to raise taxes, so soon after the 1977 vote. It was now a tax-cutting era and many legislators were reluctant to give future challengers a sharp weapon to use against them.

Five things stand out about the 1983 rescue. First, it took the impending insolvency of the trust fund to impel action. Absent a crisis, legislators would not have made the painful modifications designed to prepare for the retirement of the baby boom generation, still decades away. Second, no group escaped cuts, not even current retirees. Third, overall support for raising Social Security taxes was lower than ever before. Fourth, the partisan divide deepened. Republicans became more concerned about the size of Social Security, more interested in restricting its growth, more worried about its effect on national savings and the economy, and more amenable to cutting benefits. Democrats were more concerned about preserving benefits and more willing to tolerate some tax increases, especially in the near term to forestall immediate cuts. Fifth, elected officials began to think of Social Security as "the third rail of American politics," meaning that touching it was as dangerous as grabbing the electrified rail that powers underground trains.[85] In short, the politics of Social Security was no longer delightful. It was perilous.

Evolution of Social Security

In 1935, few legislators were enthusiastic about enacting Social Security because it delivered no benefits in the near term. They voted for President Roosevelt's signature program not because it was politically attractive but because it was part of an omnibus bill that included other appealing programs, including old-age assistance, unemployment insurance, and financial support for expectant mothers, newborns, needy children, and the blind. By 1981, when President Reagan proposed massive cuts to Social Security, legislators had become the program's greatest champions. Not even his staunchest supporters in Congress joined the president in advocating deep reductions in Social Security benefits. Indeed, the Senate voted unanimously to reject the president's scheme to cut benefits for early retirees.

The reason for legislators' change of heart was simple: Social Security was no longer a proposed program that would start delivering benefits to a small cohort of retirees seven years after enactment. Social Security in 1981 was actually delivering $141 billion in annual benefits—4.5 percent of GDP—to 36 million retirees, disabled workers, spouses, dependents, and survivors. A program that once had just potential beneficiaries was now a program providing essential benefits to many Americans. Moreover, beneficiaries considered them *earned* benefits—earned by a lifetime of payroll contributions.

The politics of expansion between 1939 and 1973 was a happy time for leg-islators. Whenever congressional committees recommended expanding Social Security, supermajorities in both houses and in both parties voted to approve their recommendations.[86] No one should be surprised that 9 of the 12 benefit increases took effect in election years, including 4 in September, the traditional launch of campaign season. The politics of contraction between 1975 and 1983 was more difficult. Legislators hate to impose costs. And yet large costs were necessary to block automatic benefit reductions. No one should be surprised that Congress enacted both rescue plans in nonelection years.

Legislators behaved nobly in 1983 when they took actions that created a large trust fund, thus moving Social Security away from the strictly pay-as-you-go system that had operated for four decades. They could have deferred the baby boom problem to the future—that is what legislators usually do—allowing their successors to adjust tax and benefit rates when the boomers started to retire. Instead, they raised taxes moderately, cut benefits heavily, mostly by raising the retirement age, and invested the surplus revenue in the trust fund, thus creating an asset bulge that would match the demographic bulge. But the asset bulge, and therefore the movement toward advance fund-ing, was largely inadvertent. Legislators were trying to solve a long-term sol-vency problem, and they chose options that would do so. But as Alan Jacobs has shown, no one quite noticed that their actions would create a large trust fund.[87] In short, the movement toward advance funding was more accident than choice.

No one anticipated the political instability of advance-funded systems. President Roosevelt's advance-funded system lasted only four years before legislators began their successful effort to replace it with a pay-as-you-go sys-tem. Legislators in the 1940s found little appeal in taxing workers just to fill a trust fund. To be sure, the trust fund created by the 1983 reform has survived, untouched, for decades. That is to say, legislators have done nothing to threaten its existence, perhaps because AARP (previously the American Association of Retired Persons) and other groups have been vigilant watchdogs. But nei-ther have legislators done anything to augment the reserve, despite knowing that the trust fund is too small to deal with the entire demographic bulge. The basic problem is that one cohort of legislators cannot bind future legislative cohorts to maintain or enhance their policies. The forward-looking House members in 1983 were outliers. Their successors have been typical legislators—more worried more about the next election than about the judgment of history.

It is worth emphasizing that the enlarged trust fund has enhanced intergenerational equity by making boomers part of the solution to their own demographic bulge. The enlarged trust fund has also postponed the day of reckoning. But by shielding legislators from the reality that tax revenues have been insufficient to support Social Security benefits since 2010, the trust fund is allowing the fiscal cliff to reach historic levels. Tax revenues today cover 93 percent of benefits; the rest are funded by trust fund interest and trust fund redemptions. By 2034, when the trust fund finally disappears, tax revenues will cover only 79 percent of benefits.

The next chapter explores how citizens reacted to the creation and evolution of Social Security. The switch is from Washington politics to citizen politics.

3

Public Reactions

PUBLIC OPINION is an important part of Social Security's narrative. It tells us how citizens reacted to a program that officials created in 1935 and then modified over the next half century. Public opinion also acts as a stimulus and a constraint on policymakers' subsequent actions. Legislators care not only where the public stands on Social Security today, but also how the public might react if legislators enact specific remedies or if they fail to forestall insolvency. Understanding current and future opinion is a central task for this book.

This chapter begins the exploration of public opinion by focusing on how people reacted to Social Security's creation and development. Chapter 7 then focuses on how various subsets of the public reacted, comparing, for example, workers and retirees, the young and the old, the poor and the prosperous, and Democrats and Republicans. Chapters 10 and 11 investigate where citizens stand on various options to restore solvency, including raising the retirement age, increasing taxes, and privatization. These chapters also explore how the public's views might change as insolvency nears.

It helps us think about public opinion—and particularly to imagine how public opinion might change as legislators consider solvency options—if we consider how opinion relates to self-interest.[1] I consider opinion as *private regarding* to the extent that people consider what is best for themselves and their families, and *public regarding* to the extent they consider what is best for society as a whole.[2] We regularly hear both types of arguments when people are discussing Social Security. When advocates emphasize the importance of social insurance for protecting seniors from poverty, or when critics argue that social programs destroy incentives for work, saving, and investment, we are hearing public-regarding arguments. When people object to a solvency plan because the costs would be concentrated on people like them—for example, raising the retirement age would require their age cohort to work longer than previous age cohorts—we are hearing private-regarding arguments.

Policy preferences are often based on a mix of public- and private-regarding considerations that people have absorbed from the media, friends, and family. Many of these considerations are rooted in arguments initially advanced by policy experts, interest groups, and elected politicians.[3] It is not important whether individuals recognize the differing bases for their own preferences. It is important, however, that elected officials consider the distinction. The reason is that public opinion evolves differently to the extent that it rests on self-interest. For example, legislators may choose differently when deciding to raise taxes if they believe their constituents care more about their own personal taxes than about whether taxes are allocated according to some fair-minded principles for burden sharing.

The next three sections highlight Social Security's evolution from the perspective of workers and beneficiaries. These findings provide the foundation for discussing the historical development of public support for the program.

Experiencing Social Security

Soon after President Roosevelt signed the Social Security Act of 1935, government officials began planning for its implementation. According to the statute, retirement benefits would be based on each worker's lifetime taxable wages. So, the government had to record workers' wages beginning in January 1937, and it had to track those wages for decades to come, no matter how often workers changed jobs, residences, or names. It was a daunting task for a fledgling agency in a computerless world. To track the legions of Smiths, Browns, and Millers, the Social Security Board decided to assign a nine-digit number to each worker. But how could the newly created board, with little staff or budget, assign unique numbers to tens of millions of people in just a few months?

The solution was one part delegation, one part marketing. The board enlisted the post office to distribute applications, collect completed applications, and type and distribute identification cards.[4] Meanwhile, the board prepared marketing materials that explained how the program would operate and urged workers to apply for a card. By the end of the three-month campaign, the board had distributed 58 million pamphlets, issued press releases in 24 languages, and arranged 12 nationwide radio broadcasts. In movie houses across the land, 45 million people viewed the board's short film about Social Security, which was a trailer attached to the popular newsreels.[5]

One measure of the campaign's success was that 22 million workers—two-thirds of the target population—applied for Social Security cards in the first month. Another was that the post office issued 26 million cards during the first four months. Accompanying each card was a pamphlet that informed workers how Social Security operated, how the tax was split between workers and employers, and how those contributions would guarantee monthly benefits when they turned 65.[6] Wartime measures aside, it is hard to think of a more successful attempt to inform people about a government program.

Workers

Soon the marketing was over and people began to experience Social Security directly. In order to explore the link between self-interest and public opinion, we need to know when various groups began to participate in the program. Since Social Security began as an advance-funded program, the early participants were taxpayers, not benefit collectors. Nearly 24 million men and 9 million women—half the American workforce—encountered Social Security in 1937, when employers began withholding 1 percent from their wages. The median wage for those workers was $761 annually, so the typical worker contributed $7.61 annually ($136 in 2020 dollars). Of course, employers matched everything that workers contributed. Today Social Security is larger and more expensive. In the most recent year for which comparable wage data exist (2018), 91 million men and 85 million women—almost the entire American workforce—contributed 6.2 percent of their wages to the program. The median wage for these workers, including part-timers, was $31,356, so the typical worker contributed $1,944.[7]

When did these changes occur? Figure 3.1 displays the growth of contributors over eight decades. It plots workers paying Social Security taxes as a fraction of the working-age population. Notice that most growth happened in the program's first two decades, as the contributor share increased from 41 percent of the working-age population in 1937 to 73 percent in 1957. This was the period when Congress was regularly broadening the system, with notable enactments in 1950, 1954, and 1956. The original program was restricted to workers in industry and commerce. It now includes everyone except for federal workers hired before 1983, about one-quarter of state and local government workers, and members of several religious groups, including the Amish and Mennonites, who provide for their own. A contributing cause of the growth was women's increased role in the labor market. Women were 28 percent of

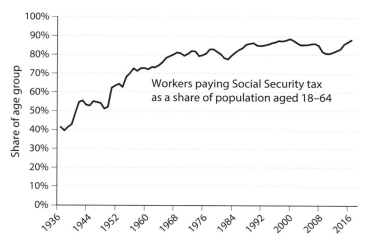

FIGURE 3.1. Social Security taxpayers compared to working-age population, 1937–2017. *Sources*: Social Security Administration 2019a, table 4.B1; Carter et al. 2006, series Bf381. Population adjustments from Carter et al. 2006, series Aa125, Aa139, Aa142, and Census Bureau 2010, 2019a.

contributors in the first year, 38 percent by the end of World War II, and 48 percent in 2017.

Figure 3.2 shows how Social Security's tax rate changed over the same period, for both employed and self-employed workers. Notice how long the initial 1 percent rate lasted (13 years), how long it took before the rate exceeded 4 percent (32 years), and how long it has been since Congress last modified the rate (39 years). After adjusting the tax rate 20 times between 1937 and 1983, legislators have not changed it since the last solvency crisis. The graph also captures the extent to which workers and their employers subsidized self-employed workers between 1950 and 1983. The subsidy is the region between the self-employed rate (dotted line) and the combined worker/employer rate (solid line). Subsidy is the appropriate term because employed and self-employed workers collect benefits under an identical earnings-based formula.

These two figures give us a sense of how contributors experienced Social Security. People who joined the Social Security system early faced low tax rates for many years. Although these rates were lower than what was required to support the original advance-funded system, they were adequate to fund what had quickly become a pay-as-you-go system. Self-employed workers did especially well until the 1983 solvency crisis, after which their subsidy disappeared.

FIGURE 3.2. Social Security tax rates for employed and self-employed workers, 1937–2020. *Source*: Social Security Administration 2019a, table 2.A3.

Beneficiaries

Figure 3.3 displays the growth of beneficiaries over nearly eight decades. Unlike tax paying, benefit collecting began later and grew slowly. A decade after the Social Security bill was enacted, only 6 percent of people aged 65 and over were collecting retirement benefits. Milestones of 25, 50, 75, and 90 percent occurred in 1953, 1957, 1964, and 1981. For disabled workers, the growth in benefit collecting was also slow, increasing from 1 percent of the working-age population in 1960 to 3 percent in 1972 and 5 percent in 2006, where it remains.

Figure 3.4 captures how the value of retirement benefits has changed since the program's inception. All values are inflation adjusted and expressed in 2018 dollars. Average retirement benefits in 1940 were $265 annually, or $4,700 in 2018 dollars. Nine years later, eroded by inflation, they were only $3,100. The following year, Congress increased nominal benefits by 77 percent, thus placing inflation-adjusted benefits 13 percent above their initial level. Never again did inflation take more than small bites from retirement benefits, as Congress gradually raised their real value to an average of $11,500 in 1972. At that point, Congress indexed benefits for inflation. So, why did average retirement benefits continue to rise, reaching $17,500 in 2018? The answer is that initial benefits—what retirees receive during their first year of retirement—reflect

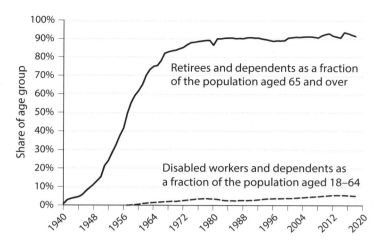

FIGURE 3.3. Social Security beneficiaries compared with target populations, 1940–2018. *Sources*: Social Security Administration 2019a, table 5.A4; Carter et al. 2006, series Bf326, Bf331. Population adjustments from Carter et al. 2006, data series Aa125, Aa139, Aa142, and Census Bureau 2010, 2019a.

FIGURE 3.4. Average annual benefits for retired workers in 2018 dollars, 1940–2018. *Sources*: Social Security Administration 2019a, table 3.C4; Carter et al. 2006, series Bf461.

average wage growth during their working years. When average wages increase, average first-year benefits increase, too.

These two figures give a sense of how beneficiaries experienced Social Security over the years. Throughout the 1940s, beneficiaries were few, benefits were small, and inflation rapidly eroded their value. At the end of this decade, there were still more seniors collecting benefits from the means-tested old-age assistance program than from dues-paying Social Security.[8] Moreover, the average benefit for old-age assistance was 70 percent greater than the average for Social Security.[9] As previously mentioned, Congress eliminated this gap in 1950, raising nominal Social Security benefits by 77 percent. But it was not until 1957 that a majority of people aged 65 or older collected benefits from Social Security. And it took a quarter century (1950–75) before retirement benefits reached a steady-state level comparable to what today's seniors enjoy. Only then did Congress stop raising benefits.

Public Support

When did people develop views about Social Security? Did they develop views while Congress and the president were designing the program? Or did direct encounters with Social Security—paying taxes and collecting benefits—induce people to support or oppose the program?

George Gallup and Elmer Roper launched the nation's first systematic opinion surveys in 1935, during the same months that Congress and the president were designing Social Security. Unfortunately, none of their early surveys asked about the program.[10] So, we have no evidence about what people thought about the program before the Social Security Board's 1936 marketing campaign, or before the Republican candidate for president Alf Landon vowed to repeal Social Security if elected.

In autumn 1936, in the middle of the Social Security Board's marketing campaign and near the end of the presidential campaign, Gallup finally asked, "Do you favor the compulsory old-age insurance plan, starting January 1, which requires employers and employees to make equal monthly contributions?" A total of 69 percent of respondents favored the plan. Six weeks later, support for Social Security was essentially unchanged (68 percent). Gallup asked a third time in early 1937, just as half the workforce began paying the compulsory tax. The survey found 77 percent of respondents favored Social Security, up 8 points from the original reading.[11] Discovering strong support for Social Security, Gallup stopped asking whether respondents approved of the program.

Support was even stronger for the other 1935 program for older people, the one that offered immediate benefits. Late that year, Gallup asked, "Are you in favor of government old-age pensions for needy persons?" This was clearly a question about the old-age assistance program, not Social Security, since it was the only nationwide program for needy retirees. Respondents were strongly supportive, with 89 percent in favor.[12] It seems that legislators had properly gauged their constituents' enthusiasm for old-age assistance when they made it their top priority.

Surveys from the 1940s showed consistent support for Social Security. After the program had been taxing workers for six years and delivering benefits for three, the National Opinion Research Center (NORC) asked, "As you may know, under the present Social Security law, workers in certain occupations have to save money so when they are too old to work they will receive money from the government, like insurance. Do you think this is a good idea or a bad idea?" That year, 95 percent of respondents declared it a good idea. The next year 92 percent agreed.[13] Social Security had become a consensus policy in less than a decade.

Another indication of support for Social Security was that people were eager to expand it. A year after the program began taxing workers, Gallup found 74 percent of respondents favored extending Social Security to include "household help, sailors, farm workers, and employees in small shops." Several years later, NORC found 82 percent of respondents favored extending Social Security to "everybody who works." Gallup asked in 1948 about extending coverage to specific occupations and found support for domestic servants (71 percent), government employees (64), farmers (59), and professional and self-employed people (58).[14]

The evidence from these and other surveys, all conducted before 1950, suggests that people were eager to be part of Social Security and eager to have everyone else part of it, too. When legislators expanded Social Security in 1950, extending compulsory coverage to domestic workers, farm workers, and some self-employed occupations, they were responding to what people wanted.

What is striking about these surveys is that they show strong support for Social Security from the very beginning. Support was strong before workers began to pay the compulsory Social Security tax, and even stronger after. Support continued to grow as seniors began to collect retirement benefits. But the benefit collectors were too few to explain the growth in support. When NORC found in 1944 that 92 percent of adults approved of Social Security, fewer than 5 percent of people aged 65 or older were collecting benefits (see figure 3.3). In fact, benefit collectors did not reach 5 percent of the adult population—that is, 5 percent of a typical opinion survey—until 1953. Although the growth in public support for Social Security might have reflected what respondents were expecting to collect later, or it might have reflected admiration for what the program promised to do for others, it had little to do with benefits that survey respondents were themselves receiving.

Legislators transformed Social Security during the 1950s. Enactments in 1950, 1954, and 1956 broadened coverage to include most occupations. Enactments in 1950, 1952, 1954, and 1958 increased retirement benefits by 141 percent. How did people respond to these changes? It is hard to know for sure. Although surveys asked 26 questions that mentioned Social Security during the 1950s, not a single one asked about programmatic improvements or about overall support for the program. One 1952 survey did ask whether creating Social Security was "a good thing or a mistake." Respondents chose the first option over the second, 90 to 3.[15] With such overwhelming support, pollsters had little reason to keep asking.[16]

Long-Term Trends

What are the long-term trends? How did public support change as Social Security matured? Unfortunately, pollsters seldom asked the same question repeatedly, the usual method for tracking opinion change. There is no Social Security equivalent of Gallup's invaluable question about presidential approval, dating from the 1940s. Beginning in the 1960s, however, pollsters started to ask similar questions, and beginning in 1984, a single question became the standard for tracking opinion change. I have stitched together 43 surveys between 1961 and 2018, where interviewers asked respondents some variant of whether we are "spending too much, too little, or about the right amount on Social Security." Figure 3.5 displays the results of my sewing project.[17]

Three things stand out. First, people were broadly supportive of Social Security throughout the entire 58-year period. Only a tiny minority, averaging 7 percent, believed we were spending too much on the program. Second, the most common response was that we were spending too little, with an average of 60 percent choosing this option. Indeed, this option was more popular than the "spending about right" alternative in 42 out of 43 surveys. Third, the discontinuities were not large when question wordings changed (noted with vertical lines). In short, the various questions seemed to be measuring the same underlying attitude about Social Security.

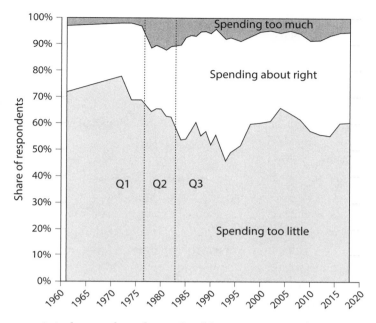

FIGURE 3.5. Attitudes toward spending on Social Security, 1961–2018. The two vertical lines show where question wordings changed. Question 1—before 1976, pollsters asked various questions about spending more money, less money, or about the same amount on Social Security. Question 2—from 1978 to 1982: "Please tell me if you would like the government to do more, do less, or do about the same as they have been on improving Social Security benefits." Question 3—from 1984 to 2018: "Are we spending too much, too little, or about the right amount on Social Security?"

Sources: Shapiro and Smith 1985; General Social Survey 2019.

How can we explain fluctuations in support for the ever-popular "spending too little" alternative? One possibility is that the shifts had nothing to do with Social Security and merely reflected changes in what James Stimson calls the *public mood*—the overall support for more or less government.[18] In fact, the correlation between public mood and support for the "spending too little" option is zero.[19] The basic problem is that the two measures moved in opposite directions during the 1980s and 1990s. Public mood was becoming increasingly liberal during the 1980s. Meanwhile, after Congress fixed the solvency problem in 1983, people were more likely than before to say that Social Security spending was "about right." Once insolvency returned to the agenda in the 1990s, people again favored more Social Security spending, but by then, the public mood was becoming more conservative. In short, opinion changes about

Social Security seem to be driven by happenings in Social Security land, not by broader forces that affect the public mood.[20]

Social Security Tax

What do people think about Social Security's payroll tax? Do they understand the direct connection between taxes and benefits? Does that connection make the tax more palatable than other kinds of taxes?

Once again, Gallup took the lead. In early 1938, just a year after workers began paying the new tax, interviewers asked, "Do you approve of the Social Security tax on wages?" A total of 73 percent approved. They next asked, "Do you think the Social Security law should be changed to make the employer pay the whole amount of the Security tax?" Only 15 percent leaped at the chance to shift the tax burden from workers to employers. A few months later, Roper asked which of several taxes was the most unjust. Only 12 percent chose the Social Security tax, placing it behind sales, real estate, and gasoline taxes. In summer 1941, Gallup asked whether "you would be willing to pay three cents of every dollar of your income until you are 60 in order to get a pension from the government of $50 a month?" Seventy-six percent said they were willing to pay the proposed levy, which was *triple* the existing Social Security tax.[21] By now, few readers will be surprised to learn that pollsters stopped asking about the Social Security tax once it was clear how few people objected.

More recent surveys show that people continue to value the Social Security tax, especially compared with other taxes. When interviewers asked whether respondents preferred cuts in the federal income tax or the Social Security tax, they chose the former 74 to 17 percent in 1978, and 78 to 14 percent in 1990. When asked about reducing one of several taxes, respondents chose income (49 percent), property (33 percent), and sales taxes (9 percent) before the Social Security tax (8 percent).[22] On seven occasions between 1978 and 2003, surveys asked which "is the worst tax—that is, the least fair?" Averaged across seven surveys, people chose local property (36 percent), federal income (30 percent), state sales (17 percent), and Social Security (17 percent) taxes.[23] The most recent survey (2015) shows little change, with income and property taxes considered least fair by 33 and 32 percent, and Social Security and sales taxes least fair by 18 and 17 percent.[24]

Why do people believe the Social Security tax is a better tax—a fairer tax— than the federal income tax? Given the actual incidence of the two taxes, we might expect that most people would prefer the progressive income tax rather than the regressive payroll tax. For instance, most people pay far more in Social Security taxes than they do in income taxes. That was true in 1937, when 32.9 million workers paid Social Security taxes, while only 3.4 million paid income taxes.[25] And it is true today, when two-thirds of taxpayers pay more in Social Security and Medicare taxes than they do in federal income taxes.[26] Moreover, the income tax is progressive, with rates ranging from 10 to 37 percent, whereas Social Security imposes an identical 6.2 percent tax on everyone. The income tax also avoids taxing earnings until they exceed the standard deduction ($25,100 in 2021 for joint filers), whereas Social Security taxes begin with the first dollar earned. Finally, Social Security exempts all wages above the maximum taxable wage base, so the rich pay an effective tax rate that is lower than the rate for everyone else. In short, the income tax bites the rich; the Social Security tax bites the poor.

The puzzle of why so many people prefer the regressive Social Security tax to the progressive income tax has a simple answer. Paying the Social Security tax entitles the payer to collect valued benefits. It is the price of admission. Paying the income tax delivers nothing so personal. It is what people do to avoid fines, prison, and public humiliation. It is easy for people to applaud cuts in the income tax because they believe government wastes money doing many disagreeable things. But few people think Social Security does disagreeable things.

A second explanation is that many people misperceive the size of Social Security's payroll tax. Vanessa Williamson, the leading expert on how Americans think about taxes, first interviewed by phone a sample of 49 adults for about an hour in 2013 and 2014, and then conducted a more typical fixed-choice survey of 1,000 adults in 2014. Although most respondents were aware of the payroll tax, knew that it supported Social Security benefits for current retirees, and valued the overall program, they were more likely to believe that their own income taxes exceeded their own payroll taxes, even when their reported incomes made it clear that the opposite was true. Williamson believes this pattern reflects the higher visibility of income taxes. Although employers withhold both income and payroll taxes from workers' wages, the income tax requires that workers subsequently file tax returns, but not before considering other income sources and various deductions, while the payroll tax requires no effort at all. Indeed, the more Williamson pressed her interviewees about the payroll tax, the more she heard about the benefits of Social Security, not about the tax. Her conclusion: "The design of the payroll tax is something of an engineering marvel—it draws attention to benefits and away from costs."[27]

Conclusion

People have shown remarkable support for Social Security over the past eight decades. Although we have no evidence about what people thought about a government-run compulsory retirement program before President Roosevelt proposed one in 1935, surveys revealed strong support for the program a year later when pollsters first inquired. Support remained strong as Congress raised the payroll tax from 1 percent to 6.2 percent. It remained strong through recessions, inflation, stagflation, and two solvency crises. Support was unchanged when President Reagan proposed deep benefit cuts in 1981, and when President Bush proposed wholesale restructuring in 2005.

It is important to note that huge majorities supported Social Security from the very start—77 percent in early 1937—even though the program was just beginning, eligibility was restricted to just half the national workforce, and the early participants were taxpayers, not beneficiaries. This early support suggests that the public liked the *idea* of Social Security, despite the exclusion of so many workers. Put differently, early support could not have been based on just the private-regarding considerations of "what's in it for me?" Support rested, at least in part, on public-regarding considerations.

Eventually, Social Security became nearly a universal program, enrolling most workers and delivering substantial benefits to most retirees. As it did, self-interest provided a second foundation for public support. Perhaps in the first few years legislators could have reversed course and terminated the program, just as they repealed, a year after enactment, the Medicare Catastrophic Coverage Act of 1988.[28] After all, there were no active Social Security beneficiaries until 1940, and not very many in the next half decade. But as time passed, more and more workers had spent years contributing to Social Security, and more and more seniors were collecting substantial retirement benefits. This gave most participants a very strong interest in the program's survival and financial health.

Widespread public support for Social Security does not guarantee that the program will continue unchanged. So far, Congress has resolved two solvency crises. In 1977, legislators protected all benefits for current and future beneficiaries by raising both the tax rate and the maximum taxable wage base, thus imposing all solvency burdens on workers and their employers. In 1983, they made the opposite choice, refusing to raise either the tax rate or the maximum taxable wage base, thus imposing large cuts on future beneficiaries and smaller cuts on current beneficiaries.

The next chapter explores the design principles for retirement systems. The aim is to understand the advantages and disadvantages of the choices that legislators made between 1935 and 1983. It also examines the reasons why some policymakers seek to reinvent Social Security.

PART II

The Policy Options

4

Reinventing Social Security

FIXING SOCIAL SECURITY is a difficult political problem because legislators hate to impose costs on their constituents. But it is not an intractable *policy* problem, like eliminating racism in society, something that no one knows how to accomplish. Fixing Social Security can be accomplished by simple things, like raising the retirement age, increasing taxes, or modifying cost-of-living adjustments. In that sense, it resembles all the other budgetary problems that legislators regularly resolve.

Fixing Social Security is a straightforward problem, however, only for legislators who believe that the program's structure is fundamentally sound. Some policymakers believe it is not. They propose reinventing the system. One argument they make is that advance funding would be a better foundation for retirement policy than pay-as-you-go financing. Since Congress has twice established, and twice effectively abandoned, advance funding for Social Security, these critics seek to design an advance-funded system that would be self-sustaining. Another argument is that retirees in the current system do not earn a fair return on what they contribute to the system. It is not just that workers could earn a better return by investing their own money, but also that overall returns decline for each successive generation. A third argument is that retirement policy needs to be better insulated from demographic changes—insulated from baby booms, baby busts, and continual increases in life expectancy.

This is the first of two chapters on policy design. My concern here is not with political questions, such as who supports and who opposes specific policy options, but rather with what the arguments are for and against each alternative. Subsequent chapters then focus on the politics of selecting options from the overall choice set.

Alternative Retirement Systems

Part of the debate about Social Security concerns whether individual responsibility or social insurance offers a better foundation for a public retirement system. This debate was central to the conflict over creating Social Security in 1935. It reappeared when Congress established Medicare for seniors in 1965. It was an important element in President Bush's campaign to reduce the scale of traditional Social Security and create personal retirement accounts in 2005. It is the principal cleavage between various plans for fixing Social Security today.

The *individual responsibility model* suggests that government should play a lesser role in preparing people for retirement.[1] Some proponents object particularly to compulsory programs such as Social Security. Why should government force people to contribute to a national retirement program rather than allowing them as free citizens to plan for their own future, whether by building businesses, assembling nest eggs, relying on their children, or working until their demise?

The *social insurance model* suggests that government should play a major role in preparing individuals for retirement.[2] Its proponents remind us that many people are not good savers for distant goals. They also underestimate what is required to support a minimum standard of living in retirement, especially as longevity continues to increase. Moreover, some people never earn enough during their working years to save for an adequate retirement. Compulsory social insurance is a mechanism to pool risks and help guarantee a minimum standard for all. It is the guiding philosophy behind not just Social Security's retirement, survivor, and disability benefits, but also Medicare, unemployment insurance, and workers' compensation.

Current retirement policy reflects a blend of the two approaches. Although Social Security rests firmly on the social insurance model, the strong relationship between years worked and benefits received underscores the importance of individual responsibility. These benefits are earned, not granted, and the longer one works, the more one collects. But coexisting with Social Security is a private retirement system that rests firmly on individual responsibility. This *private retirement system* excludes only retirement plans that federal, state, and local governments manage for their own employees. Included in the private retirement system are employer-based plans, some of them defined benefit, others defined contribution, as well as plans for self-employed workers and for people who lack access to employment-based plans.

Some experts and some policymakers propose reinventing Social Security and making it more like the private retirement system. Such proposals raise several questions. How does the private retirement system operate? Does it provide a good model for a national retirement system? And does it make sense to have both the public and private retirement systems operate according to the same design principles? This chapter addresses these questions in turn.

Private Retirement System

The private retirement system emerged in the late nineteenth and early twentieth centuries, long before Congress created Social Security.[3] The early system was small, unregulated, and concentrated in a few industries—notably, railroads, banking, and public utilities. Early retirement plans were exclusively defined benefit plans, those where employers paid retiree benefits based on some formula. Defined benefit plans grew steadily over the decades, reaching a peak of 30 million private sector participants in 1984. Since then, these plans have declined in number. Private sector defined benefit plans today have only 13 million active participants.[4]

Defined benefit plans promise a lifelong stream of retirement benefits based on an established formula, typically including years of service and recent or career-average earnings. Employers bear the costs of these pension plans, usually by setting aside funds in advance and then using investment earnings to pay retirement benefits. If investment earnings prove insufficient, employers use corporate assets to pay benefits. Defined benefit plans are attractive to retirees because employers bear both investment and longevity risks. That is, employers are responsible for paying benefits even if investments perform poorly or retirees live longer than expected.

Most private sector plans today are *defined contribution plans*, where workers, and sometimes employers, contribute to individually controlled accounts that are invested to fund each worker's retirement. Here the costs are perfectly predictable—the sum of what workers and employers contribute—while the benefits are unpredictable. Retirement benefits depend on how workers allocate their contributions among investment choices and how well their investments perform. Retirees decide how to spend down their assets without knowing how long they will live. In short, retirees bear both investment and longevity risks. Private sector defined contribution plans today have more than 83 million active participants.[5]

TABLE 4.1. Assets in Private Retirement Plans, December 31, 2020

Control	Type of Plan	Assets ($B)	Assets ($B)	Share (%)
Worker	Individual retirement accounts		12,210	48
Worker	Defined contribution plans		9,637	38
	401(k) plans	6,725		
	403(b) plans	1,189		
	457 plans	384		
	Keogh and other	600		
	Federal Thrift Savings Plan	739		
Employer	Defined benefit plans (private sector)		3,391	14
	Total assets		25,238	100

Source: Investment Company Institute 2021, tables 1 and 6.

Assets in the private retirement system total more than $25 trillion—an enormous sum. By comparison, the total value of all stocks in the S&P 500 is only one-quarter greater.[6] As table 4.1 shows, most of these retirement assets are in accounts that workers control directly. These assets include $9.6 trillion in defined contribution plans, where employers create a menu of stock and bond funds, and workers decide both how much to contribute and how to allocate contributions among funds. They also include $12.2 trillion in individual retirement accounts, where workers have even greater latitude in managing their retirement assets. Most assets enter these IRA accounts as rollovers from employment-based retirement plans, usually when workers change jobs, rather than as fresh contributions from individual taxpayers. Finally, the private retirement system contains $3.4 trillion in defined benefit plans, one-seventh of total assets. Employers manage these assets.

The private retirement system did not arise on its own. Congress shaped this system over nearly a century.[7] Working mostly through the tax code, but also with regulatory enactments like the Employee Retirement Income Security Act (ERISA), legislators created strong incentives for firms to establish private retirement plans. For example, the Revenue Act of 1926 allowed employers to treat contributions to retirement plans as business expenses and allowed assets in those plans to grow tax-free, thus encouraging the growth of employer-sponsored, defined benefit plans. Sometimes the effects were inadvertent. For example, during World War II, Congress instituted wage and price controls, while also increasing personal and corporate income taxes. These two actions sparked a rapid growth in private pension plans because employer contributions were exempt from both wage controls and taxation.

Later enactments encouraged the creation of defined contribution plans. For example, Congress amended the tax code in 1958, allowing workers at nonprofit institutions to make tax-deferred contributions to defined contribution plans, and again in 1978, allowing private sector workers to contribute to similar plans. The former, called 403(b) plans, and the latter, called 401(k) plans, are named after sections in the tax code. Congress also created incentives for self-employed workers to establish retirement plans (originally Keogh plans) and for individuals to contribute to tax-advantaged individual retirement accounts (IRAs).

There is no evidence that anyone in Congress set out to replace defined benefit plans with defined contribution plans. The initial argument for creating defined contribution plans was to give workers in nonprofit organizations access to tax-deferred retirement plans. Since their employers did not pay taxes, Congress allowed workers themselves to make tax-advantaged contributions. Later this model was extended to self-employed workers and to people working at firms that did not offer defined benefit plans. When Congress enacted ERISA in 1974, in response to several pension plan scandals, the clear intent was to strengthen defined benefit plans and prevent future malfeasance. But stricter regulation and a stronger mandate for advance funding made these plans less attractive to corporate executives. Companies gradually replaced defined benefit plans with defined contribution plans because the latter were less burdensome.[8] To be sure, some workers welcomed the switch, especially those who changed jobs frequently.

Whatever legislators may have intended, most private sector retirement plans are now designed around individual responsibility. Although most government workers still participate in defined benefit plans, most private sector workers are in charge of saving and investing during their working years, and then consuming responsibly during their retirement years.

Participation

Who participates in the private retirement system? As table 4.2 shows, only two-thirds of private sector employees work for employers that offer retirement plans. This *access rate* varies by work status. Among full-time workers, 77 percent have access to employer-sponsored plans, compared with 39 percent of part-time workers. Among union workers, 91 percent have

TABLE 4.2. Participation in Employer-Sponsored Retirement Plans, March 2020

Private Sector Workers	Access Rate (%)	Take-up Rate (%)	Participation Rate (%)
All workers	67	76	51
Full time	77	80	61
Part time	39	52	20
Union	91	89	82
Nonunion	65	74	48
Occupational Wage Group:			
Highest 10%	90	90	81
Highest 25%	88	89	78
Third 25%	79	81	64
Second 25%	67	72	48
Lowest 25%	42	52	22
Lowest 10%	29	48	14

Source: Bureau of Labor Statistics 2020, table 2PIW.

Retirement plans include defined benefit and defined contribution plans. The *access rate* is the percentage of workers who could enroll in an employer-sponsored retirement plan. The *take-up rate* is the percentage of workers who participate in a plan to which they have access. The *participation rate* is the product of the first two rates. Occupational wage group is based on the average wage for particular occupations.

access, compared with 65 percent of nonunion workers. Finally, workers in low-wage occupations are less likely to have access than those in high-wage occupations. Only 29 percent of workers in the bottom decile have the opportunity to participate in employer-sponsored plans, compared with 90 percent of those in the top decile.

Who takes advantage of this access? As table 4.2 shows, about three-quarters of workers with access to a retirement plan choose to participate. Indeed, the same factors that influence access also affect what is known as the *take-up rate*. Among part-time workers, 52 percent take advantage of access to an employer-sponsored benefit plan, compared with 80 percent of full-time workers. For nonunion workers, 74 percent take advantage of access, compared with 89 percent of union workers.[9] Finally, the relationship between wage level and the take-up rate is strong. Only 48 percent of workers in the lowest wage decile take advantage of access, compared with 90 percent in the top decile.

Participation in employer-sponsored retirement plans—that is, the *participation rate*, which is the product of the access and take-up rates—necessarily reflects the forces that drive the first two rates. As table 4.2 shows, only half the workforce participates in these retirement plans. The effects of income are particularly stark. Although 81 percent of high-wage workers participate, only 14 percent of low-wage workers do. In short, the private retirement system serves about half the private sector workforce, and largely the better-off half.

What about individual retirement accounts? Do people without access to employer-based retirement plans use IRAs to save for retirement? That was certainly the intent when Congress created these accounts in 1974. On the surface, the evidence is promising. According to the Internal Revenue Service, 14 million taxpayers contributed $70 billion to IRAs in 2018—an average of $5,000 per taxpayer.[10] But most of these contributions came from households that already had employer-based retirement plans, rather than from households that did not.[11] Moreover, these fresh contributions to IRAs are dwarfed by rollovers from existing employer-sponsored plans, amounting to $535 billion in 2018.[12] When we learn that total assets in IRAs exceed total assets in defined contribution plans (see table 4.1), we need to realize that most of these IRA assets began in employer-sponsored defined contribution plans.

Who pays for the private retirement system? Although workers and employers are the main contributors, the federal government also confers an enormous sum. The government subsidizes every plan—defined benefit, defined contribution, and IRAs—by excluding from taxable income all worker contributions, employer contributions, and investment gains. No taxes are due until money is withdrawn, sometimes late in retired life, and sometimes even later when children or grandchildren inherit accounts. The Treasury Department estimates that total federal subsidies were $193 billion in 2019.[13] By comparison, total worker and employer contributions to all private sector retirement plans—both defined benefit and defined contribution—were $630 billion.[14]

It is worth noting that these huge government subsidies are for a private retirement system where better-off workers are more likely to participate, where better-off workers contribute higher sums, and where better-off workers are subsidized at their higher marginal tax rates. These subsidies make the private retirement system heavily redistributive, though not in the usual sense of favoring the poor.

Privatization

Some experts and policymakers propose that Congress redesign Social Security to make it more like the private retirement system. Some people say these advocates seek to privatize Social Security. The generic term *privatization* means the transfer of a government service from public ownership and control to private ownership and control. For Social Security, privatization entails replacing the government-directed defined benefit program with a worker-directed defined contribution program. Partial privatization allows for a mix of government-directed and worker-directed plans.[15]

Some proponents of redesigning Social Security as a worker-directed defined contribution program bristle at the word "privatization." Surveys show that other phrases, such as personal retirement accounts, induce more favorable public reactions. My use of the term "privatization" throughout this book is strictly as a neutral descriptive term.

The principal arguments for privatization are three. First, if workers could invest their own payroll contributions in a diversified mix of stocks and bonds, they would collect more retirement income than they can with traditional Social Security. Second, a defined contribution plan would eliminate the effects of demographic booms and busts that currently afflict Social Security, because each birth cohort would fund its own retirement, not the retirement of previous generations. Third, a defined contribution plan would contribute to national savings. Since savings are the fuel for investment, reinventing Social Security as a defined contribution program would stimulate economic growth.

Rate of Return

Some people are dissatisfied with traditional Social Security because they do not think participants earn a fair return on what workers and their employers contribute to the program. They believe participants would achieve higher retirement income if they could invest their individual contributions in stocks and bonds. In this view, Social Security is a bad deal because participants do not receive their *money's worth* in retirement.[16]

Calculating the rate of return for Social Security requires great care because the program provides both insurance and retirement benefits.[17] For example, Social Security provides long-term disability benefits for workers and their families, as well as inflation protection, longevity protection, and survivor benefits for retirees. Many people value these insurance-like benefits, especially those benefits that are not adequately available in private markets, such as inflation and longevity protection. Unfortunately, many critics ignore the value of these insurance benefits. They estimate the investment yield on a lifetime of payroll contributions as if Social Security were exclusively a retirement savings program.

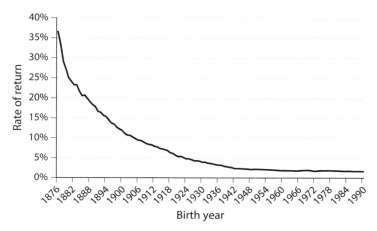

FIGURE 4.1. Real internal rates of return, by birth cohort, 1876–1990. These estimates are based on historical administrative data from 1937 to 1988, and simulated data for subsequent years. *Source*: Leimer 1994, appendix F.

One good measure for analyzing Social Security returns is the *real internal rate of return*.[18] This measure is essentially the interest rate that participants would have to earn on total worker and employer contributions in order to generate actual or expected retirement, spousal, survivor, and disability benefits. The real internal rate of return allows one to compare how various cohorts of participants, say those born in 1920, 1950, and 1980, have benefited (or will benefit) from the program. It also allows one to compare within birth cohorts to learn how participants with various earnings or marital histories have benefited (or will benefit) from Social Security.

Figure 4.1 displays estimated internal rates of return for each birth cohort from 1876 to 1990. For cohorts still working, costs include whatever tax increases are necessary to keep promised benefits flowing when the trust fund runs dry. The first portion of the figure shows that early participants earned extraordinary returns on their modest payroll contributions. Those born in 1876 earned a 37 percent return; those born in 1890, 18 percent; those born in 1900, 12 percent.[19] The rest of the figure shows that each succeeding birth cohort did (or will do) worse than its predecessors. Estimated returns are 3.9 percent for the 1930 cohort, 2.7 percent for the 1940 cohort, and 2.2 percent for the 1950 cohort. Estimated returns are less than 2 percent for every cohort born after 1957.

Why did early cohorts earn such extraordinary returns? The answer is simple: policymakers designed the system so that they would. The initial formula awarded benefits based on *average* taxable wages. Since the payroll tax began in 1937, those retiring in 1940 received benefits after only three years of contributions. For example, a man who retired in January 1940 at age 65, after earning $100 per month (then the average wage) for three years, received $25.75 per month in retirement benefits. Given that a man of that age was expected to live an additional 12.7 years, his expected lifetime benefit would be $3,924. That was a stunning return given that the worker and his employer paid only $72 in taxes during three working years. By comparison, a man retiring in 1947, with an identical wage history for ten years, would receive expected lifetime benefits of $4,191, based on $240 in taxes during the previous decade.[20] That, too, was a handsome return, although less than the return for the first retiree. In short, early cohorts received extraordinary returns because policymakers sought to give retirees benefits that would matter, not simply the modest returns from several years of contributions.

The first-generation advantage gradually disappeared as people paid Social Security taxes for their entire working years. But the second generation also profited by the fact that legislators kept postponing scheduled tax increases. It was not until 1963 that workers and their employers paid the combined 6 percent tax that the 1935 law had scheduled for 1949. Put differently, the first generation earned extraordinary returns because they contributed to Social Security for only a few years at a very low tax rate. But many second-generation participants also earned handsome returns because they faced higher tax rates only near the end of their careers.[21]

Why do current retirees earn such low rates of return? Simple arithmetic—or what two experts call the iron logic of accounting—explain the decline: since early retirees received more than they paid for, later generations must receive less.[22] When critics argue that current participants do not receive a fair return on their Social Security contributions, they are not wrong. Many people would profit—although with increased risk—by investing their contributions in a diversified mix of stocks and bonds rather than relying on the current pay-as-you-go system. But this legacy debt—the implicit debt derived from the program's generosity to early beneficiaries—is real.[23] Current retirees do not earn a market rate of return because their contributions were never invested; they were used to pay benefits for their parents' generation. And the children of today's retirees will not earn a market rate of return because their contributions are not being invested; they are being used to pay benefits for today's retirees. Until some generous generation pays off the entire legacy debt—whether by renouncing benefits for themselves or doubling their own contributions to fund both their generation's retirement and the previous generation's retirement—the debt will persist. Later generations are free to criticize what policymakers decreed in the 1930s, but they cannot escape the inevitable consequences.

Advance Funding

Some experts and policymakers favor moving from pay-as-you-go financing to advance funding because doing so would insulate Social Security from demographic booms and busts. Although pay-as-you-go systems work well with identically sized generations, or with a progression of ever-larger generations, they work poorly when a successor generation is smaller than its predecessor, because the workforce shrinks just as the beneficiary population surges. Figure 4.2 displays the magnitude of the problem in the American setting by plotting annual births from 1910 to 2018. Note the wide fluctuations, from a low of 2.3 million births in 1933 to a high of 4.3 million in 1957, then another low of 3.1 million in 1973, before returning to 4.3 million in 2007, and then declining to 3.8 million today. Advance funding would eliminate the problem of demographic booms and busts because each birth cohort would fund its own retirement.

Another attraction of advance funding is that it could contribute to economic growth. The current pay-as-you-go system contributes nothing to national savings. In contrast, an advance-funded system could increase aggregate savings as account owners purchased stocks and bonds to fund their retirements. Since savings are the fuel for investment, and investment is the foundation for economic growth, transitioning to an advance-funded system could create a stronger economy, thus improving the conditions of workers and eventually retirees. It is worth noting that this argument for advance funding predates the privatization debate.[24]

Why do some proponents of advance funding favor moving to a worker-directed defined contribution program rather than incorporating advance funding into the current government-directed defined benefit program? Why not have the Treasury Department invest payroll contributions in a single collective account rather than creating millions of individual accounts? Proponents of privatization raise two objections to a government-directed plan to invest in stocks. First, they do not want the federal government to become the dominant investor in private corporations. Even if current policymakers commit to passive investing, they cannot prevent future policymakers from becoming active and meddlesome investors.[25]

FIGURE 4.2. Births in millions, 1910–2018. The dotted line is the linear trend.
Sources: National Center for Health Statistics via Munnell and Chen 2015; Martin et al. 2019.

Proponents also worry that advance-funded defined benefit systems can easily retrogress into pay-as-you-go systems. Such reversals have already happened twice for Social Security. Recall that Social Security began as an advance-funded program, before policymakers in the 1940s transformed it into a pay-as-you-go system. In 1983, legislators took actions, including tax increases and benefit cuts, that reintroduced advance funding. But their successors forgot that advance funding requires occasional interventions to keep the coffers full. With no interventions in sight, the trust fund will disappear in 2034, thus ending advance funding's second chapter.

In contrast, defined contribution plans are immune from such backsliding. Defined contribution plans come in a single flavor, advance funded. Although employers can stop contributing to workers' retirement accounts, they cannot claw back what they have already contributed. These accounts are the property of workers, not employers. The quest for advance funding, therefore, has become a quest for worker-directed defined contribution accounts.

So, one reason for replacing a defined benefit Social Security system with a defined contribution system is to secure all the advantages—demographic and economic—of advance funding and to guarantee that those advantages persist. Unfortunately, transitioning to an advance-funded Social Security system faces the familiar problem of the legacy debt. How can workers contribute to their own investment accounts when their contributions are necessary to support current retirees?

Redistribution

Another obstacle to privatizing Social Security is that the current system is heavily redistributive. Unlike the private retirement system, where retirement benefits are roughly proportional to lifetime contributions, Social Security uses a progressive benefit formula that greatly advantages low-wage people. The formula is based on past wages, so well-paid workers collect larger benefits than poorly paid workers do. But the formula is highly progressive, so low-wage workers earn a greater return on their contributions than high-wage workers do.

A standard measure that individuals and financial advisors use in retirement planning is the *replacement rate*—retirement income as a fraction of preretirement income. The replacement rate for Social Security is defined as a worker's expected Social Security benefits as a percentage of that worker's inflation-adjusted, career-average wages.[26] Figure 4.3 plots these replacement rates over time for four hypothetical workers retiring at age 65.

Three patterns stand out. First, replacement rates increased for all workers retiring between 1950 and 1980, the period when Congress regularly expanded benefits. Second, replacement benefits declined (or will decline) for all workers retiring after that, a consequence of the 1983 solvency reforms. Third, replacement rates are highly progressive across all years. For example, the estimated replacement rate for a very low wage worker retiring in 2020 is 73 percent, nearly twice that year's replacement rate for an average worker (40 percent), and nearly thrice the rate for a maximum-wage worker (26 percent).

Social Security also redistributes income to married people. Although the original 1935 enactment promised retirement benefits only for workers, Congress added benefits for wives and widows in 1939. Spousal benefits were 50 percent of what their husbands collected; survivor benefits were 75 percent. These provisions not only redistributed income from single to married people, they also devalued tax payments from working wives, since they were entitled to substantial benefits whether or not they worked and paid taxes. Subsequent laws and court rulings broadened family coverage to include dependent husbands (1950), disabled adult children (1956), divorced wives (1965), nondependent husbands (1977), and divorced husbands (1977).[27]

All these family benefits make Social Security a worse deal for single people, and especially for single men. Table 4.3 displays internal rates of return for 20 hypothetical households where a worker and (if married) an identically aged spouse retire in 2020 at age 65. Recall from table 4.1 that the internal rate of

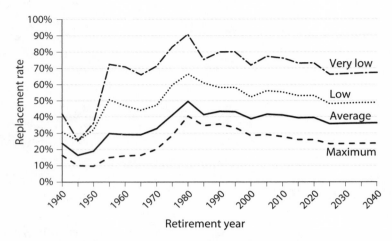

FIGURE 4.3. Replacement rates for four hypothetical retirees at age 65, 1940–2040. The rates here assume that payroll taxes increase, when the trust fund runs dry, to pay all scheduled benefits. The solid line is for a worker with average lifetime wages ($53,864 in 2019). The top two lines are for workers earning 25 percent and 45 percent of that average ($13,466 and $24,239). The bottom line is for a maximum-wage worker, defined as someone who earned the maximum taxable wage ($132,900 in 2019) consistently for 35 years.
Source: Social Security Administration 2019d, table B, column 4.

return is the interest rate that participants would have to earn on total worker and employer contributions in order to generate all retirement, spousal, survivor, and disability benefits. Not surprisingly, internal rates of return are much higher for low-wage workers than for high-wage workers. This reflects the income redistribution baked into Social Security's benefit formula. But household composition also matters. On average, one-earner couples have internal rates of return twice as large as those for single men. Two-earner couples have rates 21 percent greater than those for single men. Even single women do better than single men because Social Security benefits are based on unisex mortality estimates, although women as a group live longer and therefore collect more benefits than men. Note especially the meager 0.7 percent return for single men in the top wage group. No group is more disfavored.

It is important to put Social Security's redistribution in perspective. As previously noted, the tax code provides enormous subsidies for those who participate in the private retirement system. These subsidies, estimated to be nearly $200 billion annually, are skewed toward well-paid workers, both

TABLE 4.3. Internal Rates of Return for Workers Retiring in 2020 at Age 65, by Marital Status

Wage Level	Single Male	Single Female	Two-Earner Couple	One-Earner Couple
Very Low	4.4	4.8	4.9	6.5
Low	3.3	3.7	3.7	5.4
Medium	2.2	2.7	2.7	4.4
High	1.6	2.1	2.0	3.8
Maximum	0.7	1.2	1.1	2.8
Mean	2.4	2.9	2.9	4.6

Source: Social Security Administration 2019c, table 2.

The real internal rate of return is the interest rate that participants would have to earn on total worker and employer contributions in order to generate actual or expected retirement, spousal, survivor, and disability benefits. The estimates in this table assume that payroll taxes increase when the trust fund runs dry in order to pay all scheduled benefits.

because they contribute more to their retirement accounts than poorly paid workers, and because they receive disproportionally large tax benefits given their higher marginal tax rates. In short, the private retirement system advantages well-paid workers; Social Security advantages poorly paid workers.

What was the rationale for policymakers incorporating so much redistribution into Social Security? Why did they favor first-generation participants, poorly paid workers, and married people? Program designers clearly sought to satisfy two goals: equity and adequacy.[28] *Equity* is achieved to the extent that participants receive benefits that are proportional to their lifetime contributions. *Adequacy* is achieved to the extent that participants receive benefits that allow them to maintain a minimum standard of living in retirement. Of course, the two goals are in direct conflict: Advancing one goal impedes the other. Program designers leaned heavily toward adequacy because they sought to replace means-tested old-age assistance with a single program where retirees would collect benefits as a matter of right.

Complete privatization of Social Security would eliminate all forms of redistribution. If people had ownership rights to their individual accounts, no funds would be available to redistribute. Some proponents would welcome this change. For example, an early advocate of privatization proposed completely separating the insurance and welfare aspects of Social Security, transferring the former to the private sector, and using means-tested government programs to subsidize the poor.[29]

Most privatization advocates do not favor eliminating all redistribution. Rather, they propose partial privatization, where some fraction of all contributions would be directed to individual investment accounts, while the residual would support a scaled-back version of traditional Social Security. With this approach, policymakers could maintain some redistribution, although at the cost of even lower internal rates of return for disfavored groups.

Account Management

Another obstacle to privatizing Social Security is that people differ in their skills, interest, and temperament for financial management. This is not a problem with defined benefit plans because professionals administer everything. For defined contribution plans, however, individuals make the investment choices. Those who choose badly earn poor returns.

One guide to how people might manage their individual accounts if Social Security were privatized is to examine how people currently manage their individual accounts in the private retirement system. Several problems are evident. First, many workers are not good savers. More than one-quarter of private sector workers with access to defined contribution plans fail to participate in those plans.[30] Lack of participation is common even when employers offer matching contributions. Second, people often withdraw funds from their retirement accounts for other purposes. One study found that one-third of workers who switched jobs withdrew all their retirement assets as taxable cash, rather than preserving the assets in the original plans or transferring them to other tax-deferred plans.[31]

A third problem is that people often make poor investment choices. For example, Enron employees chose to invest 60 percent of their retirement assets in Enron stock.[32] When the company collapsed in 2001, they simultaneously lost their jobs and their retirement assets. Although most retirement plans no longer offer company stock as an option, when they do, nearly 40 percent of workers select it.[33] Research also shows that many people violate best practices when managing their retirement assets. They fail to diversify appropriately across stocks and bonds. They choose high-cost actively managed funds even when lower-cost index funds are available. They fail to revise their initial investment choices or rebalance their assets. They sell stocks at market lows and rebuy them once markets recover. In short, they behave as the amateur investors that they are.[34]

The fourth problem with defined contribution plans is that some retirees will outlive their assets. Unlike Social Security and employer-sponsored defined benefit plans, which promise lifetime benefits for retirees, defined contribution plans require that people spend down their assets without knowing how long they will live. Although retirees could purchase longevity insurance in the form of lifetime annuities, most retirees do not take this simple step.[35] Thus, they assume all the financial risks of living longer than expected.

Some privatization plans seek to ameliorate these problems by restricting what individuals can do. For example, some plans would make contributions mandatory, require that participants invest in low-cost index funds, prohibit early withdrawals, and mandate annuitization at retirement.[36] Although it is easy to make a case for specific restrictions, collectively they chip away at the core privatization principle that individuals own their retirement assets from day one. If the essence of ownership is control, why should people be required to annuitize their investments at retirement? The reason, of course, is so that they will not outlive their assets. But what about sickly retirees who do not expect long retirements? Why should their monthly payments be calculated as if they had two decades to live, when they do not?

Traditional Social Security

Other experts and policymakers prefer retaining traditional Social Security. They argue that social insurance plays an important role in retirement security, one that cannot be replicated by a government-designed version of the private retirement system. Social insurance is a device for pooling risks, so that individuals—whether disabled, retired, or survivors—receive benefits that allow them to maintain a minimum standard of living. From this perspective, the redistribution that is baked into Social Security is not a flaw, but a virtue, one that helps people who had intermittent or low-wage careers retire in dignity. Social insurance also allows the pooling of risks to continue throughout retirement. With a defined contribution plan, individual retirees bear investment, inflation, and longevity risks. With social insurance, retirees are shielded from all three risks because their inflation-adjusted retirement benefits are guaranteed for life.[37]

Some defenders of traditional Social Security do support investing trust fund assets in the stock market. They differ from privatization advocates only in their belief that a collective trust fund is a better vehicle than creating millions of individual accounts. One advantage of a collective account is that professionals would manage everything. A second is that it would avoid the administrative costs of establishing and maintaining 200 million individual investment accounts. The administrative costs of privatization could be especially burdensome for part-time and low-wage workers, who could see account maintenance fees swamp their investment returns. A third advantage is that a collective account would spread investment risks widely. No matter how diligently people contribute to their retirement accounts, and no matter how carefully they invest those funds in diversified portfolios of stocks and bonds, due diligence offers little protection from worldwide cataclysmic events like the Great Recession. For example, a worker who retired and annuitized her retirement account in March 2009, a low point for the stock market, would receive far less income than if she happened to retire in March 2008 or March 2010, when the stock market, as measured by the S&P 500 Index, was 88 percent and 69 percent higher.[38] A defined benefit plan with a collective investment account would eliminate such disparities, effectively spreading investment risks over all participants, rather than concentrating them on particular individuals.

The proponents of investing a portion of the trust fund in the stock market also believe that they can design a system that would prevent the politicization of investment decisions and corporate governance. They argue that restricting investments to large index funds and delegating voting decisions to an independent agency, where members would have strict fiduciary responsibilities, would keep politicians from becoming active and meddlesome investors. Such schemes have worked for municipalities, states, and other countries that have collective stock fund investments.[39]

One obstacle to collective investing in the stock market is that the trust fund is rapidly disappearing. When experts and policymakers first proposed such investments in the late 1990s, the trust fund was growing rapidly, fueled by baby boomers entering their peak earning years. Now that boomers are retiring and the trust fund is declining, the gains from trust fund investments would be smaller. But policymakers could choose to increase the level of advance funding or even transform Social Security into a fully funded system.

Perhaps the strongest argument that defenders of traditional Social Security have against privatization is that people should never put all their eggs in one basket. Four decades ago, when advocates first began to push for privatization, defined benefit plans dominated the private retirement system. Transforming Social Security into a defined contribution program then would have diversified the retirement world, so that more people would be covered by both defined benefit and defined contribution plans. Today, however, defined contribution plans dominate the private retirement system. Transforming Social Security into a defined contribution program now would therefore *reduce* diversity in the retirement world. Since diversification is one way to reduce risk, privatization would increase overall risk. Put differently, people today should value even more how Social Security protects them from investment, longevity, and inflation risks now that the private retirement system exposes them to all three.

Broader Debate

Social Security is currently a pay-as-you-go, defined benefit program that incorporates substantial redistribution. Policymakers often speak as if the only options for fixing Social Security were incremental changes in the current system or some type of privatization. The debate would be more enlightening, however, if policymakers first addressed four foundational questions.

First, should Social Security move toward increased advance funding? The advantages of advance funding include eliminating the effects of demographic booms and busts and raising the overall level of national savings. If the answer is yes, policymakers have two routes toward that goal. They can enlarge the volume of advance funding in traditional Social Security or they can create a new defined contribution system. It makes no economic difference which path they choose. The economic effects of transferring an additional $2 trillion in worker contributions to the trust fund and investing that increment in the stock market are identical to the economic effects of parking that sum in 100 million individual accounts. Advance funding is what matters, not the number of accounts in which it dwells.[40]

To be sure, there is a legitimate fear that once again incorporating advanced funding in traditional Social Security could unravel. But policymakers could create automatic stabilizers that would preserve advance funding if circumstances change, just as they created automatic cost-of-living adjustments to preserve the real value of Social Security benefits. For example, increased longevity could trigger automatic increases in the retirement age, the tax rate, or both, in order to keep the system in balance.[41]

Second, should Social Security remain a defined benefit program or would a defined contribution program be superior? A central concern should be how the two approaches deal with the many risks associated with investing, accumulating, and spending retirement assets. Defined benefit plans shield beneficiaries from all sorts of risks—investment, inflation, and longevity—whereas defined contribution plans concentrate those risks on individuals. What balance of risks makes sense for a national retirement plan like Social Security?

Policymakers should also ask whether both the public and private retirement systems should reflect the same design principles. Should Social Security follow the private retirement system down the pathway to defined contribution accounts, or is there value in people participating in both defined benefit and defined contribution plans? And what about people—many of them poor—who do not participate in the private retirement system? Are they better off in traditional Social Security or in a new privatized system?

Third, how much redistribution should be a part of the public retirement system? Those who designed Social Security incorporated extensive redistribution because they sought to replace means-tested old-age assistance with a program that allowed all participants to retire with dignity. But decisions from the 1930s need not bind current policymakers. Does Social Security incorporate too much or too little redistribution? Does it favor or disfavor the correct groups? Along the way, policymakers might examine redistribution in the private retirement system, redistribution that favors the rich, not the poor. Are there ways to encourage more widespread participation in the private retirement system? Are there ways to make participant subsidies more equitable? For example, why are subsidies based on workers' marginal tax rates, a policy that provides well-paid workers with more generous tax subsidies than poorly paid workers?

Fourth, how should policymakers deal with the legacy debt—the lasting consequence of the 1935 and 1939 decisions to give early retirement cohorts such fabulous returns, while depressing returns for subsequent generations? Of course, Congress can continue to ignore the legacy debt by retaining pay-as-you-go financing. But if Congress moves to increase the level of advance funding, whether by replacing Social Security with a new defined contribution plan or by enlarging the trust fund and investing the increment in the stock market, it will effectively be reducing the legacy debt. In traditional Social Security, the debt would disappear once the system becomes fully funded—that is, once trust fund assets equal projected liabilities for workers, retirees, spouses, and survivors. In a privatized system, the debt would disappear once all workers are fully covered by the new defined contribution system and once all other beneficiaries die. Put differently, the cost of retiring the legacy debt is essentially the cost of transforming Social Security into an advance-funded program. It makes little difference whether advance funding is accomplished with millions of individual accounts or with a single collective account.

If Congress does choose to retire the legacy debt, what are the options for paying the enormous transition costs? Perhaps the most appealing option has already vanished. In the late 1990s, when policymakers first considered various privatization schemes, the federal government was running a large annual surplus. Some policymakers proposed allocating that surplus to Social Security, either to expand the trust fund or to jump-start privatization. In fact, Congress used the surplus to support tax cuts, war spending, and prescription drug coverage for seniors. Other policymakers proposed using the estate tax to help support advance funding, but Congress slashed that tax, too. Another option is to remove the legacy debt from the Social Security balance sheet and use general revenues to pay all accrued benefits under traditional Social Security. From that point forward, all new contributions would be used to create a fully funded defined benefit program or to create a privatized system of individual accounts. One attraction of this option is that the cost of retiring the legacy debt would be paid through the progressive income tax, rather than the regressive payroll tax.

Conclusion

Whether policymakers will make structural or just incremental changes in Social Security is an open question. We have seen legislators make structural changes in the past, most notably in the 1940s, when they transformed advance-funded Social Security into a pay-as-you-go program, and in 1983, when they reintroduced advance funding. They came close to making another structural change in 1990, when Senator Daniel Patrick Moynihan (D-NY) proposed returning Social Security to pay-as-you-go financing, a proposal that attracted majority, but not supermajority, support on the Senate floor.[42] On the other hand, when President Bush asked legislators to approve wholesale restructuring in 2005, they displayed little interest in his plan.

This chapter has highlighted the advantages and disadvantages inherent in various retirement systems. No matter what the plan, there are pluses, minuses, and trade-offs. The next chapter examines incremental options for restoring solvency to traditional Social Security.

5

Incremental Solutions

THE ALTERNATIVE TO REINVENTING Social Security is to accept the program's basic structure and simply adjust the revenue and benefits streams until they are in long-term balance. This is what legislators did in 1977 when they raised the tax rate by 25 percent and the maximum taxable wage base by 68 percent in order to protect current and future beneficiaries from benefit cuts. This is what legislators did in 1983 when they switched course and approved large benefit cuts and small tax increases.

This chapter examines the incremental options available to policymakers today. It explores the arguments for and against each option and summarizes how effective each provision would be in reducing Social Security's long-term deficit.

Score Keeping

What keeps legislators honest? What keeps them from enacting provisions that would make things worse? One answer is that legislators have delegated questions about cause and effect to policy experts. The actuaries at the Social Security Administration, who annually project the program's financial trajectory over the next 75 years, separately estimate the effects of hundreds of individual solvency provisions that would modify the revenue or benefit streams, as well as dozens of comprehensive solvency plans that would combine various revenue and benefit provisions. These are the actuaries who estimated the long-term consequences of the 1983 solvency plan before Congress approved it. Although that plan achieved solvency for only about 50 years, rather than the intended 75, the actuaries' estimate is properly regarded as a success on Capitol Hill, where long-term is more likely to suggest a half decade than a half century.

The actuaries estimate two measures that are used to evaluate both individual provisions and comprehensive plans: actuarial balance and year of insolvency. *Actuarial balance* is a summary measure of Social Security's financial status over the next 75 years. It is the sum of projected annual revenues over that period, plus current trust fund assets, minus projected annual benefits and administrative costs, expressed as a percentage of Social Security's taxable payroll over the same period. Taxable payroll includes all wages, salaries, and self-employment income that are subject to Social Security taxes, up to the maximum taxable wage base. The current (2020) actuarial balance is negative 3.2 percent.[1] That is to say, if the combined worker and employer tax rate were 3.2 percentage points higher—15.6 percent instead of 12.4 percent—Social Security would be solvent throughout the entire 75-year period. The *year of insolvency* is the year that the trust fund will likely disappear and all benefits will have to be supported by annual revenues. It is currently 2034.[2]

These two measures—actuarial balance and the year of insolvency—are the standard benchmarks for evaluating both individual provisions and comprehensive plans. For example, the actuaries might calculate that one provision would close 25 percent of the 75-year actuarial deficit, while another would close 50 percent. A successful plan in 2021 would make Social Security solvent until at least 2096 by eliminating the long-term actuarial deficit. A less successful plan would merely reduce the deficit, returning Social Security to insolvency sometime before 2096. Actuarial balance and the year of insolvency are not the only measures of Social Security's financial health.[3] But these two metrics are the most politically consequential ones. The year of insolvency tells legislators how long they can procrastinate without hurting beneficiaries. Actuarial balance tells them how painful it would be to fix the entire long-term problem today. This measure worsens with every year of delay.

Social Security's actuaries have earned the respect of politicians of every stripe—Democrats and Republicans, liberals and conservatives, incrementalists and privatizers. They all submit their solvency plans to the actuaries for scoring. They all accept the actuaries' estimates as binding. Unlike some policy areas—for example, tax or health policy—where proponents and opponents sometimes disagree on whether a particular policy would increase or decrease the deficit, Social Security policymakers have so far played ball with a single set of neutral referees who evaluate the solvency effects of every proposal.[4]

Neutral referees make clear to everyone—legislators, interest groups, and citizens—the policy consequences of each decision. They highlight the trade-offs. They frame every decision as a choice between valued things. If someone proposes to amend a solvency bill by eliminating a provision that would raise the full retirement age from 67 to 68, everyone would know that the amendment would make the next solvency crisis arrive much sooner—say, in 15 years rather than 75.[5] Legislators who support such an amendment can claim, "I blocked an unfair increase in the retirement age." But challengers can counter, "The incumbent transformed a comprehensive long-term solution into a shaky short-term fix." Both statements would be true.

Tax Rate

Some policymakers propose raising the tax rate. Under current law, workers pay 6.2 percent of their wages, up to the maximum taxable wage base; employers pay an identical sum. Roughly one-sixth of this revenue supports disability benefits; the remainder supports retirement, spousal, and survivor benefits. Aggressively raising the tax rate would close the entire 75-year actuarial deficit. Smaller increases would be less effective but might appeal to legislators as part of a comprehensive plan.

Congress has a long history of raising the payroll tax. The original 1935 legislation authorized four automatic increases to bring the rate from the initial 1.0 percent to 3.0 percent.[6] Between 1960 and 1974, Congress authorized eight additional increments, totaling 1.95 percent, both to expand retirement, spousal, and survivor benefits, and to establish and expand disability insurance. Congress approved seven more increments, totaling 1.25 percent, to deal with the 1977 and 1983 solvency crises.[7] In short, raising the payroll tax has been the primary way legislators have dealt with Social Security's finances, first to expand the program, and then to keep it solvent. What is unusual about the last four decades is that Congress has not modified the payroll tax even once.

The principal justification for raising the tax rate is that life expectancy has increased dramatically. Even in a world without baby booms and baby busts— that is, where successor generations were never smaller than their predecessors—a mature pay-as-you-go system would require additional tax revenue as people lived longer. Just as individual workers who are saving for their own retirement need to save more if they expect longer retirements, so must workers who pay into a collective pay-as-you-go system contribute more to support the longer retirements of their elders. If policymakers seek to maintain Social Security's current benefits without raising the retirement age, more revenue is essential.

One argument against raising the payroll tax is that it is regressive, especially compared with its progressive cousin, the income tax. Although the income tax begins with a rate of zero for low-wage people and then gradually applies a series of progressively higher rates, ranging from 10 percent to 37 percent, to those with higher earnings, the payroll tax begins with a rate of 6.2 percent for low-wage workers, applies the same rate for most other workers, but then applies a lower effective rate for affluent workers by exempting all their earnings above the maximum taxable wage base. Some analysts justify the regressive payroll tax with the argument that Social Security benefits are progressive. That is, lower-income workers earn a higher return on their contributions than upper-income workers do. Of course, that argument is undercut by the emergence of a large gap in life expectancies between the rich and the poor, which has reduced the progressivity of benefits. Indeed, as the next two sections show, the regressivity of the payroll tax has increased while the progressivity of benefits has declined.

The options for increasing the tax rate are many. Legislators could eliminate the entire long-term actuarial deficit by immediately (2021) increasing the worker and employer rates by 1.7 percentage points—to 7.9 percent each—with no phase-in.[8] A less aggressive plan would raise the tax almost as high (7.65 percent), but implement the change gradually between 2024 and 2090, eliminating 56 percent of the actuarial deficit. A more moderate proposal would increase the tax rate by 0.05 percentage points per year from 2026 to 2045, until the rate reaches 7.2 percent, eliminating 46 percent of the actuarial deficit. A fourth proposal would increase the tax rate by 0.05 percentage points per year from 2022 to 2031, until the rate reaches 6.7 percent. It would eliminate 27 percent of the actuarial deficit.[9]

Revenue Base

Some policymakers propose raising or abolishing the maximum taxable wage base, the sharp boundary—$142,800 in 2021—between wages subject to the 6.2 percent payroll tax and wages immune from the tax. Abolishing the base would raise substantial revenue from affluent workers. Raising the base would be less lucrative but might appeal to legislators as part of a comprehensive plan.

The maximum taxable wage base has a complicated history. Recall that the original draft of the 1935 Social Security Act offered no coverage—no taxes, no benefits—for workers earning more than $3,000 annually, then about 3 percent of the workforce (see chapter 2). When critics argued that it would be difficult to administer such a program because some workers' wages would

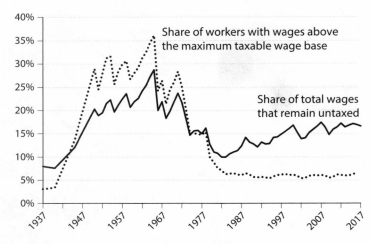

FIGURE 5.1. Share of workers and wages above the maximum taxable wage base, 1937–2017. *Source*: Social Security Administration 2019a, tables 4.B1 and 4.B4.

drift above or below the threshold from year to year, legislators transformed the $3,000 threshold for coverage into a ceiling on taxed wages. This ceiling also capped benefits because benefits were linked to taxed wages. Since the wage base was expressed in dollars, however, inflation regularly eroded its value, pushing more workers above the base and removing more wages from taxation. Although legislators raised the maximum taxable wage base eight times between 1950 and 1974, before putting it on autopilot, the base never returned to its original value.

Figure 5.1 plots how changes in the maximum taxable wage base affected both the share of workers with exempt wages and the share of untaxed wages. At inception, 3 percent of workers earned more than the $3,000 base and 8 percent of wages were untaxed. By 1965, 36 percent of workers earned more than the $4,800 base and 29 percent of wages were untaxed. Finally, during the 1977 solvency crisis, legislators raised the maximum taxable wage to $29,700 and indexed future changes to average wage growth. Those two actions reduced the share of workers above the base to 6 percent and the share of untaxed wages to 10 percent. But notice how the share of untaxed wages continued to grow, most recently to 17 percent, despite indexing the wage base. This growth is largely a consequence of increasing wage inequality. Today's affluent workers are much richer than were the affluent workers of yesteryear.

The 17 percent of wages that are currently untaxed are a tempting target for reformers. So far, policymakers have proposed 29 separate provisions that would raise or abolish the maximum taxable wage base. The most aggressive provision would abolish the tax base immediately (2021), subjecting all wages to the payroll tax, while retaining the current base for benefit calculations. Affluent workers would pay more taxes without receiving more benefits. This proposal would eliminate 73 percent of the 75-year actuarial deficit. A second proposal would abolish both the tax and benefit bases. Affluent workers would pay more taxes and receive more benefits. It would eliminate 55 percent of the actuarial deficit. A third proposal would abolish both bases but then introduce a less generous benefit formula for those above the current base. It would eliminate 66 percent of the deficit. More modest proposals would increase the tax base gradually until 90 percent of earnings were taxed, thus returning the system to where it was in the early 1940s and early 1980s. These proposals would eliminate either 22 or 31 percent of the actuarial deficit, depending on whether the current benefit base is retained.[10] In short, modifying the maximum taxable wage base can do a lot or a little to solve Social Security's problems depending on how aggressive legislators choose to be.

The principal justification for raising the maximum taxable wage base is that the percentage of total wages that escapes taxation today is more accident than choice. Although policymakers in 1935 and 1977 chose to leave 8 to 10 percent of wages untaxed, that amount has increased to 17 percent of total wages simply because they chose in 1977 to index the wage base to average wage growth. Perhaps such an indexing scheme made sense in the 1970s, when wage inequality was less pronounced, but it makes less sense when wage growth for the affluent vastly exceeds wage growth for other workers.

Whether raising the wage base should also raise retirement benefits for affluent workers is an open question. On the one hand, workers who regularly earn the maximum taxable wage base currently earn abysmal returns on their contributions—less than 1 percent for some participants (see table 4.3). Do we really want to reduce their returns even further, thus potentially alienating millions of people who currently support traditional Social Security? This argument is especially relevant for workers whose wages exceed the base by modest amounts. On the other hand, what should we do about extraordinarily rich wage earners, like a basketball star earning $30 million per season? It is one thing to welcome the additional revenue—$1.86 million each from the player and his team owner—but then do we want the player's retirement benefits to become stratospheric too? Where you stand on whether raising the

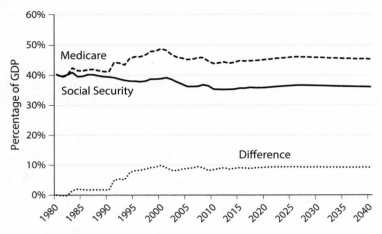

FIGURE 5.2. Taxable payroll as a percentage of GDP for Medicare and Social Security, 1980–2040. Historical data, 1980–2017; actuarial projections, 2018–40.
Sources: Centers for Medicare and Medicaid Services 2018; Social Security Administration 2020d, table VI.G5.

maximum taxable wage base should also raise retirement benefits may depend on the images in your mind. Are you picturing your daughter's pediatrician or a wealthy basketball star?

Proponents of raising or abolishing the maximum taxable wage base have one powerful precedent: Medicare. When Congress established Medicare in 1965, it made the new program's maximum taxable wage base identical to Social Security's wage base (then $4,800). Twenty-five years later, when Medicare faced financial strains, legislators decoupled the two programs by doubling Medicare's wage base. Three years later, they abolished the base completely, imposing the Medicare tax—then and now 1.45 percent each for workers and employers—on total wages. Figure 5.2 shows how these two decisions expanded Medicare's principal revenue source. In 1980, Medicare's taxable payroll was 40 percent of GDP, the same as for Social Security. Today, Medicare's taxable payroll is 45 percent of GDP, while Social Security's taxable payroll is 36 percent. The difference between the two—9 percent of GDP—is an enormous sum.

Medicare also reminds us that legislators can move beyond traditional revenue sources when financial problems become urgent. In addition to abolishing the maximum taxable wage base for workers, legislators have adopted other measures to tap higher-income people. These measures include both broader definitions of taxable income and higher premiums for Medicare beneficiaries. In 2010, legislators created a 0.9 percent surtax on wage income, reserved for individuals earning more than $200,000 and couples earning more than $250,000. Individuals and couples pay the surtax; employers do not. The same law established a 3.8 percent tax on investment income, using the same income thresholds.[11] The reach of these two provisions continues to expand because legislators chose not to index the income thresholds for inflation. Congress has also found ways to tax Medicare beneficiaries directly. For Medicare Part B (doctors), legislators established annual surcharges on premiums. The current (2021) surcharges range from $713 annually for individuals earning more than $88,000, to $4,277 annually for individuals earning more than $500,000. For Medicare Part D (prescriptions), they established similar surcharges on premiums, currently ranging from $148 to $925 annually. Both surcharges are assessed on all forms of income, including wages, capital gains, dividends, and tax-exempt interest.

Policymakers repeatedly searched for new sources of revenue to support the various Medicare programs because the financial problems were severe. Although it is too soon to tell whether policymakers will follow a similar route when they fix Social Security, Medicare provides ample precedents for finding new revenue. As already discussed, raising or abolishing the maximum taxable wage base is one option. Broadening the base to include unearned income is yet another. For example, if Social Security policymakers followed the Medicare model and applied a 6.2 percent tax on investment income for individuals earning more than $200,000 and couples earning more than $250,000, they would eliminate 30 percent of Social Security's 75-year actuarial deficit.[12]

Other policymakers propose broadening the definition of taxable earnings beyond wage and salary income. For example, taxing what workers and employers pay for group health insurance would eliminate 35 percent of the actuarial deficit. Taxing what workers contribute to various salary reduction plans—for example, flexible spending accounts—would eliminate 10 percent of the deficit.[13] Social Security's founders taxed what was then common (wages) and avoided what was then uncommon (benefits). But as benefits have become a larger fraction of total compensation, policymakers could tax some or all of those benefits, too.

Requiring newly hired employees of state and local government to participate in Social Security is another way to broaden the revenue base. Doing so would eliminate 5 percent of the actuarial deficit.[14] This requirement would help in three ways. First, state and local workers are relatively well paid, so bringing them into the system would help subsidize poorly paid workers. Second, most state and local workers already contribute to Social Security before or after their government service. This creates serious problems in calculating their Social Security benefits, since their short-term participation makes them appear poor. Although Social Security employs a modified benefit formula for these workers, it would be easier and more equitable to include them in the Social Security program throughout their careers.[15] Third, requiring state and local workers to participate in Social Security would make the program more equitable because it would spread the legacy debt—the implicit debt derived from the program's generosity to early beneficiaries—more broadly. Currently, state and local workers do nothing to pay for the program's generosity to their ancestors.[16]

Retirement Age

Some policymakers propose raising the full retirement age. Doing so would increase revenues, as participants work a year or two longer, and reduce expenditures, as retirees collect benefits a year or two less. Although the reduction in expenditures is more consequential for Social Security's finances, because a year's worth of benefits is several times greater than a year's worth of taxes, both effects are important. Aggressively raising the retirement age would close a large fraction of the 75-year actuarial deficit. More gradual changes would close less of the deficit but might appeal to legislators as part of a comprehensive plan.

The *full retirement age*—sometimes called the normal retirement age—has a special meaning in Social Security land. It is the age for which program administrators calculate participants' retirement benefits based on their work histories.[17] How much participants collect, however, depends on when they choose to retire. Those who retire early—age 62 is the earliest—receive reduced benefits. Those who retire later—age 70 is the latest—receive augmented benefits. Both adjustments are designed to be actuarially fair. They ensure that participants receive, on average, the same lifetime benefits regardless of when they choose to collect benefits.[18]

The full retirement age was 65 in the original law. In 1983, legislators decided to raise this age gradually to 67, beginning with those who were then 45 and ending with those who were then 23. Raising the full retirement age did not affect *when* participants could retire and collect benefits. It merely affected *how much* they would collect at specific ages. For example, those who chose to retire at age 62 used to collect 80 percent of what they would normally collect at age 65. As the phase-in concludes in 2022, 62-year-olds will collect 70 percent of what they would normally collect at age 67.[19] Raising the full retirement age is a simple mechanism for reducing lifetime benefits.

The principal justification for raising the full retirement age is that people are living longer. As chapter 1 showed, life expectancy for 65-year-olds has increased from 13.7 years in 1940 to 20.3 years today. It is projected to reach 24.3 years in 2095. A system designed to support retirees for 14 years cannot easily support them for 24. It does help that Congress raised the full retirement age by two years. But that decision closed only a fraction of the long-term financial gap caused by longer retirements.

How much would raising the full retirement age contribute to Social Security's long-term actuarial balance? That depends on how aggressively legislators raise the age. Several years ago, Senators Lindsey Graham (R-SC), Mike Lee (R-UT), and Rand Paul (R-KY) proposed raising the full retirement age by three months per year until it reached 70, and then indexing the age to future changes in life expectancy. They also proposed raising the early retirement age from 62 to 64. According to the actuaries' most recent estimates, this proposal would eliminate 47 percent of the long-term actuarial deficit if implemented in 2021. A much less aggressive proposal would raise the full retirement age from 67 to 68, phased in over six years. That proposal would eliminate 16 percent of the deficit. Note that the former plan eliminates nearly half the shortfall by raising the full retirement age to 72 or 73 by 2095, while the latter eliminates one-sixth of the shortfall by topping out at 68.[20] In short, raising the retirement age can do a lot or a little, depending on what age policymakers select.

The principal argument against raising the full retirement age is that some segments of society have not experienced longevity gains. Forty years ago, life expectancy for 50-year-old men in the top fifth of earners was 5.1 years greater than for 50-year-old men in the bottom fifth. Today the gap is 12.7 years. Life expectancy declined for men in the poorest fifth—by six months—while it increased for men in the richest fifth by 7.1 years. The pattern among women is even worse. Life expectancy declined for 50-year-old women in the poorest fifth of earners by 4.0 years, while increasing for women in the richest fifth by 5.7 years.[21] Why should low-wage people with declining life expectancies work longer, and therefore have shorter retirements, in order to fund increasingly lengthy retirements for affluent workers?

The second argument against raising the retirement age is that working longer is not an option for everyone. Working into their seventies seems perfectly reasonable to senators and economists—the kinds of people who design solvency plans—because appropriate jobs are still available for people like them. But working longer seems like madness to aging miners, loggers, and ditch diggers, people who labor with their backs, because they are already struggling to perform as their bodies weaken. To be sure, Social Security provides disability benefits for those incapable of gainful employment, but that hardly covers the range of people who strain to cross the finish line.

Proponents of raising the retirement age sometimes remind us that the formula for calculating retirement benefits is highly progressive: Lower-income workers receive a higher return on their contributions than affluent workers do. If the question is how much retirees of a given age receive in monthly benefits, their point is correct. But that advantage quickly erodes because affluent people collect benefits years longer than poor people do. Put differently, raising the retirement age during a period of increasing inequality in life expectancy reduces Social Security's progressivity.[22] Policymakers are free to make that choice, but they should do so knowingly.

Benefits

Some policymakers propose reducing benefits for current or future beneficiaries. Their argument is not that these people do not deserve benefits they have earned from a lifetime of contributing to Social Security, but rather that the entire burden of an underfunded system should not fall on workers and their employers. From this perspective, the question is one of balance. What role should current or future beneficiaries play in order to forestall the collapse of the system? Would it not be better for beneficiaries to suffer small, gradual, and predictable reductions rather than face huge benefit cuts in 2034 when the trust fund runs dry?

One set of proposals would reduce benefits for both current and future participants by modifying the formula for cost-of-living adjustments. Since 1975, program administrators have adjusted benefits annually according to the consumer price index. Some economists believe this index overstates inflation because it ignores how consumers alter their buying patterns—purchasing more chicken and less turkey—as relative prices change. These critics advocate using something called a chained price index, which adjusts for such substitutions.[23] According to government actuaries, adopting the chained price index would reduce cost-of-living adjustments by about 0.3 percentage points annually, and eliminate 19 percent of the 75-year actuarial deficit. Others have proposed deeper benefit cuts. For example, reducing cost-of-living adjustments by 0.5 percentage points annually would eliminate 31 percent of the actuarial deficit.[24]

Other proposals focus on future beneficiaries. Some policymakers propose adopting the method eventually included in President Bush's 2005 privatization proposal for calculating a retiree's initial benefits (see chapter 11). This provision, which would reduce initial benefits for younger workers, except for those with very low wages, would eliminate 47 percent of the actuarial deficit. Other policymakers propose changing the number of years used in calculating benefits. For example, increasing the number of working years used for benefit calculations from 35 to 38 would eliminate 9 percent of the actuarial deficit.[25] In short, reformers can save a lot or a little depending on how quickly and how deeply they choose to reduce benefits.

Other policymakers propose *increasing* benefits for all retirees or for particularly needy retirees. For example, some critics argue that the formula for cost-of-living adjustments is biased against retirees because prices for health care increase more rapidly than other prices, and because retirees spend more on health care than younger consumers do. A better index for adjusting Social Security benefits would use seniors' actual consumption patterns, rather than using workers' consumption patterns, as the current index does.[26] According to the actuaries, adopting a special price index for seniors would increase annual cost-of-living adjustments by about 0.2 percentage points. Rather than closing the solvency gap, such a change would *increase* the actuarial deficit by 13 percent.[27] Other critics argue that Social Security does not do enough to support the most vulnerable retirees. Some proposals would increase the minimum benefit for retirees with very low lifetime earnings. Others would provide extra funds for retirees aged 85 and older. All such proposals would increase the actuarial deficit.

Whether it makes sense to increase benefits when the system is already underfunded is a fair question. Most proponents recognize that increasing benefits would require policymakers to raise additional revenues beyond what is needed to fix the long-term solvency problem. But they also recognize that policymaking for Social Security is no longer a regular occurrence on Capitol Hill. The time between congressional enactments is now measured in decades, not years. In their view, the time to increase benefits is when the Social Security train is in the station, not after it departs.

Comprehensive Solvency Plans

These individual provisions—adjusting retirement ages, benefit formulas, tax rates, and the maximum taxable wage base—are the building blocks for comprehensive solvency plans. Sometimes groups of policy experts construct elaborate solvency plans and argue why their selections of particular provisions are optimal. Sometimes opinion researchers ask individual citizens to assemble their own solvency plans, with each respondent selecting from a list of individual provisions until their selections close the entire 75-year actuarial deficit. Sometimes legislators design comprehensive plans, send them to the actuaries for scoring, and then introduce bills that would adjust the statutory tax and benefit formulas. Subsequent chapters examine these plans.

The rest of the book explores the politics of fixing Social Security. Part III examines how various players view Social Security, including legislators, policy experts, interest groups, and ordinary citizens. Part IV analyzes the politics of enacting solvency plans, including the incremental options discussed in this chapter and the privatization plans disused in the previous chapter.

PART III

The Players

6

Polarized Policymakers

OVER THE PAST FOUR DECADES, policymakers have become increasingly divided over Social Security. These divisions appear in every corner of the policymaking environment. Experts disagree on the nature of Social Security's problems and how to fix them. Party platforms promise to move Social Security in opposite directions. Democratic and Republican officeholders support different remedies.

This is an enormous departure from the policymaking environment during Social Security's expansionary era. Between 1950 and 1972, Democratic and Republican officeholders were partners, not rivals. They worked together to enlarge Social Security, transforming it from a fledgling program offering meager retirement benefits for half the workforce into a mammoth program offering retirement, spousal, disability, and survivor benefits for most workers and their families. Although Democrats often initiated change, Republican officeholders were their reliable collaborators. Working together, lawmakers expanded the program, received nearly universal applause from their constituents, and expanded it again.

The fun stopped in the mid-1970s when lawmakers faced their first solvency crisis. Suddenly, the choice was between increasing taxes and reducing benefits, neither an appealing option. Only then did lawmakers begin to divide along party lines. Most Democrats preferred raising taxes. Most Republicans opposed raising taxes, preferring to pare back benefits, especially for future retirees. Democrats prevailed in the 1977 showdown, as lawmakers enacted substantial tax increases in order to protect all beneficiaries. Six years later, in the second solvency crisis, legislators compromised, but with benefit cuts vastly exceeding revenue increases. What began as mild partisan division over Social Security in the late 1970s gradually evolved into today's deeper divisions.

This chapter shows how various policymakers changed their positions on Social Security over time. Of course, actions speak louder than words. That is, we should prefer knowing what legislators *did* on important Social Security bills to knowing what they said on the campaign trail. Unfortunately, Congress last called the roll on an important Social Security bill in 1983, so this chapter rests heavily on announced positions.

Party Platforms

One way to examine how this polarization developed is to compare the quadrennial party platforms. Reading the 42 Democratic and Republican platforms from 1940 to 2020 reveals three distinct periods.[1] From 1948 to 1980, the two parties took virtually identical positions on Social Security. Both parties advocated expanding coverage and increasing benefits. Both parties claimed credit after doing so. Both parties promised to do even more—for example, creating automatic benefit adjustments for inflation. Both parties favored eliminating work restrictions so that seniors could simultaneously work and collect benefits. The only noticeable difference was that Democrats regularly favored raising the maximum taxable wage base, while Republicans never targeted high-paid workers.

Party platforms were noticeably more partisan from 1984 to 1996. The 1984 Democratic platform declared that Democrats were largely responsible for blocking President Reagan's 1981 proposal to slash benefits for early retirees. In fact, it was a bipartisan congressional effort. The 1984 Republican platform asserted that Republicans were largely responsible for forging the 1983 plan that restored Social Security to solvency. It, too, was a bipartisan effort. These partisan efforts to allocate credit and blame continued throughout the period. As late as 1996, the Republican platform claimed that the 1983 solvency reform was the result of Republican leadership.[2] Democrats maintained that Social Security's creators were its natural protectors.

Party platforms from 2000 to 2020 portrayed Social Security in deeply partisan ways. Republican platforms claimed Social Security was in dire fiscal health. They proposed replacing it with a system of personal retirement accounts for younger workers, while preserving traditional Social Security for retirees and near retirees. Democrats claimed Social Security was fundamentally healthy. Its future could be secured either by allocating the federal government's emerging surplus to cover Social Security's long-term deficit (2000 platform) or by increasing the maximum taxable wage base to raise additional revenue from well-paid workers (2008 and 2016 platforms).

The 2016 Republican and Democratic platforms capture this deep partisan polarization. Consider the following two excerpts. Republicans (2016):

> We reject the old maxim that Social Security is the "Third Rail" of American politics, deadly for anyone who would change it. The Democratic Party still treats it that way, even though everyone knows that its current course will lead to a financial and social disaster. . . . As Republicans, we oppose tax increases and believe in the power of markets to create wealth and to help secure the future of our Social Security system.[3]

Democrats (2016):

> We will fight every effort to cut, privatize, or weaken Social Security, including attempts to raise the retirement age, diminish benefits by cutting cost-of-living adjustments, or reducing earned benefits. . . . We will make sure Social Security's guaranteed benefits continue for generations to come by asking those at the top to pay more, and will achieve this goal by taxing some of the income of people above $250,000. . . . Our plan contrasts starkly with Donald Trump. He has referred to Social Security as a "Ponzi scheme" and has called for privatizing it as well as increasing the retirement age.[4]

Four years later, Republicans simply reprinted their entire 2016 platform, arguing that assembling during the Covid-19 pandemic to draft a new platform was not safe. In contrast, Democrats promised to both preserve and expand Social Security. Democrats (2020):

> Democrats will reject every effort to cut, privatize, or weaken Social Security, including attempts to raise the retirement age, diminish benefits by cutting cost-of-living adjustments, or reduce earned benefits. . . . We will enact policies to make Social Security more progressive, including increasing benefits for all beneficiaries, meaningfully increasing minimum benefit payments, increasing benefits for long-duration beneficiaries, and protecting surviving spouses from benefit cuts.[5]

One party rejects privatization; the other celebrates markets as the solution to Social Security's problems. One party rejects new taxes for anyone; the other proposes tax increases for the affluent and more benefits for all. Social Security is now a deeply partisan issue.

Presidents

Party platforms do not always capture the views of presidential candidates. The 1980 Republican platform, for example, was very protective of Social Security, calling it "one of this nation's most vital commitments to our senior citizens," and committing the party to "save, and then strengthen, this fundamental contract between our government and its productive citizens."[6] Candidate Ronald Reagan, however, offered considerably less protection. During the October debate, he completely rejected raising taxes. Instead, the future president proposed creating an expert task force to study the program's actuarial problems, promising only "no one presently dependent on Social Security is going to have the rug pulled out from under them and not get their check."[7] Clearly, the party and its standard-bearer viewed Social Security differently. Seven months later, Republican officeholders revealed how far apart they were on Social Security when President Reagan proposed enormous benefit cuts and Republican legislators quickly rejected them.

In 2016 and 2020, the Republican candidate and the Republican platform were again misaligned. But now it was the candidate, Donald Trump, who promised not to cut or change Social Security, while the Republican platform called for market-based reforms. During the first campaign, Trump promised to leave Social Security alone. And he did. During the second campaign, the president suggested that "I'm going to terminate the payroll tax, which is another thing that some of the great economists would like to see done. We'll be paying into Social Security through the general fund. And it works out very nicely."[8] Although it was not clear if the president meant switching to general funds permanently or only during the pandemic, either position would be a huge departure from Republican orthodoxy. By his actions, President Trump also made clear that Social Security was not a priority. He never once proposed or endorsed a solvency reform during his four years in office.

More commonly, the candidate's platform *is* the party platform. For example, the 2000 and 2004 Republican platforms outlined how George W. Bush planned to replace a portion of traditional Social Security with personal retirement accounts. These two Republican platforms were excellent guides to what the president formally proposed in 2005. But the platforms were poor guides to what Republican legislators were willing to approve. Despite Republican control of the House and Senate, and despite enormous presidential pressure, neither chamber embraced the president's privatization plan. The huge transition costs made the plan politically risky for most lawmakers (see chapter 11).

The only other recent president to recommend that Congress enact a specific solvency plan was Bill Clinton. His party's platforms offered little guidance for what he would eventually propose. The 1992 Democratic platform never mentioned Social Security. The 1996 platform simply declared, "We will fight to save it." The actual impetus to Clinton's proposal was the unexpected surplus in the federal budget, a surplus that experts projected would continue for many years (assuming Congress did not increase spending or cut taxes). In his 1999 State of the Union address, the president proposed committing "60 percent of the budget surplus for the next 15 years to Social Security, investing a small portion in the private sector, just as any private or state government pension would do," and using the investment earnings to "keep Social Security sound for 55 years."[9] The Republican Congress showed little interest in his plan, arguing that cutting income taxes was a higher priority. Two years later, a Republican president and a Republican Congress did cut income taxes, thus eliminating both the surplus and the lifeline to Social Security.

Three of the last six full-term presidents—Reagan, Clinton, and Bush—proposed solvency plans during their time in office. The Reagan plan involved cutting both benefits and taxes. The Clinton plan recommended using general funds to shore up Social Security. The Bush plan proposed reinventing Social Security for younger workers, while borrowing trillions of dollars to fund the transition. Without the bother of hearings, markups, or roll call votes, Congress rejected all three plans. Republican lawmakers refused to support any of the plans. Democrats were united in opposing the Reagan and Bush plans, but seemed open to the Clinton plan.

The only solvency plan that Congress found acceptable during the past four decades was the 1983 Greenspan plan. Its advantages were two. First, bill drafting was the work of a bipartisan commission, not a partisan president. Second, and more importantly, the clock was running down. Failure to approve the commission's plan—and there were no others on the table—would force immediate cuts in everyone's Social Security benefits.

Legislators

Where do legislators stand on fixing Social Security? It is always challenging to determine where 535 members of the House and Senate stand on any issue, especially one that is not on the active decision agenda. It is even tougher to show how their positions have changed over time. Although roll call votes are often a good way to chart changing positions, the last significant vote on Social Security was in 1983.

Here I summarize a collection of policy statements that individual House members made on Social Security prior to the 2014 congressional elections. The interest group AARP assembled this collection by searching legislators' speeches, writings, and websites for their views on how they would "protect Social Security for today's seniors and strengthen it for future generations."[10] The organization then produced 471 four-page color flyers, one for each House and Senate contest, and shared them with the media, its own members, and voters.[11]

Reading the policy statements of the 367 House members running for re-election in 2014 reveals several fault lines.[12] The statements by the 188 Republican incumbents were especially good at capturing Social Security's gloomy future if Congress failed to act. Republican legislators often mentioned the exact year when expenditures would first exceed revenues and the trust fund would start to shrink, or the exact year when the trust fund would run dry and retirement benefits would be cut. The drumbeat of pessimism seemed to suggest that Social Security needed wholesale reinvention. In contrast, the statements by the 179 Democratic incumbents were more optimistic. Democratic legislators acknowledged the seriousness of Social Security's problems, but mostly as a prelude to the need for solutions that would preserve the program. They repeatedly emphasized a search for "common-sense" solutions. Democrats—but never Republicans—praised President Reagan for accepting bipartisan solutions during Social Security's 1983 solvency crisis. Republican legislators seemed to recall Reagan exclusively as a tax cutter. But Democrats remembered a president who accepted some tax increases as part of the Greenspan Commission's share-the-pain compromise.

Republican legislators seldom endorsed specific solutions that would impose costs on anyone. For example, Martha Roby (R-AL) was clear with her objections—"I oppose raising the retirement age; I oppose cutting benefits; I oppose increasing payroll taxes"—but she never mentioned how she would close the growing gap between expected revenues and promised benefits.[13] Many others shared both her objections to imposing costs on anyone and her reluctance to endorse specific solutions.[14] How many Republicans supported raising the retirement age? I counted seven, but mostly for temporally distant cohorts.[15] How many Republicans supported reducing benefits for current retirees? That would be one, Speaker John Boehner (R-OH), who supported reducing benefits for well-off retirees.[16] How many Republicans supported raising the maximum taxable wage base that limits taxes for well-paid workers? Just two: Mark Meadows (R-NC) and John Shimkus (R-IL).[17] Several Republicans advocated ideas that would *worsen* the solvency crisis. For example, three legislators proposed eliminating the income tax on Social Security benefits for some retirees, a crucial source of revenue introduced by the Greenspan Commission.[18]

Democratic legislators were more willing to impose costs to save Social Security. Twenty-two Democrats explicitly endorsed raising the maximum taxable wage base, a solution that would close much of the solvency gap. Two legislators proposed raising the tax rate for all workers. Several Democrats endorsed package proposals, like the Simpson-Bowles plan, which included raising the retirement age, raising the wage base, and lowering cost-of-living adjustments.[19] Other Democratic legislators were less specific about who should pay, but by praising past deals, such as those between President Reagan and Speaker O'Neill in 1983, they signaled a willingness to impose costs.

Nearly half the Democratic legislators explicitly opposed privatizing Social Security. I counted 77 Democratic legislators who opposed privatization by name, while 5 others clearly had privatization on their minds when they disparaged "Wall Street solutions" to Social Security's insolvency.[20] Republican House members displayed more complicated views. Nineteen Republican legislators opposed privatization by name, while only two Republicans explicitly endorsed it.[21] A more careful reading of their statements, however, reveals many closet supporters. I counted forty Republicans who praised elements of privatization—eliminating mandatory contributions, giving workers an ownership stake, allowing young workers to control their nest eggs, diverting payroll contributions into personal retirement accounts, investing in the stock market—or who endorsed specific plans, like the Roadmap for America's Future, that embraced privatization. For Republicans, the term "privatization" is now a toxic word. But many Republican legislators still favor the central tenet of privatization—namely, that workers should own their payroll contributions and invest them as they wish.

While speaking about reinventing Social Security, Republican legislators were careful to assure current retirees that their benefits were secure. As John Fleming (R-LA) put it, "comprehensive reform can be achieved without adversely affecting any current or near-retiree."[22] I counted 86 Republicans who made similar assurances to current retirees and 47 who did so for near retirees. Although legislators offered no details about how they might insulate current and future beneficiaries from the trust fund's inevitable disappearance, such assurances were necessary for politicians who spoke of reinventing the system. Democratic legislators seldom offered such assurances because they promised to preserve Social Security for everyone.

Democratic and Republican legislators talk about Social Security in very different ways. Democrats seek to preserve traditional Social Security for everyone. They accept that additional revenues are necessary. Republicans seek to reinvent Social Security for younger workers, advocating something like privatization, though avoiding that toxic word. Republicans also seek to protect retirees and near retirees from harm, but they seldom discuss where they would find the revenue to do so.

Policy Experts

The partisan conflict among candidates and officeholders on Social Security did not arise on its own. It began in Social Security's broader policy community. When policy experts were largely united in support of the program, as they were throughout the 1950s, 1960s, and early 1970s, elected politicians were themselves united. But as the policy community fractured in the 1980s and 1990s, politicians followed divergent paths.[23]

Martha Derthick's classic account of policymaking for Social Security, covering the period from 1935 to 1972, found little conflict among policy experts.[24] Expertise was concentrated among the program administrators and actuaries at the Social Security Administration. Administrators had a vision for expanding the program incrementally and a talent for selling their ideas to lawmakers of both parties. The chief actuary, who estimates the financial soundness of proposed policy changes, developed a reputation among lawmakers for neutral competence. In fact, Congress never hired its own Social Security experts, preferring to rely on program administrators and the chief actuary for advice. Although several university-based economists were critics of the program, their objections were often philosophical—Milton Friedman rejected the whole enterprise—rather than being helpful to politicians considering incremental changes to a popular program.

The mature Social Security system eventually attracted the attention of various Washington think tanks, most notably the Brookings Institution and the Urban Institute on the left and the Cato Institute, the American Enterprise Institute, and the Heritage Foundation on the right. Although both liberal and conservative experts criticized aspects of Social Security, the conservative critics changed the conversation. The liberal critique—that the payroll tax was regressive and that retirement benefits were too meager for some recipients—gained little traction in the 1970s once the central problem became insufficient revenue to support the current system.[25] In contrast, the conservative critique, which focused on what critics called design flaws in Social Security—lack of advance funding, excessive redistribution, a worse deal for each successive generation, ever-increasing taxes to support promised benefits—found fertile soil in an increasingly conservative Republican Party.[26]

By 1980, conservatives were offering alternatives, not just critiques. An early Cato plan proposed replacing traditional Social Security with privatized individual accounts. The private sector would establish and manage personal retirement accounts for workers, while the government would use general revenues to support poverty-stricken retirees.[27] Later plans were less radical, offering to retain traditional Social Security for retirees and near retirees, while creating a new advance-funded system of personal retirement accounts for younger workers.

Expertise on Social Security is no longer one-sided or concentrated in the executive branch. In addition to the dozen or so think tanks that employ or convene experts on Social Security, Congress employs its own specialists, located in the Congressional Budget Office, the Congressional Research Service, and its financial committees. There are now experts inside and outside government to advise policymakers of every political persuasion, whether they seek to expand, contract, refashion, or replace traditional Social Security.

Interest Groups

Interest groups once played only a minor role in Social Security policymaking. Derthick called organized labor merely a "collaborator" for program administrators, as they worked to expand Social Security between 1950 and 1972.[28] Business groups, most notably the Chamber of Commerce and the National Association of Manufacturers, were also active, but they mostly sought to slow the program's expansion and to block automatic benefit increases. They were unsuccessful in both quests.[29] It is hard to see how labor, business, or any other interest group left a distinct imprint on Social Security during the expansionary years.

Interest groups are now central players in Social Security policymaking. The most important group is AARP, once known as the American Association of Retired Persons. Founded in 1958, the organization originally offered its members not policy advocacy, but access to services, and particularly discounted health insurance. Although access to services provided the fuel for growth—a million members by 1966, 5 million by 1974, 10 million by 1978, 20 million by 1985—and access to various services is still the primary reason why people join the organization, AARP did not become a serious political force in Washington until the late 1970s.[30] Engaging in both direct and grassroots lobbying, its influence on Social Security policymaking is now unrivaled. AARP distributes both a monthly news bulletin and a bimonthly magazine to its 38 million members, so it can quickly alert them to Washington happenings and encourage them to contact their representatives. AARP also lobbies policymakers directly. In 2017, it employed 51 lobbyists—27 on staff and 24 in outside firms—to monitor what lawmakers were doing and communicate the organization's official positions. Although AARP takes positions on scores of issues, nothing is more central than protecting Social Security and Medicare. When policymakers threaten these programs, it pulls out all the stops. After President Bush proposed privatizing Social Security, AARP quadrupled its lobbying budget, from $8 million in 2004 to $36 million in 2005.[31]

Some interest groups are more concerned with taxes than benefits. The National Federation of Independent Business (NFIB), founded in 1949, became active on Social Security beginning in the early 1980s. Since then, the organization and its 350,000 members have stood firmly against increasing Social Security's payroll tax. The dispersion of federation members across all congressional districts facilitates grassroots lobbying. The group also lobbies lawmakers directly. In 2017, it employed 20 lobbyists—9 on staff and 11 in outside firms.[32] The federation enjoys an additional advantage because so many candidates for elective office come from the business community. During the 117th Congress, for example, 22 House members and 6 senators were themselves members of the federation.[33] What better way to influence policy than to have two dozen seats at the table?

An important newcomer is Americans for Tax Reform (ATR), founded in 1985 by Grover Norquist, who still heads the group. By Washington standards it is a tiny organization, with annual expenditures of only $6 million, compared with $100 million for NFIB and $1.5 billion for AARP.[34] Its influence flows principally from the Taxpayer Protection Pledge, known informally as the Norquist pledge. The organization asks all candidates for legislative office to sign a pledge promising that they will *never* vote to increase taxes. Most Republican candidates quickly agree. It is the best way to avoid alienating Republican voters or donors. Who wants to be the lone candidate in a Republican primary who did not sign the pledge? Consequently, most Republican legislators today have pledged to oppose one of the principal alternatives for restoring Social Security's solvency.[35] The organization devotes more than one-quarter of its annual budget to obtaining the pledge from candidates running for state and national offices, nearly triple what it spends on direct lobbying.[36] It seems like money well spent. It takes vulnerable candidates, perhaps running in their first primaries, and commits them to ATR's principal goal. No wonder the organization spends so little on direct lobbying. Its lobbyists need only identify congressional votes that would violate the pledge and remind legislators of their signed commitments.

These three groups make solvency reform vastly more difficult because they oppose the principal alternatives for achieving solvency: raising taxes or cutting benefits. But these groups are far from alone. The Chamber of Commerce, the National Association of Manufacturers, and many other employer groups work with Americans for Tax Reform and the National Federation of Independent Business to oppose raising Social Security's payroll tax. So, too, does the Club for Growth, an influential antitax organization. On the benefit side, more than 70 advocacy organizations, joined together as the Leadership Council of Aging Organizations, work to coordinate and magnify AARP's efforts to protect traditional Social Security.

Most groups are nonpartisan. They work with members of both parties to advance their interests. That said, many groups find a greater affinity with one party or the other. Three scholars—Jesse Crosson, Alexander Furnas, and Geoffrey Lorenz—developed a method for measuring partisan affinity by examining both how 950 legislators voted on 1,035 bills between 2005 and 2016, and where nearly 2,600 groups stood on those bills. They place both sets of findings on a standard left–right scale, which allows a direct comparison between the positions of legislators, parties, and groups. By this measure, the Chamber of Commerce and the National Federation of Independent Business took positions very close to the median Republican legislator during this period—or, equivalently, the typical Republican legislator voted almost exactly the way these two groups preferred. In contrast, Americans for Tax Reform and the Club for Growth were more conservative than the typical Republican. These groups aim to pull Republicans even further to the right of their regular positions. By the same measure, AARP took positions to the left of the median Democrat. Its absolutist positions on Social Security and Medicare—no cuts ever—as well as its consistent support for regulating things like prescription drug prices are part of a strategy to pull legislators to the left of their regular positions.[37]

Advisory Councils

Advisory councils once played an important role in Social Security policymaking. Created intermittently in the first two decades, and then established by statute beginning in 1956, these councils brought together representatives of business, labor, and the public to consider proposals to modify Social Security. According to Derthick's account, these deliberations mattered because they helped create consensus among stakeholders in advance of congressional action.[38] To be sure, consensus was partly achieved by appointing council members who were favorably disposed toward the program, and then reappointing those who were especially effective. Three individuals—an economist who served on five of the first six councils, a labor leader who served on four, and a business leader who served on three—groomed newly appointed members, helped forge compromises within the councils, and testified as experts before congressional committees.[39] Indeed, creating new experts on Social Security, at a time when there were few experts outside the Social Security Administration, was an important role for the early councils.

The advisory councils gradually lost influence in the late 1970s. One reason was the proliferation of policy experts in think tanks and academia. A second was that many groups with divergent interests became active on Social Security. The notion of a consensus view among business, labor, and the public was no longer tenable. A third reason was that solvency replaced expansion as the principal agenda item. Since most solvency proposals required policymakers to impose costs, achieving consensus was extremely difficult. As the law prescribed, successive secretaries of health and human services appointed new councils every few years, but the councils accomplished little.[40]

The final advisory council (1994–96) included the statutorily required balance of business, labor, and public representatives. But as the solvency conflicts of 1977 and 1983 revealed, organized labor and organized business no longer viewed Social Security through the same lens. The divergence was even greater among the so-called public representatives. Robert Ball, perhaps the leading architect of Social Security's expansion from the late 1940s to the early 1970s, was a member. So, too, was Carolyn Weaver, an economist with two decades of books and articles criticizing the program as unsustainable.[41] The 13-member council split into factions and offered three alternative solvency plans. The largest faction proposed incremental changes to preserve traditional Social Security. The next largest proposed replacing a portion of the current program with advance-funded, individually directed retirement accounts. A third faction proposed adding smaller individual accounts, while preserving more of traditional Social Security.[42]

This final advisory council was consequential. By embracing advance funding and partial privatization, the council transformed the Washington debate. It helped legitimate the notion that individual retirement accounts could be part of Social Security reform. It stimulated a wave of new proposals featuring individual accounts, with both Democrats and Republicans as sponsors.[43] Privatization was no longer a fringe idea advanced by libertarians and academics. It was now a legitimate alternative to traditional Social Security.[44]

Deficits

Republicans were once fiscal hawks who abhorred deficits. Actually, when they are out of power, Republicans still abhor deficits—Democratic deficits, Obama deficits, Biden deficits. When they control the White House, however, Republicans are increasingly tolerant of deficits. Republicans in Congress eagerly supported the Bush 2001 tax cuts and the Trump 2017 tax cuts without much concern for the deficits that were sure to follow. The same was true for the wars in Iraq and Afghanistan, the recent defense buildup, and the congressional response to the 2020 pandemic. The root cause of Republicans' newfound tolerance for deficits is their promise—their signed promise—*never* to increase taxes. Deficits are the principal alternative to taxes for those with a taste for ships, wars, and reelection.

What makes fixing Social Security so difficult for Republicans is that the program cannot run deficits. Of course, Congress could change the law and allow general funds to fund a portion of Social Security benefits. That was actually the plan of Roosevelt's 1934 Committee on Economic Security, before the president insisted that Social Security be self-supporting. One argument for using general funds today is that the program is heavily redistributive and redistribution works better with a progressive income tax than a regressive payroll tax. Another argument is that Medicare, which is also redistributive, has been funded since inception with both general funds and a dedicated payroll tax. Although some Democratic legislators find these arguments appealing, most Republicans do not.

Some Republicans have come to accept deficit financing as an option, not to preserve traditional Social Security, but to finance the transition to private retirement accounts. For example, the government could borrow money to pay benefits for current retirees, while diverting workers and employers' contributions to individual accounts. The transition costs would be enormous. For example, if all contributions were diverted to individual accounts, except for those used to fund disability benefits, the government would need to borrow nearly 5 percent of GDP in the initial year to pay that year's retirement, spousal, and survivors benefits, followed by a slightly smaller sum the second year, as death begins to cull the benefit rolls, and so on for four decades, until the last beneficiary dies. If near retirees were included in the transition—as seems likely—the total cost would be higher and the transition period even longer. Partial privatization would require less borrowing.

Polarization

Why did officeholders polarize on Social Security? Why did Democratic and Republican legislators—once collaborators on Social Security's expansion—come to see the program's future so differently? It is important to understand that the movement was asymmetric. Republicans moved right; Democrats stood pat. Today many Republican officeholders speak of reinventing Social Security, a path not considered during the 1977 and 1983 solvency crises. Republicans' once enthusiastic support for traditional Social Security is now more limited, applying more to retirees and near retirees than to younger workers. Moreover, their positions on taxes have hardened. In 1983, Republican legislators supported some tax increases as part of a plan that mostly relied on benefit cuts. Today they insist on tax-free solutions. In contrast, most Democratic legislators remain enthusiastic supporters of traditional Social Security. Indeed, they appear open to the same types of incremental solutions that Democrats supported during previous crises.

Republican officeholders moved right not just on Social Security but on many other issues, including taxes, spending, immigration, climate change, and the environment. Scholars who study legislative voting have discovered that a single ideological scale summarizes overall voting patterns quite nicely. Republican legislators have been shifting rightward on this scale since the 1970s, with each Republican caucus more conservative than its predecessor. In contrast, the leftward drift among Democrats has been quite modest. This asymmetric polarization among legislators is a general phenomenon. It is not something unique to Social Security.[45]

The forces that pushed Republicans rightward on so many issues are well known. First, the Southern realignment increased the overall congruence between district and member ideology. As Republicans replaced Democrats in conservative Southern districts, the House Republican caucus moved right. Second, ideologically oriented outside groups did more to recruit, train, and fund conservative candidates than they once did. Third, candidates became more reliant on ideologically motivated campaign contributors than on access-oriented political action committees.[46] In short, as Republican districts, activists, and donors became more conservative, so too did the candidates who ran and won.

The rightward shift on Social Security is distinctive only because it also involves the creation of a novel solution. Since the 1983 solvency crisis, policy experts developed privatization as a credible alternative to traditional Social Security. This allowed policymakers to break free of the incremental options— adjusting the revenue and benefit streams—and advocate a new course. In fact, wealthy conservatives funded both the experts who worked out the de- tails of privatization and the organizations and candidates who championed those plans. For example, Charles Koch founded the Cato Institute, which published the first book-length study of privatization in 1980, just as his brother David was running for vice president on the Libertarian ticket, which advocated the repeal of Social Security. Later the two brothers joined forces to create an extraordinarily well-funded network of organizations that engage in policy advocacy, constituency building, and candidate support, helping to push Republican candidates toward free-market solutions like privatization.[47]

How did citizens react to this increasing polarization among policymakers on Social Security? That is the subject of the next chapter.

7

Supportive Citizens

PUBLIC OPINION is often shaped by the actions of politicians, experts, activists, and journalists.[1] When these actors agree on some issue—for example, believing that the 9/11 attacks were acts of terrorism—most people follow their lead. When elite actors divide, however, people tend to follow the lead of those actors with whom they identify most closely. People who identify with a particular party often follow the lead of that party's elected officials. For example, party polarization among people on climate change is largely a consequence of Democratic and Republican politicians taking opposite positions on whether or not climate change is real.[2] The same patterns are evident for people's attitudes on welfare, health care, defense, foreign assistance, and the environment.

This chapter explores whether Republicans followed the lead of Republican policymakers and became increasingly hostile toward traditional Social Security, and whether Democrats followed the lead of Democratic policymakers and remained steadfast supporters. It also examines how support for Social Security varied among other groups, including workers and retirees, the young and the old, the poor and the better-off.

Overall Support

We need a measure of citizens' support for Social Security that covers the period when policymakers began to divide and that includes recent polling. Only one measure meets this standard. Twenty-two times between 1984 and 2018 the General Social Survey (GSS) asked respondents, "Are we spending too much, too little, or about the right amount on Social Security?" As figure 7.1 shows, the most frequent response was "too little." On average, 57 percent of respondents chose this answer.[3] The next most frequent answer

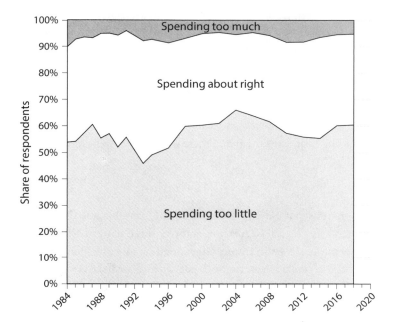

FIGURE 7.1. Citizens' attitudes toward spending on Social Security, 1984–2018. Question: "Are we spending too much, too little, or about the right amount on Social Security?"
Source: General Social Survey 2019.

was "about right," with 37 percent choosing this option. Only 6 percent thought we were spending too much, with a high of 10 percent in 1984 and a low of 4 percent in 1991. Support in the most recent survey (2018) was above the long-term average, with 61 percent responding "too little," 34 percent "about right," and 5 percent "too much."

This evidence suggests that overall support for Social Security has not changed much over the past 34 years. To be sure, the GSS question is not a perfect way to track changing attitudes toward a complicated program. Given that Social Security revenues are the product of a dedicated payroll tax, expenditures are the result of an intricate benefit formula, and the flow of revenues and expenditures must be kept in reasonable balance over time, a single question about spending levels provides an incomplete guide to the range of issues about Social Security's taxing and spending. But we have no better alternative. Only one other organization (American National Election Studies) repeatedly asked people about Social Security and it, too, asked a single question about spending levels. Although the results of the GSS and ANES surveys are similar, the infrequency with which ANES asked about Social Security in the last two decades makes the GSS question the better choice.[4]

The GSS question offers respondents three options: spending too much, spending about right, or spending too little. In order to simplify the presentation, the rest of this chapter ignores the middle option and focuses on respondents' net preference for increasing rather than decreasing Social Security spending. The *net preference* is the difference between the percentage who prefer spending more and the percentage who prefer spending less.

Party Polarization

Figure 7.2 charts separately for Democrats and Republicans their net preference for increasing Social Security spending. Three patterns stand out. First, both Democrats and Republicans prefer spending more to spending less. That is, net preferences are positive for both parties in all years. Averaged across the 22 surveys, 62 percent of Democrats preferred spending more and 4 percent preferred spending less, for a net preference of 58 points. The comparable averages for Republicans were 49 percent for spending more, 9 percent for spending less, with a net preference of 40 points. Second, the trend lines are positive for both groups. The net preference for Democrats increased from 53 points in 1984 to 63 points in 2018. The net preference for Republicans increased from 23 points to 52 points over the same period. Third, party polarization declined over time. This decline is revealed in the bottom line, which plots the difference between Democratic and Republican net preferences. By this measure, party polarization declined from 30 points in 1984 to 11 points in 2018.

The message is inescapable. Although policymakers have become increasingly polarized on Social Security over the past few decades, citizens have not followed their lead. In fact, people today are *less* polarized on Social Security than they were decades ago.

What should we make of the current level of party polarization on Social Security? Is an 11-point gap between Democrats and Republicans big or small? Fortunately, the General Social Survey asks questions about many spending programs, so we can make appropriate comparisons. Figure 7.3, which plots the differences between Democrats' and Republicans' net spending preferences for 21 issues, shows that Social Security in 2018 was among the *least* polarized issues. Huge gaps between Democrats and Republicans exist for welfare (59 points), assistance to Blacks (57), national defense (49), the environment (38), foreign aid (38), and assistance to the poor (35). But only four

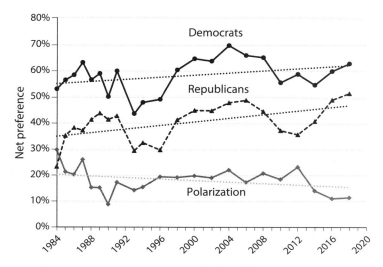

FIGURE 7.2. Party polarization on spending more for Social Security, 1984–2018. Net preference is the difference between the percentage who prefer spending more and the percentage who prefer spending less. Polarization is the difference between the net preferences for Democrats and Republicans. Partisans include those who lean toward a party. Dotted lines are linear trends. *Source*: General Social Survey 2019.

issues had smaller partisan gaps than Social Security: crime (3 points), the space program (5), bridges and highways (8), and drug addiction (10). In short, Social Security stands out for its relatively low level of partisan polarization.

How did Social Security escape the forces of party polarization? For a while, it seemed that it had not. If one were to construct a 1984 version of figure 7.3—that is, rank-order spending issues according to how much Democrats and Republicans disagree—one would find the usual suspects near the top of the polarization scale: assistance to the poor (39 points), assistance to Blacks (29), welfare (27), defense (27), health (26), and the environment (23). In short, the 1984 rank order would look similar to the 2018 rank order, although the differences between Democrats and Republicans would be smaller in 1984. The only surprise is that Social Security would be the second-most polarized issue on the 1984 list, with a 30-point difference between Democrats and Republicans.[5]

Why did Social Security move from the second-most polarized issue in 1984 to one of the least polarized issues in 2018? Are such movements common

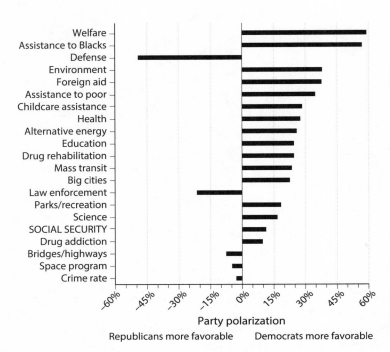

FIGURE 7.3. Party polarization on 21 spending issues, 2018. Polarization is the difference between the net preferences for Democrats and Republicans.
Source: General Social Survey 2019.

or uncommon? Figure 7.4 puts things in perspective by plotting—in two separate panels for clarity—changing levels of polarization over 34 years for six of the most polarized issues in 1984: welfare, assistance to Blacks, national defense, health, the environment, and Social Security. Several patterns stand out. First, short-term variation is common. For example, substantial declines in polarization occurred over the first six years for health, the environment, and Social Security. Second, most long-term trends are toward increased polarization, notably for defense, assistance to Blacks, welfare, and the environment, where a linear trend line captures most of the variation.[6] Third, Social Security is the only issue among the six for which polarization declined over the long term.

In order to understand why popular polarization declined for Social Security, it helps to analyze both short-term variations and long-term trends for the other issues. First, how can we explain short-term fluctuations in polarization? Such variation typically follows changes in the way officeholders speak, campaign, and govern. For example, consider the differences in how President

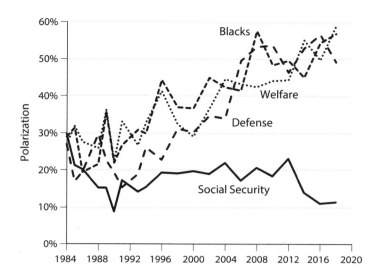

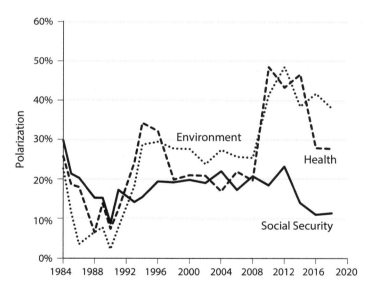

FIGURE 7.4. Changes in party polarization for six issues, 1984–2018. Polarization is measured as the absolute value of the difference between the net spending preferences for Democrats and Republicans. The issues are welfare, assistance to Blacks, national defense, improving and protecting the environment, improving and protecting the nation's health, and Social Security. The trends are plotted in two panels for clarity.

Source: General Social Survey 2019.

Reagan and the first President Bush discussed environmental policy. The former appeared unfriendly to the environment; the latter proposed sweeping improvements in the Clean Air Act, improvements that Congress approved with bipartisan majorities. Notice how quickly party polarization on the environment declined among citizens, from 23 points in 1984 to 2 points in 1990 (figure 7.4, bottom panel). In contrast, polarization among citizens increases when policymakers clash along partisan lines. For example, when President Clinton and Republican legislators split on health-care policy, party polarization on health increased from 12 points in 1991 to 34 points in 1994. When President Obama and Republican legislators battled on the same issue, polarization increased from 20 points in 2008 to 48 points in 2010. In short, intense conflict among Democratic and Republican officeholders increases party polarization among citizens.

But what about long-term changes in polarization? These trends typically follow *persistent* changes in the way candidates and officeholders speak, campaign, and govern. Democratic and Republican officeholders split on race, welfare, and national defense decades ago. Those divisions intensified over time and they persist today. By the mid-1990s, officials had also split on the environment. These partisan disagreements affected how candidates campaigned for office. They affected what politicians did in office. And they affected how Democratic and Republican citizens viewed these policies.

Social Security is unusual in that intense partisan polarization appeared only at the start of the time series. One stimulus for this divergence was President Reagan's 1981 attempt to cut Social Security benefits, which Democrats quickly used to tar other Republicans. A second stimulus was the 1983 solvency crisis itself, where Democratic and Republican officials disagreed on how to fix the program. Although legislators from both parties eventually approved the Greenspan plan, the partisan clashes leading up to that compromise left a clear imprint on public opinion when pollsters asked about Social Security the following year. Once solvency was restored, and politicians stopped bickering, partisan differences quickly declined, from the initial 30 points in 1984, to 20 points in 1986, 15 in 1988, and 9 in 1990.

Party polarization on Social Security ticked up again in subsequent years— averaging 20 points from 1996 to 2012—as policymakers tangled over whether to use the budget surplus to shore up the program in the late 1990s, whether to approve President Bush's privatization plan in 2005, and whether to modify cost-of-living adjustments during the Obama years. More recently, polarization declined again—averaging 12 points in the three most recent surveys—as policymakers largely ignored Social Security. To be sure, Democratic and Republican candidates and officeholders still take divergent positions on Social Security, but they do so relatively quietly, outside the glare of actual policymaking. Apparently, quiet talk does little to divide a public that remains largely content with the status quo.

Workers and Retirees

Political party is one of several cleavages that could affect whether people support a program. Another is whether people currently benefit from the program. During the 2012 presidential campaign, for example, candidate Mitt Romney argued that what mattered in politics was whether a citizen was a "maker" or a "taker." In his view, the 47 percent of citizens who collect governmental benefits (the takers) were natural supporters of President Obama, while those who pay the bills (the makers) should flock to Romney. Applied to Social Security, this suggests that workers and retirees would have divergent views on the program.

Figure 7.5 reveals no such difference in how workers and retirees evaluate Social Security.[7] Between 1984 and 2018, workers' net preference for increased spending was actually 5 points *greater* than retirees' net preference.[8] To be sure, the difference has narrowed in recent years—and even reversed in one recent survey—but that is a long way from suggesting that current workers and current beneficiaries differ significantly in their support for Social Security. In short, the evidence provides no support for the notion that workers and retirees have fundamentally different views of Social Security.

Work status is a crude indicator of how people feel about spending on Social Security because it lumps together workers of many ages. Perhaps younger workers oppose expansion because retirement is distant and they prefer current to deferred compensation. Perhaps older workers focus more on Social Security's solvency and accept the need for more revenue to shore up the system because they will soon rely on the program for retirement. Figure 7.6 examines this question by exploring respondents' net preference for Social Security by their exact chronological ages, 18 to 80.

The results for the most recent five surveys (solid line in figure 7.6) suggest that age does matter. Its effects are relatively small, however, involving only the youngest and oldest participants. Between 2010 and 2018, net spending preferences averaged 35 points for respondents under age 30, compared with

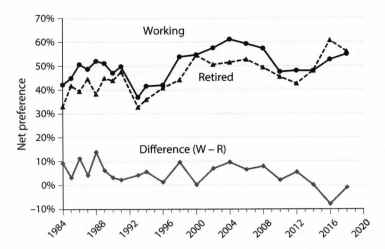

FIGURE 7.5. Net preference for spending more on Social Security by work status, 1984–2018. Workers include full- and part-time workers.
Source: General Social Survey 2019.

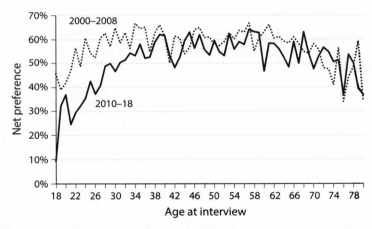

FIGURE 7.6. Net preference for spending more on Social Security by age, 1984–2018. Does not include respondents older than 80.
Source: General Social Survey 2019.

54 points for those between 30 and 80. Within the younger group, there was a relatively steep gradient, as support increased from 9 points at age 18, to 50 points at age 29. Within the older age group, there was no obvious relationship between age and support, with the exception of a small decline after 70. Exactly why younger people are less supportive of Social Security than their

elders is not clear. It appears, however, to be a recent phenomenon. Between 2000 and 2008, the differences between the two age groups were much smaller (dotted line in figure 7.6). Net spending preferences averaged 52 points for respondents under age 30, compared with 58 points for those between 30 and 80.

Overall, the evidence for Romney's makers-and-takers hypothesis is thin. Workers and retirees seem equally supportive of Social Security. Although age matters a bit, it mostly matters within the youngest age cohort, which includes people still in college and people just beginning their careers. By the time respondents have worked for a few years, their views are indistinguishable from respondents in their thirties, forties, fifties, sixties, and seventies. In short, the notion that the politics of Social Security is fundamentally a zero-sum conflict between makers and takers, workers and retirees, or the young and the old, enjoys little empirical support.

Income

Another possibility is that respondents vary in their support for Social Security depending on their income. Most Social Security participants are, sequentially, makers and takers, contributing to the program during their working years, and later collecting benefits as retired or disabled workers. It may not matter where they are on life's trajectory as long as they earn—or expect to earn—a reasonable return on their contributions. But as chapter 4 demonstrates, Social Security is a much better deal for low-income workers than it is for high-income workers. So perhaps affluent citizens are disaffected about Social Security because they earn poor returns on their contributions.

Figure 7.7 examines whether attitudes toward spending on Social Security relate to total family income. It tracks the net preferences for four groups of respondents: the poorest 30 percent, the middle 30 percent, the next 30 percent, and the richest 10 percent.[9] Several patterns stand out. First, all four income groups supported spending more on Social Security in all 22 surveys. Second, the extent of support varied across the income groups. In the lowest income group, the net preference for increased spending averaged 57 points, compared with 55 points for the next higher group, 47 points for the following group, and 30 points for the top group. Third, the differences among income groups narrowed considerably in the most recent survey (gray line in the bottom panel of figure 7.7). People in the top decile—those earning $170,000 or more—were only 10 points less supportive of increased spending in 2018 than

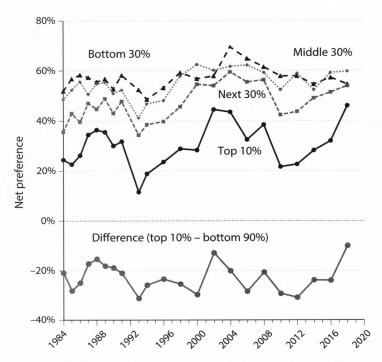

FIGURE 7.7. Net preference for spending more on Social Security by income, 1984–2018. Total family income categories in the original surveys have been recoded into four groups: bottom three income deciles, middle three deciles, next three deciles, and top decile.
Source: General Social Survey 2019.

those in the bottom nine deciles. In short, income does affect the strength of support for more Social Security spending, but the differences among income groups are not large. It would be a mistake to conclude that high-income folks are seriously disaffected with the program.

A separate targeted survey suggests that very wealthy people may be less supportive of Social Security than the typical well-off folks who populate the top income decile in ordinary surveys. In 2011, investigators interviewed a random sample of the top 1 percent of wealth holders in the Chicago area. One-third of these respondents reported annual household incomes over $1 million.[10] When asked whether spending on Social Security should be "expanded, kept about the same, or cut back," wealthy respondents' net preference for expansion was *negative* 33 points—that is, more respondents wanted to cut spending than expand it. By comparison, the net preference for expansion was positive 46 points for a national sample of citizens asked the exact same question several months earlier. The wealthy respondents were more negative about spending on Social Security than they were about spending on environmental protection, health care, food stamps, or job programs.[11]

The overall evidence on income effects is reasonably clear. Respondents in the top income decile support increased Social Security spending, although not quite as enthusiastically as lower deciles. Only the uber-wealthy seem to oppose spending more on Social Security. Unfortunately, we have no information about where along the income continuum from $170,000 to $1 million the shift from support to opposition takes place.[12]

My overall assessment is that citizens' support for Social Security is remarkably unaffected by age, work status, income, or party identification. Yes, there are differences to note, but some results are counterintuitive (work status) and others are diminishing (income and partisanship). The most striking finding is that partisan polarization among citizens is declining, largely driven by increased support for Social Security among Republicans. Some scholars might wonder if any of these conclusions change in a multivariate analysis. They do not.[13]

Policy Priorities

Do people consider fixing Social Security a priority? After all, nothing bad happens until 2034, so what is the hurry? In fact, people regularly emphasize the importance of doing something soon. Since 1997, the Pew Research Center has asked people every January what policy priorities Congress and the president should pursue in the coming year. Interviewers mention issues one by one from a list of about 20, and ask whether that issue should be a "top priority, an important but lower priority, not too important, or should not be done." One issue is always "taking steps to make the Social Security System financially sound." In the first year (1997), respondents put Social Security top on the list, tied with education. Only four times in 25 years has it been lower than fifth.[14] The only issues that regularly outrank Social Security are the economy, education, and terrorism. In short, people want Congress and the president to fix Social Security's solvency problem soon.

One advantage of the Pew question is that it allows us to revisit the issue of party polarization. Given the aforementioned limitations of the GSS question on spending levels, it is helpful to have a second measure to determine if the unexpectedly low polarization on Social Security in the GSS survey appears

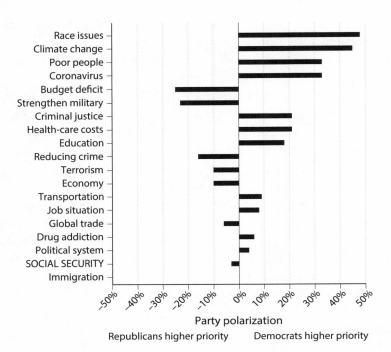

FIGURE 7.8. Party polarization on the nation's top priorities, 2021. Party polarization is the difference between the percentages of Democrats and Republicans who believe an issue should be a top priority.
Source: Pew Research Center 2021.

in other surveys. Figure 7.8 displays the differences between the percentages of Democrats and Republicans who believed various issues should be a top priority in 2021. Like the previous ordered list from the GSS survey (figure 7.3), the 19 issues are rank-ordered from the most polarized to the least polarized issue. Race tops the list, with 72 percent of Democrats, but only 24 percent of Republicans, believing it should be a top priority (difference of 48 points). Immigration is at the bottom of the list, with 39 percent of Republicans and 39 percent of Democrats believing it should be a top priority. Notice that Social Security is second from the bottom, with 54 percent of Republicans and 51 percent of Democrats believing it should be a top priority (difference of 3 points). In short, both the GSS and Pew surveys underscore how *little* Democrats and Republicans disagree about Social Security.

Figure 7.9 explores how party polarization as measured in the Pew surveys has varied between 1997 and 2021. The top two lines display the percentages

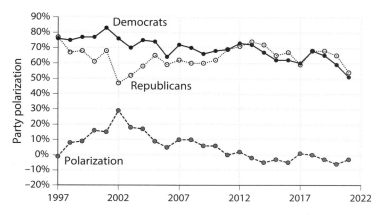

FIGURE 7.9. Party polarization on Social Security as a top priority, 1997–2021. Party polarization is the difference between the percentages of Democrats and Republicans who believe Social Security should be a top priority.
Sources: Pew Research Center 2020 and 2021.

of Democrats and Republicans who believe Social Security should be a top priority, while the bottom line shows the difference between the top two. According to this measure, polarization was essentially zero in 1997, increased steadily during the next five surveys, and then returned to essentially zero near the start of the Great Recession. When polarization first appeared, it was largely because Republicans lost interest in immediate action. The stimulus was probably President Clinton's proposal to use the budget surplus to save Social Security, which Republican leaders strongly opposed. The larger story, however, is that both Democrats and Republicans regularly place Social Security near the top of their lists of what they want Congress and the president to address. Moreover, the current difference between the two partisan groups is negligible.

Citizens do differ in how urgently they want Congress and the president to fix Social Security. For example, it matters how old they are. Dividing a recent (2018) Pew sample by age reveals that only 54 percent of those between 18 and 29 identify Social Security as a top priority, compared with 60 percent of those 30 to 39, 71 percent of those 40 to 49, 74 percent of those 50 to 59, and 80 percent of those 60 to 69—a difference of 26 points between the youngest and oldest age groups.[15] It also matters how well-off they are. Dividing the Pew sample by income reveals that 77 percent of those earning less than $20,000 identify Social Security as a top priority, compared with 60 percent of those earning $150,000 or more—a difference of 17 points.[16] Presumably, age and income matter because they reflect how much more important Social Security benefits are for the old and the poor than they are for the young and the rich. But do not lose sight of the principal message: Majorities of every age and every income group believe that fixing Social Security should be a top priority for Congress and the president.

Officeholders

People have views about Social Security. But as citizens, they have no direct role in choosing policy alternatives. Instead, voters choose among House, Senate, and presidential candidates, who offer various packages of positions, priorities, and accomplishments. How do officeholders' records on Social Security affect how people evaluate their performance?

Early evidence about how people viewed presidential performance on Social Security is thin. Pollsters asked five times in the 1950s whether the Eisenhower administration was doing "a very good job, a fairly good job, or a poor job in improving Social Security." Respondents gave the president high marks, with 41 and 39 percent selecting the first two options and only 10 percent selecting the last.[17] Having learned that most people were content with the first Republican president in two decades, pollsters asked no more questions about how presidents were handling Social Security for 24 years. Perhaps that was not surprising, given that Presidents Kennedy, Johnson, Nixon, Ford, and Carter consistently supported the program.[18]

During the 1980 presidential campaign, however, some pollsters must have sensed that Social Security was becoming more controversial. They asked whether candidate Ronald Reagan was "for or against guaranteeing the continuation of the Social Security System." Of the respondents, 55 percent declared he was for, 22 percent against, and 23 percent were not sure.[19] Although hardly a ringing endorsement, given the poll's language about keeping Social Security, it was still a positive reading. The next year, after President Reagan proposed massive cuts for early retirees, pollsters returned to the field to gauge citizens' reactions. They were livid. Respondents remained unhappy with President Reagan in 22 polls conducted in 1981, 1982, and 1983, where an average of 65 percent rated him negatively and only 30 percent rated him positively.[20] Near the end of his administration, when pollsters asked whether President Reagan's policies had "helped or hurt people on Social Security," only 8 percent selected helped, while 47 percent selected hurt.[21] The Reagan case shows that threatening Social Security—even unsuccessfully—can inflict long-term damage on a president's reputation.

The case of the second President Bush reinforces this conclusion. Near the end of the 2000 presidential campaign, a pollster asked in three separate polls, "Which presidential candidate, Al Gore or George W. Bush, do you trust to do a better job protecting the Social Security system?" Respondents favored Gore by one point in the first two polls and Bush by two points in the third.[22] In short, the two candidates were tied. In subsequent years, the same pollster asked, "Do you approve or disapprove of the way George W. Bush is handling Social Security?" Over twelve polls during his first term in office, the president's approval level on Social Security exceeded his disapproval level by two points.[23] After the 2004 election, however, when the president campaigned for partial privatization of Social Security, the public quickly soured. Over six polls during the year after reelection, Bush's average disapproval level on Social Security exceeded his approval level by 21 points.[24] At one point, 64 percent disapproved of his performance on Social Security, while only 31 percent approved.[25] People turned against the president because he threatened to dismantle a popular program that was fiercely defended by its advocates.

Democratic candidates and Democratic presidents enjoy no natural advantage on Social Security. When pollsters asked during the 1992 campaign, "Which candidate for president would do the best job protecting the Social Security system?" they found a virtual tie between Bill Clinton, Ross Perot, and President Bush.[26] Two years later, after Republicans seized control of the House and elected Newt Gingrich (R-GA) as their leader, pollsters found that people trusted Republicans in Congress more than they trusted President Clinton to protect Social Security.[27] This probably reflected overall declines in presidential approval and overall improvements in Republicans' standing, since nothing much was happening on Social Security.[28] But once Speaker Gingrich and his lieutenants proposed cutting many domestic programs, including Medicare, people repeatedly chose President Clinton as the more trustworthy protector of Social Security. The president beat the Republicans in Congress in seven polls spanning four years, with Clinton averaging 53 percent trust and the Republicans averaging 33 percent.[29]

The next Democratic president also had to earn citizens' support. Early campaign polls that asked whether Barack Obama or John McCain would better handle Social Security showed Obama with only a modest, 4-point advantage.[30] By the end of the campaign, however, Obama's advantage had grown to 16 points.[31] His advantage at the end of campaign season did not last long. In late 2010, when pollsters asked whether people trusted President Obama or the Republicans in Congress more on Social Security, they chose the Republicans in three polls by an average of 4 points.[32] Again, this probably reflected overall declines in presidential approval, given the lack of specific actions on Social Security. People changed their views again, however, after Republicans threatened in 2011 not to raise the debt ceiling unless Congress and the president approved massive spending cuts. Not raising the debt ceiling could have interrupted the delivery of Social Security benefits. Two polls in the midst of the crisis gave President Obama a 12-point advantage over Republicans about who would better handle Social Security.[33]

People seem to give presidential candidates of both parties a fair chance to reveal their true colors on Social Security. Once in office, however, people seem to judge presidents by their actions. When citizens believe that presidents are threatening Social Security, as they did with Reagan in 1981 and Bush in 2005, or when they believe that Republicans in Congress are threatening Social Security, as they did in 1995 and 2011, they turn to Democrats for protection.

Presidents are easy to study. Pollsters love to ask about the country's most visible elected official. Unfortunately, we have no systematic evidence about how citizens evaluate legislators' positions and actions on Social Security. Partly this reflects the cost and difficulty of interviewing sizable samples in 50 states and 435 House districts. It also reflects the care with which legislators have managed their voting records. No legislator has voted on a Social Security solvency plan—or, indeed, on anything that would significantly affect Social Security taxes or benefits—since 1983.

Parties

We do have systematic evidence about how people evaluate party teams. Pollsters have regularly asked respondents, "When it comes to dealing with Social Security, which party do you think would do a better job?"[34] Figure 7.10 shows how citizens answered this question between 1981 and 2018.[35] The first thing to note is that pollsters never asked the question before 1981. The figure begins that year because that is when the data series begins. So, we have no evidence from the early decades about whether people gave extra credit to Democrats for inventing Social Security, gave extra credit to Republicans for supporting the other party's proud creation, or gave both parties equal credit for maintaining and expanding it. Once polling on political parties began, however, people

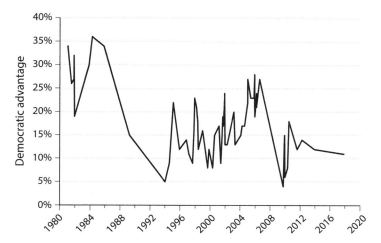

FIGURE 7.10. Democratic advantage on which party can better handle Social Security, 1981–2018. The Democratic advantage is the percentage of respondents who believe Democrats would do a better job dealing with Social Security minus the percentage who believe Republicans would do a better job.
Source: Roper Center: 62 polls from 10 polling organizations.

invariably claimed that Democrats would do a better job dealing with Social Security than Republicans. The *Democratic advantage*—the difference between the fraction of respondents who thought Democrats were the better stewards and the fraction that chose Republicans—varied widely, from a 36-point margin in February 1985, to a 4-point margin in August 2010.[36] The most recent poll gives Democrats an 11-point advantage.

What seems to account for variations in the Democratic advantage? The advantage widened when Republicans proposed major changes in Social Security. Indeed, it was President Reagan's proposal to cut benefits for early retirees by nearly a third, and Democrats' swift denunciation of his proposal, that first inspired pollsters to ask people which party they trusted more dealing with Social Security's problems. The results were startling. Eight polls conducted during the Reagan administration showed that Democrats had, on average, a 30-point advantage over Republicans (figure 7.10). The first President Bush proposed nothing on Social Security; the one poll during his administration showed that the Democratic advantage had diminished to 15 points. The Democratic advantage persisted during the Clinton administration and the early years of the second Bush administration. Soon after President Bush proposed partial privatization of Social Security in 2005, however, the Democratic advantage surged to 28 points, where it remained until legislators from both parties abandoned the president's proposal (see chapter 11). The Democratic advantage averaged 11 points during the Obama years as some Republicans in Congress resumed their attacks on Social Security.[37] The only poll from the Trump administration gave Democrats an 11-point advantage.

It is striking that in 62 polls taken over 38 years, citizens always claimed that Democrats were better stewards of Social Security than Republicans were. Not once did they choose Republicans. This consistent issue advantage for the Democratic team is probably a consequence of Democrats consistently championing Social Security.[38] People apparently give new presidents clean slates on Social Security, waiting to see what they write on them. But the parties have sticky reputations that are tough to shed. Even when people claim to trust Republican presidents on Social Security, they do not trust Republicans.

Interest Groups

In addition to the partisan divide on Social Security, there is discord among various interest groups that care about fixing Social Security. The most central player is AARP, the Washington-based organization that puts protecting both Social Security and Medicare at the top of its political agenda. But dozens of other groups have interests at stake, including various groups that seek to block tax increases (see chapter 6). What do people think about these organizations? Are they known? Are they respected? Do people see them as allied with one party or the other?

Although pollsters frequently ask questions about the National Rifle Association, and sometimes about unions or big business, they seldom inquire about other interest groups. Fortunately, they have asked several useful questions about AARP, the 38-million-member organization for people aged 50 and older.[39] Several findings stand out. First, AARP is very visible. In December 2004, 88 percent of adults aged 30 and older claimed that they had heard about the organization. Second, most people respect it. In the same survey, 74 percent of those who had heard about AARP had a favorable opinion of the group; only 15 percent had an unfavorable view. Third, most people trust it. When asked in the same survey which of five groups they would trust on how to reform Social Security, respondents gave AARP the highest marks, with 64 percent trusting and 23 percent not trusting, for a net approval of 41 percent. By comparison, the net approval was 18 percent for financial planners, 5 percent for the Democratic Party, negative 9 percent for the Republican Party, and negative 21 percent for Wall Street investment firms.[40]

Some people in Washington characterize AARP as a Democratic-leaning group. Indeed, the organization does support many core Democratic priorities, not only protecting Social Security and Medicare but also promoting generic drugs and regulating prescription prices. On the other hand, AARP collaborated with President Bush to enact the 2003 Medicare Prescription Drug Act, much to the annoyance of Democratic leaders. What about AARP's membership? Does it have a partisan or bipartisan complexion? In fact, political party is unrelated to membership. A 2003 survey of adults aged 50 and over found that 47 percent of Republicans and 45 percent of Democrats were dues-paying members. Age, not party identification, affects the decision to join AARP. The same survey found that 39 percent of respondents between 50 and 64 were members, compared with 58 percent of those aged 65 and older.[41]

Finally, AARP seems to be effective communicating its messages to target voters. After Congress approved the 2003 Medicare Prescription Drug Act, pollsters asked, "Do you happen to know what the position of the AARP was on the new Medicare plan? Did they favor the plan, were they neutral, or did they oppose the plan?" Three-quarters of respondents aged 65 and over claimed to know the group's position, and more than 80 percent of them were correct. By comparison, less than half of respondents younger than 30 claimed to know the group's position, and most of them guessed incorrectly.[42]

Conclusion

How can it be that party elites are increasingly polarized on Social Security, while partisan citizens are not? One explanation is that Social Security is more immediate and real to people than most other issues. Few people have personal experience with defense, climate change, foreign assistance, or the environment. What people know about these issues is largely third-hand, perhaps beginning with elite discourse, and then filtered through family, friends, or the media. In contrast, most people have extensive personal experience with Social Security. Most children first encounter the program by watching their grandparents collect benefits. Later they experience it as young workers, watching part of their wages diverted to Social Security. Later still, they begin to think about their own retirement, perhaps around the time their parents begin to collect benefits. Finally, people experience the program as retirees, discovering how central these benefits are to their well-being. Unlike most government programs, Social Security is not something that people learn about principally through the media. People experience Social Security through daily living and family life.

Michael Tesler differentiates between attitudes that are *crystalized*—very stable over time and largely resistant to change, for example, attitudes about abortion or race—and those that are heavily influenced by elite communications.[43] Public attitudes toward Social Security may not be fully crystalized. After all, we saw some evidence of party polarization in the early 1980s, stimulated by President Reagan's efforts to reduce it, and again around 2005, stimulated by President Bush's effort to restructure it.[44] But because attitudes on Social Security rest on a sturdy foundation—life experience—they are much more resistant to change than attitudes on ordinary issues.

A second explanation for why elite polarization has left such a light imprint on attitudes toward Social Security is that elite messaging has been relatively quiet over the past decade. The media covered Social Security extensively in the early 1980s, as Congress considered a solvency bill, and again in 2005, as Congress considered privatization. But Social Security has slipped off the congressional agenda, and therefore slipped off the media agenda. The evidence in the previous chapter about polarized legislators was based on their written statements. But we have no evidence on whether legislators featured these messages in their speeches, mailings, websites, and advertisements, or whether they remained largely hidden to all but the diligent staffers who were tasked with finding at least one statement on Social Security for each legislator.

Moreover, legislators' words are not particularly threatening. Although Republicans regularly propose "repealing Obamacare," they never advocate "repealing Social Security." Republicans also avoid scary words, like privatization, in favor of market-tested phrases like giving workers "a choice" or an "ownership stake" in their retirement contributions. They assure retirees and near retirees that nothing would change for them. Meanwhile, Democrats emphasize "commonsense solutions" to the solvency problem, like those used in the past. Neither side says anything to alarm voters. They merely differ in how they would approach fixing the retirement system.

Yes, recent party platforms have become more strident on Social Security. But legislative candidates have nothing to do with drafting party platforms. And even presidential candidates sometimes break free of these party promises. Donald Trump, for example, campaigned for office and for reelection largely as a supporter of the current Social Security program rather than as a champion of the changes outlined in his party's 2016 and 2020 platforms.

All this is to say that party polarization among citizens is currently low. Of course, that could change quickly if Democratic and Republican officeholders go to war over fixing Social Security. But the ability of politicians to split citizens on Social Security is limited by the strong reservoir of public support that is based on extensive real-world experience.

8

Motivated Voters

THE BROAD PUBLIC SUPPORT for Social Security does not mean that every-one agrees on how to fix the system. It is one thing to assert that we are spend-ing too little on Social Security, as citizens repeatedly do in national surveys. It is quite another to think that everyone would tolerate large tax increases in order to prevent huge benefit cuts. Although some people would accept what-ever tax increases are required to preserve the promised flow of benefits, others would prefer a blend of tax increases and benefit cuts. People would also divide on how to allocate tax increases and benefit cuts among various groups of taxpayers and beneficiaries.

Central to politics is the allocation of costs and benefits. What makes fixing Social Security politically perilous is that participants already ex-pect a statutorily defined flow of benefits. We are not talking about the political joy of allocating new benefits. The problem is the insufficiency of revenues to fund already-promised benefits. Fixing Social Security, then, is all about allocating costs—about choosing how workers, employers, and beneficiaries will share the burden of making the system solvent. Some people propose privatizing Social Security because it seems less costly than fixing the current system. But that is partly because the principal cost of privatization—massive borrowing to fund the transition—pushes costs into the future.

Allocating costs is politically perilous because elected officials fear that either unhappy beneficiaries or unhappy taxpayers might punish them for whatever actions they take. Legislators seek ways to minimize unhappiness among various participant groups in order to reduce the chances of electoral retribution. This chapter explores the factors that affect electoral retribution from the perspective of citizens. The next chapter explores the subject from legislators' point of view.

Beneficiaries

How might beneficiaries react to benefit cuts? Their reactions would likely depend on how much they currently receive, how long they expect to collect those benefits, and what other sources of income they happen to have. An affluent retiree, for whom Social Security is a small fraction of total income, may react differently than a poverty-stricken retiree who is totally dependent on program benefits.

Social Security currently pays monthly benefits to 65 million participants. As table 8.1 shows, 72 percent of those participants (46.7 million) are retirees collecting benefits based on their own earnings records. The retirement program also provides monthly benefits for 2.2 million spouses and 700,000 children. But Social Security is more than a retirement program. The survivor program supports 5.9 million beneficiaries, including surviving spouses, children, and aged parents, and the disability program supports 8.1 million disabled workers and 1.4 million spouses and children. Disability, spousal, survivor, and children's benefits are an important and costly part of Social Security, constituting 28 percent of beneficiaries and 22 percent of expenditures.

Total adult beneficiaries (62 million) are about one-quarter of the nation's voting-age population (255 million). Table 8.1 provides median ages for various adult participants.[1] Note especially the median ages for retirees (72) and retiree spouses (70)—both relatively young in a world where longevity continues to increase. Note also that most disabled workers—median age 57—are nearing retirement age. In fact, the number of disabled 60-year-olds is 16 times the number of disabled 30-year-olds.[2] Finally, note that nearly one-third of beneficiaries who qualify for benefits as the children of retired, disabled, or deceased workers are themselves voting-age adults.[3]

Figure 8.1 moves beyond medians to show the distribution of the beneficiary and nonbeneficiary populations by exact age, 18 to 98. First, note how many young and middle-aged people collect some type of Social Security benefits. For example, 1 percent of 27-year-olds are already beneficiaries.[4] After that, benefit collecting increases with age, from 3 percent of the adult population at age 40 to 5 percent (age 49), 7 percent (age 53), 9 percent (age 55), and 11 percent (age 57). Most younger beneficiaries are disabled workers, but they also include spouses of disabled workers, surviving spouses, and disabled adult children. The explosion of beneficiaries occurs at age 62, when workers first become eligible for retirement benefits. Social Security beneficiaries increase from 14 percent of the adult population at age 60 to 34 percent at age 62, then

TABLE 8.1. Social Security Beneficiaries, June 2021

Program	Number of beneficiaries (thousands)	Share of beneficiaries (%)	Mean annual benefit ($)	Median age (years)
Retirement				
Retired workers	46,738		18,663	72
Spouses of retired workers	2,241		9,547	70
Children of retired workers	698		8,817	*
Total	49,677	76.4	18,113	
Survivor				
Surviving spouses	3,572		17,541	76
Children of deceased workers	1,954		11,062	*
Disabled surviving spouses	232		9,252	60
Widowed mothers and fathers	112		12,673	44
Parents of deceased workers	1		15,779	87
Total	5,870	9.0	14,964	
Disability				
Disabled workers	8,076		15,365	57
Children of disabled workers	1,309		4,818	*
Spouses of disabled workers	102		4,309	63
Total	9,486	14.6	13,791	
Grand Total	65,033	100.0	17,199	
*Beneficiaries who qualified as the children of retired, disabled, or deceased workers				
Children under age 18	2,737	69.1		
Students, aged 18–19	111	2.8		
Disabled adult children	1,113	28.1		
Total	3,961	100.0		
Total beneficiaries aged 18 and older	62,296			

Sources: Social Security Administration 2021b, table 2; 2021a, tables 5.A1.1–5.A1.8.

All data are for June 2021, except for median ages and the breakdown of children by age, which are calculated from December 2019 data.

49 percent (age 64), 82 percent (age 66), 88 percent (age 68), and 94 percent (age 70). Those who never collect Social Security benefits include infrequent workers, late-arriving immigrants, members of several religious groups, including the Amish and Mennonites, and people in jobs not covered by Social Security, primarily in state and local government.

Two patterns stand out. First, benefit collecting is not something that begins at age 65, the original retirement age for Social Security. Despite the

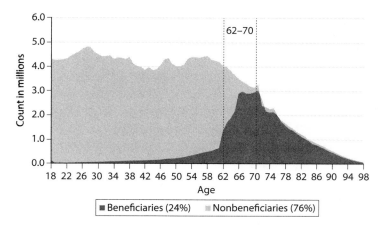

FIGURE 8.1. Social Security beneficiaries and nonbeneficiaries by age, 2018. Population by age as of July 2018. Beneficiaries by age as of December 2018. Nonbeneficiaries are the difference between the two. The box from ages 62 to 70 highlights the period when participants can file for retirement benefits.

Sources: Social Security Administration 2019a, tables 5.A1.1–5.A1.8; Census Bureau 2019a.

financial penalties for retiring before the so-called full retirement age (currently 67 for those born after 1959), and the financial rewards for postponing retirement until age 70, the most common retirement age is still 62. In 2018, 37 percent of women and 33 percent of men began collecting retirement benefits at that age. In all, 63 percent of workers began collecting benefits before reaching age 66.[5] Most of this early benefit collecting is voluntary, as workers choose to retire soon after they become eligible. Second, most people are beneficiaries for a very long time. This is clear from the fact that life expectancy at age 65 is now 19 years for men and nearly 22 years for women.[6] There are now 5.8 million beneficiaries aged 85 or older.

For other people, however, benefit collecting begins less happily, in their thirties, forties, or fifties, when they become disabled. Although some disabled people return to work, most do not.[7] The typical exit from the disability rolls occurs at a person's full retirement age, when retirement benefits replace disability benefits.[8]

Social Security beneficiaries are already a quarter of the adult population. But that share will continue to increase, as the overall population gets older. Figure 8.2 displays how the age composition of adults has changed since 1930, and how demographers project it will change in the next four decades. When

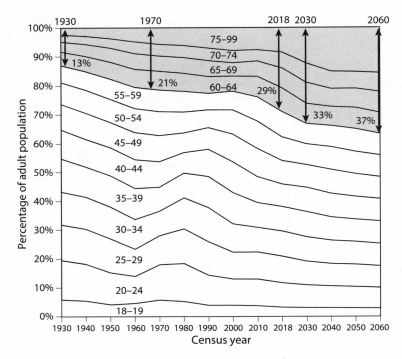

FIGURE 8.2. Age composition of adults, 1930–2060. Census data, 1930–2018; projections, 2030–60.

Sources: Census Bureau 1939, 1943, 1954, 1991, 2001, 2011, 2015b, 2019a.

Congress first created Social Security, people aged 60 or older were 13 percent of adults.[9] Their share of the adult population increased to 21 percent in 1970 and 29 percent in 2018. Experts project that seniors will be 33 percent of adults in 2030 and 37 percent in 2060—nearly triple their share at Social Security's inception.

This rapid growth in the senior population—fueled by both increasing longevity and the aging of the oversized baby boom generation—is the principal reason that Social Security is headed towards insolvency. But this growth also complicates the politics of fixing Social Security. When Congress last faced a solvency crisis in 1983, seniors, aged 60 or older, were 22 percent of the voting-age population. By 2034, seniors will be 34 percent of the voting-age population. Given that seniors vote at a much higher rate than younger people do (see evidence later in this chapter), the pressure on Congress to preserve benefits will be enormous.

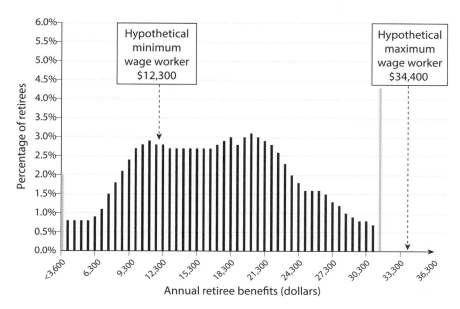

FIGURE 8.3. Distribution of annual retiree benefits from Social Security, December 2018. The 46 vertical black bars show the percentage of all retirees receiving annual benefits within each $600 range (say, $21,300 to $21,900). The left gray bar shows the percentage with benefits less than $3,600. The right gray bar shows the percentage with benefits greater than $31,200. The left dashed line shows the estimated retirement benefit for a hypothetical full-time, full-career, minimum wage worker who retired in 2018 at age 66. The right dashed line shows the estimated retirement benefit for a hypothetical full-career worker who earned the inflation-adjusted maximum taxable wage for each of 35 years before retiring in 2018 at age 66. The actual scale extends to $45,408, which is what the hypothetical full-career, maximum wage worker would collect for retiring at age 70.

Source: Social Security Administration 2019a, table 5.B6.

Benefits

How much do beneficiaries have at stake? For a first cut, table 8.1 (above) provides the mean annual benefits for 11 categories of beneficiaries in 2021. Retired workers collect, on average, $18,663 annually, surviving spouses $17,541, disabled workers $15,365, and so on. Figure 8.3 then provides the full distribution for retiree benefits, the largest category of Social Security benefits, in 2018. The range of benefits is broad, with 2 percent of retirees receiving less than $3,600 annually and 4 percent receiving more than $31,200. The overall distribution, however, is remarkably symmetrical, with median annual benefits ($17,100) almost identical to mean annual benefits ($17,536).[10]

What gives rise to the particular distribution of benefits in figure 8.3? Note first the dotted arrows for two hypothetical retirees collecting $12,300 and $34,400. The former is the approximate annual retirement benefit for someone who worked 40 hours per week for at least 35 years, earning exactly the federal minimum wage each year, before retiring in 2018 at age 66 (then the full retirement age).[11] The latter is the approximate annual benefit for someone who earned the inflation-adjusted maximum taxable wage for each of 35 years before retiring in 2018 at age 66.[12] These two hypothetical examples provide the complete range of retirement benefits for full-time, full-career, full-retirement-age workers. Those who consistently earned the minimum wage (now $7.25 an hour, or $15,080 annually), collect about $12,300 in annual benefits. Those who consistently earned the maximum taxable wage ($128,400 in 2018) collect about $34,400 in annual benefits. Full-time, full-career, full-retirement-age workers cannot do worse than the former or better than the latter. These two examples also underscore how progressive the benefit formula is. The maximum wage person earned 8.5 times as much as the minimum wage person during the final working year, but collected only 2.8 times as much during the initial retirement year.

Who are the people in the left quarter of the distribution in figure 8.3? Why did they collect less than our diligent minimum wage worker did? First, some people worked fewer than 35 years. The benefit formula, which calculates average inflation-adjusted earnings based on the 35 highest-earning years, uses zeros for nonworking years. Zeroes lower average wages, which then lower average benefits. Second, some people worked part-time for some or all of their working years. Third, some people retired in advance of the full retirement age (then 66). For example, someone who retired at age 62 would collect 75 percent as much annually as someone with the same earnings history who retired at age 66. Our hypothetical minimum wage worker would collect only $9,225 at age 62. Of course, people could also increase their annual benefits by working longer. Someone who delayed retirement until age 70 would collect 132 percent as much as he or she would at age 66. At age 70, our diligent minimum wage worker would collect $16,236; our maximum wage worker would collect $45,408.

How central are Social Security benefits to retirees' well-being? Do they constitute a large or a small portion of their total income? If Social Security benefits were cut by 21 percent, how much would retirees' total income fall? These are difficult questions to answer. One problem is that most retirees live in households with other people, usually spouses or partners. This means that

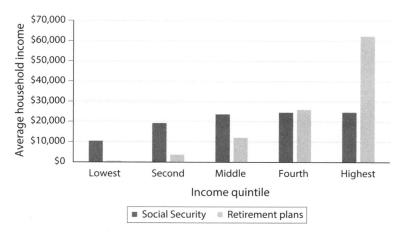

FIGURE 8.4. Average household income from Social Security and retirement plans by income quintile, 2016. Excludes all income from household members younger than 65. Retirement plan income includes distributions and withdrawals from all defined benefit and defined contribution retirement plans.
Source: Health and Retirement Study 2016 via Chen, Munnell, and Sanzenbacher 2018.

we need to shift our focus from individuals to households. A second problem is that retiree households have diverse sources of retirement income, some of them difficult to track, including withdrawals from defined contribution plans, such as 401(k) and IRA plans, and payments from traditional pension plans, known as defined benefit plans. The Social Security Administration—my principal data source in this chapter so far—does not collect individual-level data about income from other retirement plans. For evidence on these matters, we need survey data. I have chosen a survey that has a good track record in matching the known aggregate measures of pension distributions, IRA withdrawals, and Social Security benefits, and that is accurate across the entire income distribution.[13]

Figure 8.4 displays information about household income from both Social Security and all other retirement plans for people aged 65 and older. The data were collected by the University of Michigan's Health and Retirement Study. Notice first that average Social Security benefits are only $10,316 in the lowest income quintile—less than our diligent minimum wage worker would collect. Average Social Security benefits are considerably higher across the other four quintiles, ranging from $19,099 for the second quintile to $24,574 for the highest one. The more startling differences are for retirement plan income. These plans provide very little income in the first two quintiles, averaging $513 in the lowest one and $3,629 in the next. But after that, they really matter: $11,970 for the middle quintile, $25,804 for the next, and $62,448 for the highest.

Clearly, the importance of Social Security varies widely by income. It provides 95 percent of total retirement income in the lowest income quintile, and 84 percent in the next, but only 66, 49, and 28 percent in the top three quintiles. Put differently, if Social Security benefits were suddenly cut by 21 percent, those in the lowest quintile would lose, on average, 20 percent of total retirement income. For the next four quintiles, total retirement income would decline by 18, 14, 10, and 6 percent.

Some retirees have other sources of income besides their retirement plans and Social Security. These sources include wages, interest, dividends, capital gains, and the Supplemental Security Income program (SSI), a federal program for disabled, blind, and aged people of limited means. Currently, 11 percent of people aged 72 and older still work, most of them part-time, with median earnings of $10,600 annually.[14] Although the ability to work does not vary much across the income distribution, it does decline with age, so even retirees who continue to work cannot be certain how long that option will last. The other income sources are heavily concentrated by household income. For example, the SSI program is for very poor people. The 4 percent of seniors who receive SSI benefits are, therefore, from the lower portion of the lowest quintile.[15] Interest, dividends, and capital gains are concentrated in the top quintile. In short, Social Security and retirement plans are the main sources of income for most retirees, with the exception of the poorest of the poor, the richest of the rich, and the 11 percent who are still working.

One last question deserves investigation. If Social Security benefits are cut, could retirees simply make up the difference by withdrawing more from their 401(k) and IRA plans? As a legal matter, the answer is simple. In all IRAs, and in many defined contribution plans, retirees may withdraw as much as they please. The more urgent question is whether withdrawing more would be financially prudent. The last thing we want is millions of retirees draining their retirement accounts long before their demise. An appropriate benchmark for prudence, therefore, is how much annual income an individual or couple would receive if they converted their current retirement assets into an inflation-adjusted annuity, a financial instrument that guarantees benefits for as long as the policy owners live. Three experts who compared potential household income—the annual payments from joint-survivor annuities that protect both retirees and spouses—to what the same people were withdrawing from their retirement accounts found that households in the lowest three quintiles were already withdrawing a bit more than prudent, while those in the highest quintile were withdrawing about 78 percent of what an annuity would pay.[16] Put differently, it makes financial sense only for the rich to withdraw more from their retirement accounts. Many others are already living at or over the prudential edge.

Mobilizing Beneficiaries

More than 62 million adults now collect Social Security benefits, nearly one-quarter of the nation's voting-age population. Once baby boomers are fully retired, Social Security beneficiaries will be closer to a third of the voting-age population. After that, the beneficiary share of the population will continue to rise as long as longevity continues to increase.

As I have shown, most beneficiaries are heavily dependent on Social Security. Although these benefits matter less to the affluent, they are central to the well-being of most beneficiaries, and crucial to the poorest ones. Reducing benefits by 21 percent—the automatic reduction scheduled for 2034—would be devastating for the bottom third of recipients and challenging for many others.

Would cuts of this magnitude impel citizens to punish their senators and representatives? This partly depends on how well legislators play their cards, a topic addressed in the next chapter. But these cuts share several important attributes with issues that are known to be politically perilous. The cuts are large, perceptible, and clearly the consequence of governmental action.[17] Large and perceptible effects stimulate citizens to search for people to blame. Since everyone knows that Social Security is a federal program, the search for villains will begin on Capitol Hill. Assisting citizens in their search will be the media, interest groups, and electoral challengers. In short, legislators have much to fear from slashing Social Security benefits.

Taxpayers

One way to avoid large cuts in Social Security benefits is to increase payroll taxes. How might taxpayers react to these increases? Their reactions would likely depend on how much their own tax payments increase and whether they think the overall tax assessments are fair.

Recall from chapter 1 that four sets of taxpayers fund Social Security. Employed workers pay 6.2 percent of their wages, up to the maximum taxable wage base. Employers pay an equal sum. Self-employed workers pay both sums—12.4 percent in all—subject to the same wage limit. Seventy percent of Social Security beneficiaries pay income taxes on a portion of their benefits.[18]

Most economists do not differentiate between what workers and employers contribute to Social Security. In their view, the two taxes are really a single 12.4 percent tax on workers because workers, in effect, pay the so-called employers' share with forgone wages. Although economists may be correct about the *incidence* of these taxes, the distinction between workers' and employers' shares matters politically. It matters because neither workers nor employers think like economists.

Workers notice the visible costs that they pay directly rather than the invisible costs that employers pay on their behalf. We see this regularly with health insurance. Unions fight tenaciously to keep workers' health-care premiums low, not to keep the combined worker/employer premiums low. Similarly, many firms act as if the employer share of the payroll tax is a direct tax on them, not an assessment that they can foist on workers. For example, the National Federation of Independent Business, an influential Washington group, argues that *its members* cannot afford higher payroll taxes, not that its workers cannot afford them. Apparently, they are blind to the magic of labor markets that deftly shifts employer costs to workers. Finally, what matters politically is how much workers and employers pay before the next election. Even if workers eventually pay the so-called employer share by receiving smaller than usual wage increases, in the near term workers pay, and therefore notice, the worker share, while firms pay, and therefore notice, the employer share. Electoral retribution, if it happens, is for visible things like direct taxes, not for invisible things like forgone wages.

How might the 162 million employed workers—ignoring for now self-employed workers—respond to proposals to increase payroll taxes? Here I consider the effects of three proposals that would put Social Security on the road to solvency. All three would take effect in 2021. One proposal would increase the payroll tax rate from 6.2 percent to 7.9 percent. The second would eliminate the maximum taxable wage base, so that all wages and salaries would be fully taxed. A third would modify both parameters, increasing the tax rate to 7.0 percent and the wage base to $250,000. These proposals would eliminate 101 percent, 73 percent, and 85 percent, respectively, of the 75-year actuarial deficit.[19]

Table 8.2 illustrates how the three proposals would affect four hypothetical workers: (a) a full-time minimum wage worker, making $15,080 annually;

TABLE 8.2. Projected Tax Increases under Three Solvency Proposals

Proposal	Annual Wage ($)	Payroll Tax (%)	Wage Limit ($)	Payroll Tax ($)	Tax Increase ($)	Tax Increase (%)	Wage Reduction (%)
0: Keep the 2020 tax rate and wage limit	15,080	6.2	137,700	935			
	137,700	6.2	137,700	8,537			
	250,000	6.2	137,700	8,537			
	1,000,000	6.2	137,700	8,537			
1: Raise just the tax rate	15,080	7.9	137,700	1,191	256	27	1.7
	137,700	7.9	137,700	10,878	2,341	27	1.7
	250,000	7.9	137,700	10,878	2,341	27	0.9
	1,000,000	7.9	137,700	10,878	2,341	27	0.2
2: Eliminate the entire wage limit	15,080	6.2	none	935			
	137,700	6.2	none	8,537			
	250,000	6.2	none	15,500	6,963	82	2.8
	1,000,000	6.2	none	62,000	53,463	626	5.3
3: Raise the tax rate and the wage limit	15,080	7.0	250,000	1,056	121	13	0.8
	137,700	7.0	250,000	9,639	1,102	13	0.8
	250,000	7.0	250,000	17,500	8,963	105	3.6
	1,000,000	7.0	250,000	17,500	8,963	105	0.9

Source: Social Security Administration 2020a, provisions E1.1 and E2.1.

(b) someone earning the 2020 maximum taxable wage base, $137,700; (c) someone with wages of exactly $250,000; and (d) someone with wages of exactly $1,000,000. The first proposal would increase everyone's payroll taxes by 27 percent. The minimum wage worker would pay an additional $256; the others would pay an additional $2,341. The second proposal would increase taxes for the two high-wage workers by 82 percent and 626 percent, while protecting others from any increases. The third proposal would increase taxes for the two high-wage workers by 105 percent and for the others by 13 percent.

How would these three proposals affect the 20 million self-employed workers? There is no need for a separate table for this group, since the percentage increases for self-employed workers would be identical to those for employed workers. Of course, the dollar-value increases would be twice as large, since self-employed workers pay both the employer and employee shares. Depending on the solvency plan, self-employed workers in the top two earnings categories in table 8.2 would face tax increases ranging from $4,682 to $106,926.

The various comparisons show how much is at stake for workers. The first solvency plan would increase the tax rate for all employed workers from 6.2 percent to 7.9 percent, effectively cutting most workers' after-tax wage income by 1.7 percent, with smaller reductions for affluent workers. The second plan would protect everyone with wages at or below the maximum wage base, while increasing the payroll tax for two hypothetical high-wage workers by 82 to 626 percent, effectively cutting their after-tax wage income by 2.8 to 5.3 percent. The third plan would split the difference, imposing smaller tax increases for those below the current wage base, and higher tax increases above that base, thereby reducing after-tax wage income by 0.8 percent to 3.6 percent. For self-employed workers, all reductions in after-tax income would be twice as large.

How many workers would feel the effects of raising or eliminating the maximum taxable wage base? In 2018, 6.2 percent of 164 million employed workers earned more than the wage base, as did 3.7 percent of 20 million self-employed workers.[20] That is, 10 million employed workers and 740,000 self-employed workers would be directly affected if Congress raised or eliminated the wage base. Of course, many of these workers are not very far above the base, so they do not have that much at stake. In fact, nearly 20 percent of all workers earn more than the wage base at least once in their careers.[21] But their occasional good fortune hardly gives them a shared interest in keeping the base low. Still, several million workers would face significant tax increases if the maximum taxable wage base were eliminated, including 4.3 million workers with wage income greater than \$200,000, over 650,000 workers with wage income greater than \$500,000, nearly 170,000 workers with wage income greater than \$1,000,000, and 12,000 workers with wage income greater than \$5,000,000.[22] These are the taxpayers with much at stake if Congress considers raising or eliminating the maximum taxable wage base.

Politics

The notion that everyone is opposed to tax increases is clearly false. Local voters regularly support tax increases for constructing and operating local schools. Although voters with school-age children may be stronger supporters of school budgets than voters without children, public education would not survive without the support of both groups. The same is true for Social Security. Many workers support spending more on Social Security, in part because they are workers today but beneficiaries tomorrow (self-interest), in part because today's workers have parents and grandparents who are already beneficiaries (familial interest), and in part because they accept Social Security as a valuable part of society's safety net (altruism).

Restoring solvency to Social Security, however, is a very expensive endeavor. We are talking about reallocating 1.2 percent of GDP annually. Would tax increases of the magnitude outlined in the previous section impel citizens to punish their senators and representatives? Should legislators fear the wrath of taxpayers more than the wrath of beneficiaries? Would a mix of tax increases and benefit cuts be a safer alternative, or would such a mix simply enrage both sides?

Taxpayers will certainly have views about how the tax burden should be allocated. To be sure, self-interest will play a role. Taxpayers will notice how much they are asked to pay. But notions of equity and fairness will matter, too. Some people argue that affluent workers should shoulder all the solvency costs because they can afford it. Others counter that insolvency threatens everyone and that no taxpayers should be immune from paying some fraction of the costs.

Workers clearly outnumber beneficiaries. If this were a tug of war, nearly 180 million workers would easily overpower more than 60 million beneficiaries. In politics, however, intensity matters more than raw numbers, and intensity depends on how much is at stake. If Congress never acts, all Social Security beneficiaries would face a 21 percent benefit cut. For the poorest retirees, that would equal a 21 percent reduction in total income; for others, the reductions would be smaller, but still substantial. In contrast, if Congress adopts the first solvency plan, most taxpayers would face a 27 percent increase in the Social Security tax, but only a 1.7 percent reduction in wage income. In short, most Social Security beneficiaries have vastly more at stake than most workers do. Of course, intensity matters within the overall group of taxpayers, too. If Congress adopts the second solvency plan, well-off self-employed workers would face Social Security tax increases from 82 to 626 percent—and wage reductions from 6 to 11 percent—while lower paid self-employed workers would suffer no declines in wages. One might guess that many people in the first group would feel aggrieved by such disproportionate income reductions.

Voting

How do workers and beneficiaries differ in their propensity to vote? Age is a good proxy for collecting Social Security benefits, so figure 8.5 plots how voter turnout varies by citizens' exact chronological ages.[23] In three recent elections—2014 midterm, 2016 presidential, and 2018 midterm—the relationship between age and voting participation was linear and steep. Voting was least common for 18-year-olds, where 13 and 24 percent voted in the two midterm elections and 34 percent in the presidential election. Voting then increased steadily with age, peaking for citizens in their seventies, where 62 and 68 percent voted in the two midterm elections and 73 percent in the presidential election. Although participation then declined for the very old, it is remarkable how small the drop was.[24] Citizens in their early eighties voted at the rate of people in their early sixties. Citizens in their late eighties and early nineties voted at the rate of people in their fifties. In short, the very oldest people, who tend to be the most dependent on Social Security, are some of the nation's most dedicated voters.[25]

Do older people always vote at higher rates than younger people do? Or was there something special about these three elections? Figure 8.6 explores this question by plotting turnout by age group for all midterm elections between 1974 and 2018. The evidence shows that age has become increasingly important over time. In 1974, turnout for people in their fifties was highest, followed by people in their sixties, forties, seventies, thirties, twenties, and teens. Two decades later, all seven age groups were rank ordered as they are today, largely because turnout increased the most for people in their seventies, and the second most for those in their sixties. By 2014, people in their seventies voted at rates 21 points higher than people in their forties, and

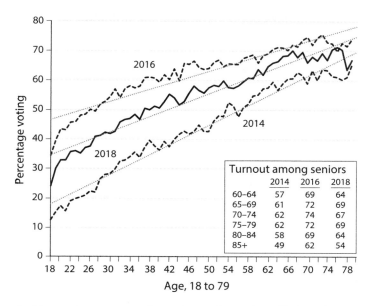

FIGURE 8.5. Turnout in 2014, 2016, and 2018 elections by age. Dotted lines are linear trends. *Sources*: Census Bureau 2015c, 2017, 2019b.

41 points higher than people in their twenties.[26] Figure 8.6 also demonstrates that there *was* something special about the 2018 midterm election—turnout was unusually high among all age groups—but this surge did nothing to alter the fact that older people continued to vote more regularly than younger people did.

In order to understand how voting participation might vary by age in the future—say in 2024, or 2034, or whenever Congress gets serious about fixing Social Security—we need a better sense of how and why chronological age affects turnout.[27] How much is the relationship between age and participation a *life-cycle effect*: people becoming more interested in voting as they grow older? How much is it a *cohort effect*: people raised in different times becoming more or less interested in voting when they come of age? How much is it a *period effect*: people responding together to common events? Figure 8.7, which displays voter turnout for six birth cohorts over four decades, helps disentangle these three effects. The steep and positive slopes for all birth cohorts reveal the importance of life-cycle effects. Aging really does affect turnout. The large surge in 2018 suggests the existence of period effects. Some elections are simply more exciting than others. Cohort effects are tougher to detect. The

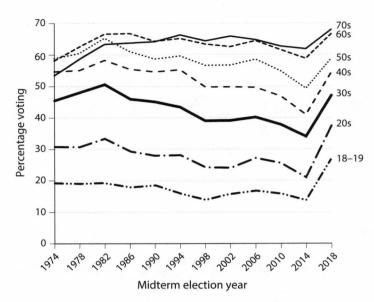

FIGURE 8.6. Turnout in midterm elections by age group, 1974–2018.
Sources: Census Bureau 2015a, 2015c, 2019b.

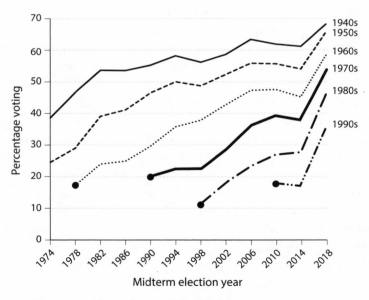

FIGURE 8.7. Turnout in midterm elections by birth cohort, 1974–2018.
Sources: Census Bureau 2015a, 2015c, 2019b.

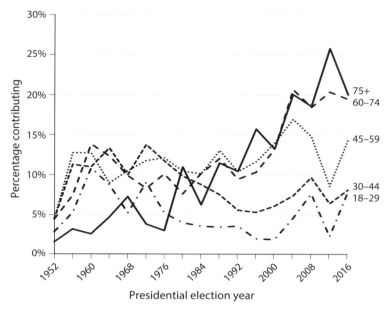

FIGURE 8.8. Campaign contributors by age, 1952–2016.
Source: American National Election Studies 2018.

black circles in figure 8.7 show that three of the four recent cohorts began voting at roughly the same level. Only the 1980s cohort began voting at a much
lower level, although it quickly caught up to previous cohorts.[28] Cohort effects
might have been greater if the time series began decades earlier and included
generations that are known for their very high voting rates.

What about other forms of political participation? Are older people more
likely to contribute to political campaigns than younger people are? Figure 8.8
reports the frequency with which people of various ages contributed to political campaigns from 1952 to 2016. Note my switch to presidential election years
because survey researchers have collected better data about campaign donors
during those years.[29] The most striking finding is among the oldest age
group—those 75 and over—who seldom contributed to campaigns in the
early years, but are now the most frequent contributors, with 19, 26, and
20 percent of them contributing during the three most recent campaigns.
People in the next age group (60 to 74) were average contributors in the early
years, but now contribute at rates—18, 20, and 19 percent—just shy of their
elders. Contribution rates for middle-aged people have not changed much

over time, while rates for the two younger groups have declined. In short, the two oldest age groups, filled with people collecting Social Security benefits, are now the most frequent contributors, while the three age groups packed with workers paying Social Security taxes are the least frequent contributors.

Why are seniors such model citizens? Not only are they the most regular voters and the most active donors, they profess greater interest in politics, display greater knowledge about public affairs, and are the most likely age group to contact government officials. All these are hallmarks of civic responsibility. And the survey evidence is clear that seniors score better on these civic metrics than younger people do.[30]

It is important to recognize that seniors have not always been active participators. In the 1950s, they voted less regularly than middle-aged people, although more regularly than young people. At the time, seniors were also less frequent campaign donors. Then, during the 1960s and 1970s, their participation rates began to climb. Seniors started to vote more consistently, contribute more regularly, and express greater interest in public affairs. By the 1980s, their age group outperformed all other age groups on most metrics of civic responsibility.

Why did seniors change? The answer, according to Andrea Campbell's careful detective work, is that collecting Social Security benefits changed how seniors viewed the political world.[31] It gave them clearer stakes in what the federal government was doing, greater motivation to monitor governmental activity, and stronger incentives to communicate with elected officials about their needs and concerns. In the early 1950s, few seniors received Social Security benefits, and what they received was modest. By the 1980s, participation was practically universal and the benefits were substantial. As seniors became more dependent on Social Security, they became more politically interested, informed, and involved.

Two findings stand out in Campbell's account of how Social Security helped mobilize seniors. First, low-income seniors became more active on matters related to Social Security than high-income seniors—the reverse of the usual positive relationship between income and participation—because low-income seniors were more dependent on Social Security benefits. Second, an analysis of the exact months in which people contacted legislators between 1973 and 1994 discovered huge jumps in contact rates for seniors around the time of the 1977 and 1983 solvency crises, while contact rates for other age groups held steady or declined. In short, as Social Security became more central to the lives of seniors, they became more interested in politics—or at least the politics of Social Security—and more involved in campaigns, elections, voting, contributing, contacting, and lobbying. Seniors became the most politically active group because they had the most at stake.[32]

Should we expect the impact of age on participation to change again as Social Security approaches the solvency cliff? It is very hard to imagine that senior citizens would lose their participatory zeal just as the program faces its most serious crisis ever. But what about taxpayers? Might young workers march in the streets or march to the polls insisting that Congress protect them from increased taxation? Of course, anything is possible. But the principal impediment to mobilizing young workers is that their stakes in Social Security reform are relatively small. For most workers, the most onerous solvency plan would reduce their wage income by about 1.7 percent. That reduction seems minor as a motivating force compared to low-income seniors who would face a 21 percent reduction in their already-meager incomes.

If there is mobilization among those who pay for Social Security, three groups of taxpayers are more likely candidates than younger workers. First, some affluent workers might mobilize to block efforts to eliminate the maximum taxable wage base. Modest increases in the wage base would impose modest costs, but very large increases would impose very large costs on several million workers. Second, self-employed workers appear to be more sensitive to Social Security taxes than employed workers, not only because their tax rate is double the rate for employed workers, but also because they calculate and pay these taxes directly, rather than having them quietly withheld from their wages. Vanessa Williamson discovered, with her in-depth interviews, that independent contractors were much more likely to complain about Social Security taxes than employed workers were.[33] Third, business firms may work to block excessive increases in either the tax rate or the wage base. Social Security taxes are very visible to management. They first withhold these taxes from workers' wages and then transmit double that amount to the government.

Affluent workers may be few in numbers, but their influence is magnified by what they contribute to parties and candidates. In a Pew survey, 32 percent of people with family incomes exceeding $150,000 made campaign contributions in 2016—precisely matching the contribution rate for those aged 65 and over—compared with 22 percent of respondents with incomes between $75,000 and $150,000, 16 percent of those with incomes between $30,000 and $75,000, and 7 percent of those with incomes less than $30,000.[34] Moreover, the richer they are, the more they give. At a minimum, large campaign contributions provide affluent people with greater access to elected politicians—that is, more opportunities to share their grievances and subtly remind legislators that they do more than merely vote. They provide the wherewithal for candidates to attract other voters. Employers have interest groups to remind legislators of their grievances and their importance to local economies. Many of these groups—including the National Federation of Independent Business, the Chamber of Commerce, and the National Association of Manufacturers—regularly remind legislators how opposed they are to all tax increases.

Conclusion

The dangerous people in politics are not the ones who get irritated by congressional action. The dangerous people are those who get hopping mad—so mad that they search for politicians to punish. Citizens can punish legislators by voting against them in primary and general elections, by withholding funds from legislators or contributing funds to their challengers, or by working to mobilize family, friends, neighbors, and workmates.

Senior citizens—here defined as those aged 60 or older—enjoy several advantages in the upcoming battle to reform Social Security. First, they are a large and growing share of the adult population. Currently 29 percent of the voting-age population, they are slated to grow to 34 percent by 2034 and 37 percent by 2060. Second, they participate more actively in politics than other age groups. They cast 34 percent of the ballots in the 2016 presidential election and 37 percent in the 2018 midterm election. As their share of the voting-age population continues to grow, so too will their share of total votes cast. To be sure, not all senior citizens think alike. They vary in all sorts of relevant ways, from partisanship and ideology to political interest and knowledge. What makes them distinctive is that most of them are collecting—or about to collect—substantial Social Security benefits. That makes them an unusually large and attentive audience when policymakers address the solvency crisis.

9

Cross-Pressured Legislators

WHEN SOCIAL SECURITY FINALLY REACHES the congressional agenda, how will legislators decide how to vote? Will party platforms and campaign promises be adequate guides for legislators deciding whether to support or oppose specific proposals? Or will representatives need to estimate the electoral consequences of every vote they cast? How much should they fear not just the attentive publics, who will be lobbying furiously, but also various inattentive publics, who may not learn until after a bill's enactment that their representative voted to raise their taxes or slash their benefits?

Party platforms and campaign promises are incomplete guides for decision making. One problem is that candidates routinely promise cost-free solutions. For example, some legislators have pledged never to increase taxes, cut benefits, or raise the retirement age. Such promises are not very helpful when these are the principal options for restoring solvency. To be sure, individual legislators are free to vote against every bill or amendment that would impose such costs. But if majorities of legislators follow suit, the inevitable result would be the very insolvency they seek to avoid. Moreover, once legislators vote to reject a series of solvency proposals, they create auditable records of inaction, records for which citizens may hold them accountable. In short, once solvency proposals hit the House and Senate floors, there is no place to hide. Voters can punish legislators not just for the proposals they approve but for those they reject.

Fixing Social Security is an exercise in allocating costs. Do nothing and more than 60 million beneficiaries would face a 21 percent benefit cut. Raise tax rates to cover the revenue shortfall and nearly 180 million workers would face a 21 percent tax increase.[1] Eliminate the maximum taxable wage base and some affluent workers would see their Social Security taxes increase many times over. The political problem is that legislators hate to impose costs. They fear that compelling workers to pay more or requiring retirees to accept less would mobilize aggrieved voters to oppose their reelection. The electoral threat is especially acute for House members, who face the electorate every two years.

My analysis in this chapter is based on two assumptions. First, most legislators have strong beliefs about what constitutes good public policy.[2] Second, most legislators care intensely about reelection.[3] When their electoral and policy goals coincide, life is grand. When their goals conflict, however, legislators must weigh the electoral risks of pursuing their own policy preferences. Life gets particularly complicated when events compel legislators to vote on issues that have no politically safe side.

Ideology

Most politicians have broad beliefs about what constitutes good public policy. Whether inherited from their parents, acquired at church, school, bars, or the workplace, or adopted opportunistically as they groom themselves for public office, these ideological beliefs matter. Some politicians view government as a source of good; others believe that less government is better. By convention, we call these groups liberals and conservatives. Several decades ago, ideology was only weakly related to party. That is, some Republican legislators were liberal, some moderate, some conservative. The same was true for Democrats. Today each party is more homogeneous. Most Republican legislators are conservative, some moderate, none liberal. Most Democrats are liberal, some moderate, none conservative.

Democratic and Republican legislators differ in their broad beliefs about Social Security and in their support for specific remedies. As previously shown, most Democrats are strong supporters of traditional Social Security; many Republicans are eager to lessen the role of government in retirement policy. They also differ in their attitudes toward taxation. Democrats are open to increasing Social Security taxes; Republicans remain fiercely opposed.

Ideological beliefs influence but do not dictate how legislators vote. Congress is a place where compromise regularly happens. And compromise sometimes requires that legislators suspend their ideological beliefs. Although most Republican legislators oppose raising the government's debt limit, even Republican-controlled chambers vote to raise the debt limit when default is imminent. Although most Democratic legislators oppose cutting funds for health and education programs, even Democratic-controlled chambers vote to approve such cuts in order to avoid government shutdowns. Ideology is only one of the forces that affect legislators' decisions. It is important, not determinative.

Position Taking

Most legislators have already staked out positions on fixing Social Security. Their position taking, however, has been largely free-form. Unlike roll call voting, where they face an up or down choice on a fixed package of costs and benefits, individual legislators frame their own alternatives when they discuss future policy choices. Not surprisingly, they emphasize protecting benefits rather than imposing costs. When legislators promise to protect current beneficiaries from any cuts, they seldom mention who would pay the costs of that protection. When legislators propose that workers invest their individual contributions in personal retirement accounts, they seldom identify what revenue source would support current beneficiaries after workers' contributions are diverted elsewhere. When legislators oppose raising the retirement age, they seldom explain how an already-struggling system can support retirees for ever-lengthening retirements.

Most campaign talk is happy talk. But as Governor Mario Cuomo (D-NY) once said, "You campaign in poetry; you govern in prose."[4] When actual solvency bills reach the House and Senate floors, they will be written in very precise prose. Provisions to raise the retirement age will specify exactly when and by how much. So, too, will provisions to increase tax rates, raise the maximum taxable wage base, or modify the benefit formula. These real-world bills will severely restrict legislators' options for position taking. Voting in favor of a solvency bill would be a vote to enact a precise menu of tax increases and benefit cuts. Voting against a solvency bill would be a vote to allow the status quo to prevail—that is, to allow for automatic 21 percent benefit cuts. None of these will be happy votes.

Cross Pressures

Whether voting on comprehensive solvency plans or individual provisions, most legislators will feel cross-pressured. That is to say, some of their constituents and some of their donors will prefer A, while others prefer not A. Nowhere will the cross pressures be greater than within the Republican caucus. Many Republican legislators have raised campaign funds from wealthy donors who criticize traditional Social Security and who promote privatization. In contrast, most Republican voters are relatively content with traditional Social Security and care more about the program's solvency. In 2005, when a Republican president proposed partial privatization to a Republican-controlled Congress, the result was not elation that Republican policymakers could finally enact what they seemed to favor, but rather panic that they would need to choose between their elite and mass supporters. As chapter 11 will show, stalemate was the inevitable result. Congress never held hearings, never drafted a comprehensive plan, and never called the roll. Although inaction was a safe choice in 2005, when insolvency was three decades away, inaction in 2034 would be politically perilous. It would impose enormous costs on beneficiaries, many of them Republicans.

Republican legislators will not be alone. Most legislators will face cross pressures of some sort. Despite people's broad support for traditional Social Security, restoring solvency is a zero-sum game. One person's gain is another's loss. Unlike some policy areas—agriculture is a good example—where policy beneficiaries are concentrated in a few districts while cost payers are widely distributed, every congressional district contains hundreds of thousands of taxed workers and tens of thousands of Social Security beneficiaries. In each district, every possible solution to the solvency crisis would help some constituents while hurting others.

Incidence of Costs and Benefits

In thinking about legislators' decision making, it helps to think about the incidence of costs and benefits. For any particular proposal, the *incidence of costs and benefits* refers to (a) who would profit and who would pay, (b) how much the beneficiaries would reap and the contributors would suffer, and (c) when the various beneficiaries would receive their benefits and the contributors would suffer their losses. I refer to these three components of incidence as the *concentration, magnitude,* and *timing* of costs and benefits.[5]

The incidence of costs and benefits offers legislators a rough guide to how constituents might react to particular proposals. For example, the magnitude and timing of costs affect the probability that various voter groups would notice their plight and seek to punish those responsible. Large and immediate costs provoke voters more easily than small, gradual, or distant costs. As a consequence, legislators are more likely to fear the wrath of constituents who would bear large and immediate costs compared with those who would bear smaller and more distant costs.

The incidence of costs and benefits also offers policy designers a template for making proposals more appealing. All three components—concentration, magnitude, and timing—are *variables*. Coalition leaders can manipulate any of these components to make a solvency package more attractive. Rather than raising tax rates immediately, raise them gradually over time. Rather than eliminating the maximum taxable wage base, which would concentrate all costs on the most affluent, use a combination of wage base increases and tax rate increases so that all workers contribute something to solvency. Rather than raising the retirement age immediately, raise it very gradually, perhaps beginning a decade from now. Rather than cutting benefits immediately, reduce the value of future cost-of-living adjustments slightly. The variants are endless as coalition leaders search for the sweet spot that minimizes overall opposition.

Geographic Incidence

Most legislators care more about pleasing their own constituents than about satisfying the rest of the country. That is to say, legislators' electoral calculations are constituency based. In some policy areas, the incidence of costs and benefits varies extensively by district. Wheat growing, coal mining, and auto manufacturing, for example, are concentrated in a few districts, while consumption is widely dispersed. What about Social Security? Do some legislators face different constituency pressures than others?

Figure 9.1 shows how Social Security beneficiaries are distributed across 435 House districts. Note first the outliers. In Florida's 11th congressional district, 46 percent of adults collect Social Security benefits, compared with 12 percent of adults in Virginia's 8th district. The former is filled with retirement communities; the latter is brimming with young people attracted to the Washington metro area. Outliers aside, the differences among congressional districts are not large. In 9 out of 10 House districts, between 16 and 31 percent of adults collect Social Security benefits. In the median district, 23 percent of adults collect benefits.[6]

What about Social Security taxpayers? How are they distributed across House districts? As it happens, we do not need a separate graphical display for Social Security taxpayers because most adults are either taxpayers or beneficiaries.[7] Districts with more beneficiaries have fewer taxpayers; those with fewer beneficiaries have more taxpayers. That is, Social Security taxpayers abound in districts like Virginia's 8th but are less prevalent in districts like Florida's 11th. In the typical district, 70 percent of adults pay Social Security taxes.

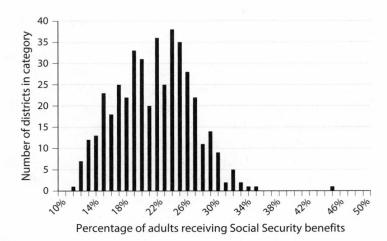

FIGURE 9.1. Percentage of adults in each congressional district receiving Social Security benefits, 2017. The data are for adults collecting benefits in December 2017 divided by total adults aged 18 or older in 2016.
Sources: Social Security Administration 2018; Census Bureau 2018.

How are high-income taxpayers—namely those with wages above the maximum taxable wage base—distributed across 435 House districts? This question deserves careful consideration because raising or eliminating the wage base would generate substantial revenue. For example, eliminating the wage base in 2021 would wipe out 73 percent of the 75-year actuarial deficit.[8] Of course, raising substantial revenues in this way would impose significant costs on small, often influential groups of workers. Legislators need to consider whether doubling, tripling, or quintupling some workers' Social Security taxes might induce those workers to punish legislators by redirecting both their votes and their campaign contributions to other candidates.

Estimating the geographic distribution of high-income taxpayers requires clearing one small hurdle. Although individual workers pay Social Security taxes, the Census Bureau reports household income—not individual income—by congressional district. My solution is to focus on the 6 percent of households with 2016 incomes greater than $200,000 because 6 percent of individual workers earned more than the Social Security wage base that year ($118,500). This method identifies, though imperfectly, the districts where disproportionate numbers of workers would suffer from raising or eliminating the maximum taxable wage base.[9]

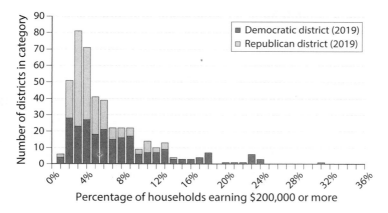

FIGURE 9.2. Percentage of adults in each congressional district earning $200,000 or more, 2016. The reported data are for 7.6 million households earning $200,000 or more in 2016 out of 118.6 million total households.
Source: Census Bureau 2018.

Figure 9.2 shows that the distribution of households earning more than $200,000 is skewed. Although high-income households are 4.7 percent of households in the median congressional district, the range is from less than 1 percent in three districts—Detroit, the South Bronx, and the Dallas/Fort Worth corridor—to 31 percent in one Silicon Valley district.[10] In 80 districts, high-income households are 10 percent or more of households; in 30 districts, they are 15 percent or more; and in 13 districts, they are 20 percent or more. These are the districts where affluent workers would pay dearly if legislators choose to eliminate the maximum taxable wage base.

The distribution of high-income households by congressional district is odd in one respect. Although Republican legislators consistently oppose raising the maximum taxable wage base, few high-income districts elect Republicans to Congress. In the 116th Congress (elected 2018), Democrats represented all 30 districts where 15 percent or more of households earned more than $200,000, and 78 percent of the 80 districts where 10 percent or more of the households earned that much.[11] High-income households are 6.0 percent of households in the median Democratic district, but only 3.8 percent of households in the median Republican district. In short, the people who would suffer most from raising or eliminating the wage base reside in Democratic, not Republican, districts. The refusal of Republican legislators to support raising the maximum taxable wage base says more about their ideological beliefs, their pledges never to increase taxes, and their donor base than it does about their constituents' pecuniary interests.

Electoral Calculations

How would legislators calculate the electoral risks of supporting or opposing particular solvency plans? Do they have more to fear from beneficiaries, ordinary workers, or affluent workers? To be sure, most people interviewed by pollsters assert that we should spend more on Social Security. Moreover, their support for the program is remarkably unaffected by age, work status, income, or party identification (chapter 7). So, perhaps the electoral risks of raising taxes to protect beneficiaries are not very large. But most workers probably underestimate what it would cost to restore solvency—1.5 percent of GDP— and underestimate the taxes required to raise that sum. Legislators need to know more than simply where their constituents stand on an abstract issue about spending. They need to know how workers would react to the actual imposition of new taxes sufficient to restore solvency. Would they notice the new taxes? Would they accept them as legitimate? Would they be furious, angry, annoyed, indifferent, pleased, elated, or oblivious?

The magnitude and timing of costs provide a first cut at the question. Legislators have more to fear from participants who bear large costs than those who bear small ones. And they have more to fear from those who bear immediate costs than from those who face costs far in the future. It also matters whether people regularly participate in politics. Legislators have more to fear from those who regularly vote in congressional elections than from those who have yet to acquire the habit.

Despite the fact that workers outnumber beneficiaries in most districts, most legislators would view beneficiaries as the greater electoral threat. As the previous chapter demonstrated, the typical beneficiary has vastly more at stake than the typical worker. Recall that a 21 percent benefit cut would reduce total income in the lowest three income quintiles by 20, 18, and 14 percent, thus threatening retirees' ability to meet basic living expenses. By comparison, closing the 75-year actuarial shortfall exclusively by raising the tax rate in 2021 would reduce most workers' after-tax wage income by only 1.7 percent. Losing 20 percent of one's income is a much stronger motivating force than losing 1.7 percent. Moreover, seniors vote at much higher rates than younger people do. In short, the prospects for electoral retribution are much greater from furious seniors than they are from ordinary workers.

It is tougher to know how legislators would view the electoral threat from affluent workers. First, it would probably depend on whether Congress eliminates the maximum taxable wage base—forcing high-income workers to pay virtually all the solvency costs—or whether increasing the wage base is one of several measures to close the solvency gap. The former singles out affluent workers; the latter asks them to pay their share. Second, the electoral threat would probably vary by congressional district. I count 15 wealthy districts—in places like Manhattan, Silicon Valley, and suburban Washington, DC—where the number of workers above the maximum taxable wage base exceeds the number of Social Security beneficiaries.[12] Perhaps legislators from these places need to be especially careful. Most legislators, however, face far fewer affluent workers.

Not all electoral threats are constituency based. Most legislators raise campaign funds nationally, including from interest-oriented political action committees (PACs) and from networks of ideologically motivated people. The latter are increasingly important. The threat is not just that these donors might stop funding a legislator's campaign if the legislator disappoints them in office, but that these donors might switch sides and fund a challenger's campaign. Since most districts are relatively safe for one party or the other, such threats often center on party primaries. Many donors are not shy about communicating their policy views. For example, some conservative donors repeatedly tell Republican candidates how strongly they oppose tax increases and how much they admire privatization. Cautious legislators listen to their donors as well as their constituents.

Many legislators also care how various interest groups assess their performance, especially groups that affect how their constituents and donors perceive them. Republican legislators face a particular challenge with AARP. From a Washington perspective, it looks like any another Democratic-leaning group. Recall that AARP's positions across the entire range of policy issues place the group to the left of the median Democratic legislator (see chapter 6). But from a constituency perspective, Republican voters are just as likely as Democratic voters to be dues-paying members of this 38-million-member organization. Not even the most conservative Republican legislators would relish AARP labeling them as enemies of Social Security.

In a world without interest groups, it is hard to know how the owners of small businesses might react to a half point increase in the payroll tax. Would they notice? Would they care? Would they be furious or resigned? In the real world, however, they would be bombarded with messages from business groups. For example, the National Federation of Independent Business (NFIB) scores legislators based on their roll call votes, identifying small business heroes and villains. Many legislators, especially Republicans, watch carefully where the NFIB stands on specific issues, not wishing to tarnish their reputations with ill-chosen votes. Republicans are equally attentive to the antitax views of Americans for Tax Reform, the Club for Growth, and the Chamber of Commerce.

Legislators' electoral calculations, then, are both constituency based and resource based. Although only constituents vote directly in primary and general elections, others provide material resources that legislators deploy to attract voters. And still others affect legislators' political reputations. In short, legislators consider how their constituents, donors, and other groups would react when they choose how to vote on solvency plans.

Urgency

How do legislators' electoral calculations vary depending on the urgency for action? When legislators are deciding how to vote, does it matter whether insolvency is two months away rather than two decades away? Indeed, it does. Strong, principled stands are easier to maintain when tragedy is in the distant future. When tragedy is at the door, legislators are more willing to compromise.

Defaulting on the national debt, for example, is a consequence so calamitous that Congress has never allowed it to happen. Although many legislators have taken principled stands against raising the debt limit, when total debt nears the statutory limit, when the Treasury Department cannot borrow even to pay current bondholders, and when the first-ever national default is imminent, legislators consider whether they want to be personally blamed for default and its economic consequences. So far, majorities have flinched—often at the last moment—and agreed to raise the statutory limit.

Sometimes the consequences are less dire than default, so legislators tolerate failure for a few days or a few weeks. When Congress and the president cannot agree on how much to appropriate for government spending, they usually approve a short-term fix, called a continuing resolution. When they cannot agree on such a fix, the government shuts down, although some essential functions, like air traffic control, continue. Then each side dances an elaborate jig, trying to persuade the public that the other side is to blame.[13] Twice in the mid-1990s, Speaker Newt Gingrich (R-GA) and his Republican House shut down the government—for 5 and 21 days—before learning that President Clinton was the better dancer. House Republicans closed the government again in 2013—for 16 days—this time over the Affordable Care Act, before conceding to President Obama and Senate Democrats. The longest shutdown to date—35 days—occurred in 2018 when Senate Democrats refused to fund President Trump's wall along the Mexican border. That shutdown ended with no funds for the wall. These shutdowns are an important part of civic education. They remind citizens of government's myriad functions. Eventually, the public turns against one side or the other. Citizens demand that legislators settle their differences so that the government can reopen parks, renew passports, and resume processing applications for Social Security benefits.

Compromise is vastly more difficult when the consequences are distant. Why should today's representatives violate their principled stands when another six House elections will take place before the Social Security trust fund runs dry? Why should today's legislators risk being blamed for raising the retirement age, increasing the maximum taxable wage base, or increasing tax rates when Social Security has adequate funds to pay all benefits until 2034? Insolvency just before the next election would be a political tragedy. Insolvency a decade hence threatens no one.

If compromise is so difficult, why did Congress resolve the 1977 and 1983 solvency crises so quickly? Recall that Congress resolved both crises in two years (chapter 2). Of course, what today seems like swift action was then thought to be agonizingly slow. In 1977, the House held 12 roll call votes, and the Senate 21, before agreeing to increase the tax rate by 25 percent and the wage base by 68 percent. In 1981, conflict was so intense that Congress and the president created the Greenspan Commission to broker a deal. The reason that decision making was relatively quick both times was that the trust fund was rapidly vanishing. Legislators approved the 1983 plan just a month before insolvency. So, what in retrospect appears to be swift was right on schedule from the perspective of legislators who act only when the wolf is at the door. The only thing different about today's solvency crisis is that legislators have had four decades from the first doomsday prediction (1994) to doomsday itself (2034). Unfortunately, having more time does not change legislators' natural proclivity for delay.[14]

Inattentive Publics

When legislators decide how to vote, they need to consider both attentive and inattentive publics. *Attentive publics* are people who are aware that an issue is on the congressional agenda, know what alternatives are under consideration, and have firm preferences about what Congress should do. *Inattentive publics* are people who have neither firm preferences about the alternatives under consideration nor knowledge of what Congress is doing.

The importance of attentive publics is obvious. Often organized into interest groups, they communicate to legislators not only where they stand on issues but also how intensely they feel. Intensity helps to signal how these people would react if legislators cast displeasing votes. But why should legislators worry about inattentive publics? By definition, these are people without knowledge or preferences. But having no preferences prior to congressional action does not mean that these people will not develop preferences sometime before Election Day. Prudent legislators consider in advance how a wrong vote might rouse inattentive publics against them.

Consider two tax bills. The first would modify hundreds of narrow tax provisions, helping or hurting a wide range of groups from investment bankers and hedge fund managers to steel makers and pharmaceutical companies. The second would impose a $5 per gallon gasoline tax to curb carbon emissions. Although attentive publics would be active for both bills, it is hard to imagine how enacting the first bill would galvanize inattentive publics against special tax breaks for hedge fund managers. In contrast, the second bill would quickly enrage automobile owners when gasoline prices tripled. Perhaps their first instinct would be to blame oil companies, but those companies would quickly counter, "Don't blame us; blame Congress." In primary and general election campaigns, challengers would inform citizens about legislators' dastardly votes to triple the price of gas. To be sure, we seldom see such reactions in the real world. But that is because legislators rarely give challengers such powerful campaign weapons. Legislators do everything they can to avoid provoking sleeping giants.

What kinds of policy enactments would galvanize inattentive publics to punish their representatives? Such enactments have three essential features.[15] First, they impose large, *perceptible costs* on constituents. Perceptible costs include 10 percent inflation, losing one's job, or tripling the price of gasoline. Imperceptible costs include paying a penny more for milk or marginal changes in air quality. Without large, perceptible costs, there is nothing to galvanize inattentive publics. Second, these costs are a direct consequence of a single *identifiable governmental action*. Costs that arise from dozens of enactments do not count. Without an identifiable governmental action, there is nothing to suggest that Congress is to blame. Third, legislators must have made a *visible individual contribution* to the enactment. Bill sponsorships and recorded roll call votes are good examples. Without visible individual contributions, citizens cannot know whether to blame legislators for working to pass a bill or praise them for working to block it. When all three features are present—large, perceptible costs; identifiable governmental actions; and visible individual contributions—inattentive publics can trace unpleasant costs back to legislators' actions. To avoid such traceability, rational legislators consider in advance whether their individual actions could rouse inattentive publics against them.

These three features underscore why fixing Social Security is so dangerous for most legislators. First, every solvency plan would impose large, perceptible costs on constituents. Take your pick: Would you rather infuriate retirees, ordinary workers, affluent workers, or small employers? Second, Congress cannot delegate the enactment of tax laws to other branches of government. Although legislators can delegate bill drafting to a body like the Greenspan Commission, only Congress can enact a bill into law. Third, enacting a solvency plan without a recorded vote would require virtually all legislators to agree to secrecy. The prospects for a bipartisan conspiracy of silence on such a high-stakes bill are not high.

It should now be clear why legislators need to anticipate the reactions of both attentive and inattentive publics when voting on a solvency plan. Attentive publics lobby in advance, so there is no question where they stand. Inattentive publics lie dormant until roused by activists who object to what legislators have enacted. Both attentive and inattentive publics can punish legislators retrospectively for their actions. Savvy legislators anticipate the reactions of both groups and vote carefully.

Conclusion

Sometimes observers notice how strongly people support Social Security and conclude that it would be easy to restore solvency by simply raising taxes. To be sure, it is easier for legislators to fund popular programs, such as Social Security or public education, than it is to fund unpopular programs, such as welfare or foreign assistance. But popularity is no guarantee that voters will accept whatever tax increases policymakers enact. For example, when we hear that local voters rejected a local school budget—a common occurrence in communities where such votes are required—we do not conclude that voters dislike public education. We conclude that voters were unwilling to accept the proposed tax rate. When the school board returns with a lower tax rate, voters generally adopt the revised budget. Social Security differs from this example only in the procedures required for approval. For Social Security, voters do not have an opportunity to approve or reject a solvency plan. That is a job for Congress. Instead, voters have an opportunity to remove legislators based on whether they supported or opposed a solvency plan. That is why legislators struggle to find the least treacherous path.

When voting on real-world solvency bills, legislators have the most to fear from Social Security beneficiaries. The reasons are three. First, retirees have more at stake than taxpayers do. Some retirees would lose 21 percent of their total income if Congress does nothing to forestall insolvency. Second, most retirees are politically active. They vote and donate more regularly than younger people do. Third, retirees are a large and growing share of the voting-age population. Already more than a third of the active electorate, seniors are far too numerous to ignore.

Legislators have far less to fear from ordinary workers. One reason is that Social Security provides benefits for two much-admired groups—self and kin. Most workers have parents or grandparents who are already collecting benefits. Moreover, today's workers are tomorrow's beneficiaries. Second, ordinary workers have less at stake in solvency reform than current beneficiaries do. Even if policymakers raised the tax rate high enough to cover all solvency costs, ordinary workers would face income losses no greater than 1.7 percent of their wages, a far cry from the huge losses facing retirees. Mobilizing inattentive workers after a tax increase would be much tougher than mobilizing inattentive beneficiaries after a benefit cut. Third, although workers have the numerical advantage over beneficiaries, they diminish that advantage by their disinclination to participate in politics, as either voters or donors.

Three groups of taxpayers stand out as potentially troublesome. Affluent workers would bear large costs if Congress eliminated the maximum taxable wage base. Nothing stimulates opposition faster than large, concentrated costs. Also, business owners, and especially small business owners, are vocal opponents of increasing either the tax rate or the wage base. Finally, voters who are antitax absolutists—no new taxes, ever—are a persistent problem because they consider small violations to be just as egregious as large ones.

As this chapter makes clear, Republican legislators face heavy cross pressures. They have spent years promising voters and donors that they would oppose all tax increases. Indeed, most of them have given signed pledges to the antitax crusader Grover Norquist. At the same time, Republicans have assured current beneficiaries that their own retirement benefits would remain safe. Satisfying retirees, near retirees, taxpayers, and donors is not easy. Some believe that privatizing Social Security would do the trick. But when President Bush proposed such a solution in 2005, both the Republican-controlled House and the Republican-controlled Senate displayed little enthusiasm for his plan.

Democratic legislators face cross pressures, too. Although Democrats are more comfortable raising taxes than Republicans are, enacting large tax increases is never easy. Moreover, affluent workers are heavily concentrated in Democratic districts. Indeed, party leaders often cater to their interests. When the Democratic House passed a $3 trillion economic stimulus package in May 2020 in response to the Covid-19 pandemic, some people were surprised that the bill contained an enormous tax break for high-income people. The bill would have suspended for two years the $10,000 cap on deducting state and local taxes on federal tax returns, costing the government $137 billion in lost revenues. One surprise was that this tax provision was in a bill allegedly designed to benefit 30 million unemployed Americans. A second surprise was that 57 percent of the tax savings would go to the top 1 percent of taxpayers and 83 percent would go to the top 5 percent.[16] Roughly speaking, these are the same taxpayers who earn more than Social Security's current maximum taxable wage base. It is not a huge leap to imagine that Democratic legislators, having catered to affluent workers during the pandemic, might consider their interests when deciding whether to eliminate the maximum taxable wage base.

Democratic legislators also face increasing pressures from the left, where activists are pushing to expand various benefits, including health care, education, and Social Security. The support for Senator Bernie Sanders (I-VT) in the 2020 presidential primaries is one measure of this leftward drift. Although many Democratic legislators represent safe Democratic districts, meaning that Republican challengers are not a big threat, primary challengers are a growing threat. Two progressive candidates, Ayanna Pressley and Alexandria Ocasio-Cortez, toppled two 10-term Democratic incumbents in 2018. Another pair, Cori Bush and Jamaal Bowman, overpowered Democratic incumbents serving their tenth and sixteenth terms in 2020. When long-term incumbents fall, surviving legislators often consider what they could do to forestall future challenges.[17] Supporting Sanders and DeFazio's Social Security Expansion Act is one option. Of course, the political downside of that bill is that it derives all new revenues from affluent taxpayers.

This chapter has presented a framework for analyzing how legislators anticipate the electoral repercussions of their decisions on Social Security. The next three chapters employ this framework to analyze the politics of fixing Social Security. Chapter 10 examines the incremental solutions available today. Chapter 11 examines the politics of reinventing Social Security. Chapter 12 explores how politics will change in 2034, when further delay would threaten the immediate well-being of 83 million beneficiaries.

PART IV

The Politics of Choice

10

Adjusting Taxes and Benefits

MANY POLICYMAKERS advocate incremental solutions to fix Social Security's solvency problem. These remedies—discussed in detail in chapter 5—adjust the tax and benefit formulas without modifying the program's basic structure. The history of policymaking for Social Security rests largely on incremental adjustments. From 1939 to 1972, legislators expanded the program by repeatedly adjusting the tax and benefit formulas. They enacted similar adjustments in 1977 and 1983 to resolve serious solvency problems. Even when legislators have made what in retrospect seem like large structural changes in Social Security—most notably the transformation from the original advance-funded program to the 1950-era pay-as-you-go program—they have done so with a series of incremental steps. The transformation to pay-as-you-go financing, for example, was the consequence of eight laws that legislators enacted between 1939 and 1947.

This chapter explores the politics of various incremental solutions. It begins by exploring the politics of *individual solvency provisions*, such as raising the retirement age, increasing the tax rate, or modifying the benefit formula. It then examines the politics of *comprehensive solvency plans*. These are plans that incorporate several individual provisions, sometimes with a mix of tax increases and benefit cuts.

Public Opinion

What do people think about the various incremental solutions to restore solvency? Do they prefer raising taxes or cutting benefits? Here I report results from two kinds of surveys. First are traditional polls—think Gallup—where pollsters ask quick questions about multiple topics, including one or more questions about Social Security. Second are in-depth surveys, where interviewers ask dozens of questions about Social Security, often preceded by background information about how the program operates and how particular proposals would restore solvency. Both types of surveys are informative. The former capture how inattentive publics react to specific triggers—"raise the retirement age" or "tax the wealthy"—while the latter suggest how attentive publics might react when Social Security reaches the decision agenda and people begin to hear politicians, interest groups, and journalists debate the pros and cons of specific proposals.

I found ten surveys containing 15 questions about raising the retirement age, administered between 2012 and 2019.[1] In two in-depth surveys, respondents first learned how much life expectancy had increased since 1940, and how and why Congress previously raised the full retirement age from 65 to 67. The respondents then viewed two arguments in favor of raising the retirement age again, and two arguments opposed, both sets of arguments vetted for fairness and accuracy by majority and minority staffers from the congressional committees that handle Social Security. Finally, respondents answered successive questions about whether they would support gradually raising the normal retirement age to 68, 69, or 70, each time with information about how much a proposal would reduce Social Security's shortfall.[2] Two other surveys offered a few sentences of background information before asking about raising the retirement age to 68 or 70, each time with an estimate of how much the shortfall would decline.[3] Six traditional surveys asked about raising the retirement age without offering any additional information.

Table 10.1 presents the results.[4] Four surveys that asked about gradually raising the full retirement age by a single year (to 68) showed modest support, with an average of 41 percent favoring and 39 percent opposing. Four surveys that asked about gradually raising the retirement age by two years revealed much less support, with the opponents 20 points greater than the supporters. Asking about raising the retirement age by three years increased the difference to 30 points. Finally, three surveys asked about raising the retirement age without specifying how high. Not hearing a precise age, respondents apparently presumed the worst and opposed it overwhelmingly. In short, people support a small increase in the retirement age by a narrow margin, but oppose larger increases by wider margins. Table 10.1 also explores whether Democrats and Republicans reacted differently to proposals to raise the retirement age. Evidence from seven surveys that reported party identification reveals only modest differences: Democrats were 6 points more likely to oppose raising the retirement age than Republicans were.[5]

TABLE 10.1. Attitudes toward Raising the Full Retirement Age, 2012–16

Number of Surveys	Proposal	Mean % in Favor	Mean % Who Oppose	Difference
4	Raise to 68	41	39	2
4	Raise to 69	33	53	(20)
4	Raise to 70	27	57	(30)
3	Raise retirement age	37	60	(23)

Number of Surveys	Proposal	Mean % Who Oppose		Party Difference
		Dem	Rep	
2	Raise to 68	38	33	5
2	Raise to 69	53	47	6
3	Raise to 70	63	57	6

Sources: Program for Public Consultation 2013a, 2016a; Tucker, Reno, and Bethell 2012; Walker, Reno, and Bethell 2014; Roper Center.

TABLE 10.2. Attitudes toward Raising the Maximum Taxable Wage Base, 2012–16

Number of Surveys	Proposal	Mean % in Favor	Mean % Who Oppose	Difference
4	Raise the wage base	61	26	35
4	Eliminate the wage base	66	19	47

Number of Surveys	Proposal	Mean % Who Oppose		Party Difference
		Dem	Rep	
2	Raise the wage base	18	28	(10)
3	Eliminate the wage base	15	21	(6)

Sources: Program for Public Consultation 2013a, 2016a; Tucker, Reno, and Bethell 2012; Walker, Reno, and Bethell 2014; Roper Center.

Pollsters also asked about raising or abolishing the maximum taxable wage base, the sharp boundary—$142,800 in 2021—between wages subject to the 6.2 percent payroll tax and wages immune from the tax. As table 10.2 shows, both proposals were very popular.[6] In four surveys, respondents supported raising the wage base by a wide margin, with an average of 61 percent favoring and 26 percent opposing. They were even more enthusiastic about abolishing the wage base, with 66 percent favoring and 19 percent opposing. Again, there were modest differences between the parties, with about 10 percent more

TABLE 10.3. Attitudes toward Raising the Tax Rate, 2012–16

Surveys	Proposal	Mean % in Favor	Mean % Who Oppose	Difference
NASI 2012, 2014	Raise rate from 6.2 to 7.2 (20 years)*	76	14	62
NASI 2012, 2014	Raise rate from 6.2 to 8.2 (40 years)	60	27	33
PPC 2013, 2016	Raise rate from 6.2 to 6.6 (8 years)	44	31	13
PPC 2013, 2016	Raise rate from 6.2 to 6.9 (14 years)	41	34	7
PPC 2013, 2016	Raise rate from 6.2 to 7.2 (20 years)*	35	41	(6)

Surveys	Proposal	Mean % Who Oppose		Party Difference
		Dem	Rep	
PPC 2013, 2016	Raise rate from 6.2 to 6.6 (8 years)	27	32	(5)
PPC 2013, 2016	Raise rate from 6.2 to 6.9 (14 years)	29	36	(7)
PPC 2013, 2016	Raise rate from 6.2 to 7.2 (20 years)	36	46	(10)

Sources: Program for Public Consultation 2013a, 2016a; Tucker, Reno, and Bethell 2012; Walker, Reno, and Bethell 2014.

NASI, National Academy of Social Insurance; PPC, Program for Public Consultation.

*Identical proposals.

Republicans than Democrats opposed to raising the wage base, and about 6 percent more Republicans than Democrats opposed to abolishing it. The only survey with information about a respondent's income showed that it did not matter. Of those with incomes greater than $100,000 10 percent opposed raising the wage base, as did 10 percent of those with incomes less than $30,000.[7] In short, partisanship mattered a little, but income not at all.

Two pollsters asked 10 questions about raising the tax rate. Table 10.3 presents the results. Two surveys conducted in 2014 and 2016 by the National Academy of Social Insurance (NASI) found overwhelming support, both for raising the rate from 6.2 percent to 7.2 percent over 20 years, and for a separate proposal to raise the rate to 8.2 percent over 40 years. On average, 68 percent of respondents favored the two proposals, while 21 percent opposed them. Two surveys conducted in 2013 and 2016 by the Program for Public

Consultation (PPC) found much less support. Respondents favored by small margins gradually raising the rate to 6.6 percent or 6.9 percent, but opposed by small margins gradually raising the rate to 7.2 percent. As with the previous questions on raising the retirement age or the wage base, there were modest differences between the parties, with about 7 percent more Republicans than Democrats opposed to raising the tax rate. The only survey with information about respondents' incomes revealed no differences.[8]

The differing results from the NASI and PPC surveys on raising the tax rate underline how much framing matters. Following are descriptions, shared with respondents, of two *identical* proposals to raise the tax rate from 6.2 percent to 7.2 percent over 20 years.[9]

> Workers currently pay 6.2 percent of their earnings to Social Security, matched by the employer. One proposal would raise the Social Security tax rate very gradually over 20 years, by 1/20th of 1 percent (5 cents per $100 of income) per year for workers and employers each. Example: For a worker earning $50,000, this would mean an increase each year of 50 cents per week, matched by the employer. This change would reduce the financing gap by 52 percent.

> A third proposal raises the payroll tax rate 0.05 percent a year for 20 years so that it would ultimately rise to 7.2 percent. A person earning $32,000 a year would see their monthly payroll tax go up by $32, from $202 to $234. This would reduce the Social Security shortfall by 49 percent.

The differences between the question wordings are subtle, but consequential. The first version (NASI 2014) summarizes the weekly increase in the first year: just 50 cents. The second question (PPC 2016) summarizes the monthly increase in the twentieth year: a more noticeable $32. Both descriptions are true—or mostly true—but people who are responding quickly to dozens of queries might consider the first proposal more affordable than the second.[10] And so they did: respondents favored the NASI-worded proposal by 66 points (83 to 17), while opposing the PPC-worded proposal by 8 points (35 to 43).[11] Respondents were much more supportive of two other PPC proposals, one increasing the tax rate to 6.6 percent, with a monthly cost of $13 in year 8, and another increasing the rate to 6.9 percent, with a monthly cost of $22 in year 14. When the sticker prices were lower, support was greater.

Several pollsters asked directly about the trade-off between raising taxes and cutting benefits. Although the results vary depending on question wording, majorities clearly prefer raising taxes. A 2013 McClatchy/Marist survey found that 60 percent of respondents preferred to "mostly increase taxes," while 33 percent preferred to "mostly cut spending." A 2015 Gallup poll found that 51 percent of respondents favored raising taxes, while 37 percent favored curbing benefits for future recipients. A 2015 AARP survey of adults who were not yet retired reported that 68 percent of respondents "would be willing to contribute more to Social Security to make sure it will be there for me when I retire." A 2014 NASI survey found that 79 percent of respondents agreed, "we should ensure Social Security benefits are not reduced, even if it means raising taxes on some or all Americans," while only 21 percent agreed, "we shouldn't raise taxes on any American, even if it means reducing Social Security benefits."[12]

Collectively, these surveys demonstrate remarkable realism among citizens. They do not expect money to fall magically from the clouds to fill Social Security's empty coffers. They are willing to raise the retirement age, but not too much. They are willing to raise the tax rate, but not too high. They are more than willing to raise or abolish the maximum taxable wage base. It would be a mistake, however, to conclude that citizens believe taxing the rich is a complete solution to the solvency problem. One survey found that 83 percent of respondents agreed with the statement "it is critical that we preserve Social Security benefits for future generations, even if it means increasing the Social Security taxes paid by top earners." But when asked the same question for "working Americans," 77 percent of respondents agreed that increasing taxes on that group was also acceptable.[13]

It is worth noting that all these surveys were administered when Social Security was not on the congressional agenda. Presidents were not peddling their favorite plans. Legislators were not debating the proper course forward. Interest groups were not doing battle. Nothing was happening to split the public along party lines. Respondents were merely reacting to straightforward questions about incremental solutions. Without any partisan cues, the differences between Democratic and Republican respondents were small.

Legislators

What do legislators think about the various incremental solutions? Do they prefer raising taxes or cutting benefits? Here the search for answers is more complicated. Although we have many surveys of ordinary people answering fixed-choice questions about Social Security, senators and representatives do not answer fixed-choice surveys. Legislators decide whether, when, and how to express their policy views. That makes it tougher to know exactly where they stand on specific provisions. Chapter 6 presented some evidence on where Democratic and Republican legislators stood in 2014 on some incremental options, most notably raising Social Security taxes—Democrats seemed willing, Republicans were not—but the evidence was thin on other options, precisely because many legislators refused to take positions on how they would allocate the costs of restoring solvency.

The evidence is stronger if we focus on comprehensive solvency plans—collections of individual provisions that together would close the actuarial deficit. As it happens, most Democratic legislators and some Republican legislators have sponsored or cosponsored comprehensive solvency plans. Unlike campaign rhetoric, bill sponsorship requires legislators to specify exactly how they would modify tax rates, benefit formulas, and retirement ages. Vagueness and contradictions fit poorly into the precise legal language of tax bills. Moreover, every claim that a sponsor makes about a bill's effects is tested by Social Security's actuaries, who project how the incidence of taxes and benefits would change for various income and age groups, and how much each bill would contribute to closing the 75-year actuarial deficit.

Here I examine 20 comprehensive solvency plans that representatives or senators submitted to the Office of the Chief Actuary for scoring between 2010 and 2020. This is the universe of all submitted congressional plans that the actuaries forecast would close at least three-quarters of the long-term actuarial deficit. Roughly speaking, closing three-quarters of the long-term deficit means funding Social Security for an additional three decades (until 2064). Although this would be a considerable accomplishment, it is less impressive than funding Social Security for the entire 75-year period (until 2095). Table 10.4 shows that Democratic legislators submitted five unique plans and seven previous versions of those plans.[14] Republicans submitted seven unique plans and one precursor.[15]

The most striking finding is that House Democrats have now converged on a single plan that would eliminate the solvency problem for at least 75 years. Entitled the Social Security 2100 Act, Representative John Larson (D-CT), now chair of the Social Security subcommittee of House Ways and Means, first introduced the plan in 2014, and then refined and reintroduced it in 2015, 2017, and 2019. The original bill attracted 2 Democratic cosponsors, the 2015 version 105, the 2017 version 174, and the most recent bill 205.[16] Nearly 90 percent of House Democrats cosponsored the 2019 version. The companion Senate bill, sponsored by Senator Richard Blumenthal (D-CT), has 1 cosponsor. An

TABLE 10.4. Bills That Would Close 75% or More of the Actuarial Deficit, 2010–20

#	Lead Sponsor	Chamber	Year	Share of Deficit	Cosponsors		Previous Versions
					House	Senate	
D1	Larson	H/S	2019	114%	205	1	**3**
D2	Sanders	S/H	2019	78%	25	4	**3**
D3	Moore	H	2019	76%	4		**1**
D4	Crist	H	2017	75%	1		
D5	Deutch	H	2010	93%			
R1	Johnson	H	2016	100%			
R2	Ribble	H	2016	101%	6		
R3	Hutchison	S	2012	100%			**1**
R4	Chaffetz	H	2011	109%			
R5	Coburn	S	2011	108%			
R6	Graham	S	2011	108%		2	
R7	Ryan	H/S	2010	103%	14	1	

Sources: Social Security Administration 2020b; Congress.gov.

Previous versions: Larson (2014, 2015, 2017); Sanders (2015, 2016, 2017); Moore (2013); Hutchison (2011).

alternative plan, entitled the Social Security Expansion Act, first introduced by Senator Bernie Sanders (I-VT) in 2015, and refined and reintroduced three times, has 4 cosponsors. The companion House bill, sponsored by Representative Peter DeFazio (D-OR), has 25.

Republicans have drafted more solvency plans than Democrats. But most of their plans are quite old, with five drafted between 2010 and 2012, and none more recently than 2016. Moreover, only 1 of the 7 sponsors, Senator Lindsey Graham (R-SC), still serves in Congress. Graham has neither revised his 2011 plan nor resubmitted it to the actuaries for scoring. Also, notice how few legislators have endorsed the Republican plans. Representative Paul Ryan's (R-WI) 2010 plan attracted 14 cosponsors in the House and 1 sponsor in the Senate. Representative Reid Ribble's (R-WI) 2016 plan had 6 cosponsors; Senator Graham's 2011 plan had 2.[17] The other four plans had no cosponsors. In short, these seven plans are too old, and the cosponsorships too few, to teach us much about where today's Republican legislators stand on fixing Social Security.

Representative Larson's Social Security 2100 Act promises not only to preserve but also to expand Social Security benefits.[18] The expansionary provisions include increasing benefits for new retirees, providing a higher minimum benefit for retires with low-wage careers, shielding from taxation the Social Security benefits of middle-income retirees, and using the more generous

TABLE 10.5. How Two Democratic Bills Would Affect Social Security's 75-Year Actuarial Deficit

Provision	Larson (%)	Sanders (%)
Revenue Increases		
Tax wages above $250,000 (later all)		77
Tax wages above $400,000 (later all)	67	
Tax investment income for affluent		33
Gradually increase tax rate from 6.2 to 7.4 percent (by 2043)	64	
Benefit Increases		
Adjust benefits with price index for seniors	(14)	(14)
Increase benefits for all new retirees	(8)	(13)
Higher minimum benefit for new retirees	(4)	(4)
Eliminate taxation of benefits for middle-income retirees	(6)	
Continue benefits for students until age 22		(2)
Total of all provisions	99	77
Adjustments for interactions among provisions	10	1
Estimated share of 75-year deficit eliminated	109	78

Source: Social Security Administration 2020b (Larson: January 30, 2019; Sanders: February 13, 2019).

Each cell shows how a provision would affect the 75-year actuarial deficit. Positive entries reduce the deficit by the given percentage; negative entries increase it. Estimates are based on the intermediate assumptions of the 2018 Trustees Report.

price index for seniors to adjust benefits for inflation. By themselves, these four provisions would increase the long-term actuarial deficit by nearly a third (see table 10.5).[19] But the plan's revenue measures would not only pay for the new benefits, they would also eliminate the 2034 solvency cliff. One revenue provision would gradually raise the tax rate on workers and employers from 6.2 percent each in 2019 to 7.4 percent each in 2043. This alone would close 64 percent of the long-term actuarial deficit. The other revenue provision would eventually eliminate the maximum taxable wage base, first by immediately taxing all wages above a new $400,000 threshold—leaving wages between the current $142,800 base and the new threshold untaxed—and then, once the wage base gradually increases with inflation to equal the new threshold (around 2048), taxing all wages. This provision would close 67 percent of the actuarial deficit.

Senator Sanders's Social Security Expansion Act proposes similar benefit increases. But it is much less aggressive on the revenue side. His bill proposes taxing, at the existing 6.2 percent rate, the investment income of high-income taxpayers (something Medicare already does). It also proposes eliminating the maximum taxable wage base in a manner similar to Larson's bill, but with a $250,000 threshold. Although these two revenue measures could have closed the entire 75-year actuarial deficit, they are insufficient to achieve that goal and to fund the plan's expensive new benefits. Under his plan, insolvency would return in 2070. Notice that Sanders proposes no changes in the tax rate itself. His bill raises all revenues from affluent workers and affluent retirees.

Both Larson and Sanders introduce a new approach for taxing wages above the current maximum taxable wage base. So far, Congress has dealt with un-taxed wages by simply raising the wage base, first with 15 legislated steps, bring-ing it from $3,000 in the original law to $29,700 in the 1977 law, and then with automatic annual increments, bringing it to $142,800 in 2021. But, as previously shown, the share of total wages that remain untaxed continues to grow—from 10 percent under the 1977 law to 17 percent today—largely because of increas-ing wage inequality (see figure 5.1). Both legislators target this inequality di-rectly. By immediately taxing all wages above a new $250,000 or $400,000 threshold, and then waiting patiently for the current wage base to rise gradu-ally with inflation to equal the new fixed threshold, they avoid explicitly raising the wage base, while nevertheless engineering its demise.[20]

The politics behind their new approach is simple: tax the richest workers first and then wait for inflation to spread the tax more broadly. Table 10.6 shows how Larson, with a $400,000 threshold, starts by taxing only 10 percent of the 10 million workers with untaxed wages (wage intervals 9 to 11). His provision would immediately generate enormous revenues, however, because those workers earn 57 percent of all untaxed wages. With a $250,000 threshold, Sanders starts by taxing 27 percent of workers with untaxed wages (wage in-tervals 8 to 11). His provision generates even more revenue because these workers earn 79 percent of untaxed wages. Both bills avoid antagonizing 7 to 9 million workers with wages above, but not far above, the current maximum taxable wage base. These workers are an increasingly important part of the Democratic coalition. And, as previously shown, they are heavily concentrated in Democratic House districts (figure 9.2).

Republicans followed a different script. For example, Senator Kay Hutchi-son (R-TX) offered a plan in 2012 that would achieve long-term solvency with two benefit cuts and no tax increases. One provision would increase the full retirement age from 67 to 70 over 16 years, while also increasing the early re-tirement age from 62 to 64. The second would reduce cost-of-living

TABLE 10.6. Wage Distribution for Workers with 2019 Wages Exceeding $135,000

#	Wage Interval ($)	Workers with Wages over $135K		Total Wages above $135K	
		Number	%	Amount ($M)	%
1	135K to 140K	757,088	7.6	1,849	0.1
2	140K to 150K	1,299,172	13.0	12,754	1.0
3	150K to 160K	1,059,197	10.6	20,957	1.6
4	160K to 170K	853,199	8.5	25,416	1.9
5	170K to 185K	983,216	9.8	41,443	3.1
6	185K to 200K	753,954	7.5	43,135	3.2
7	200K to 250K	1,565,338	15.7	136,194	10.2
8	250K to 400K	1,688,633	16.9	291,619	21.8
9	400K to 1M	872,810	8.7	376,250	28.2
10	1M to 2M	116,043	1.2	139,249	10.4
11	2M and up	50,303	0.5	247,113	18.5
	Total	9,998,953	100.0	1,335,978	100.0
8–11	250K and up	2,727,789	27.3	1,054,230	78.9
9–11	400K and up	1,039,156	10.4	762,612	57.1

Source: Social Security Administration 2020c.

Wages as reported by employers on Form W-2. All workers in this table had wages exceeding the maximum taxable wage base ($132,900 in 2019).

adjustments by 1 percentage point annually. Senator Graham's 2011 plan was similar. It would gradually increase the full retirement to age 70 and then index the retirement age to retirees' increasing life spans. His second provision would gradually reduce benefits for new retirees, exempting only those with low career-average earnings.

The other Republican plans, although more complicated than Hutchison's and Graham's two-provision plans, were similar in character. Here I focus on the two most recent plans, both from 2016. The first plan, introduced by Representative Sam Johnson (R-TX), then chair of the Social Security subcommittee of the Ways and Means Committee, included 15 provisions that would together close the entire long-term actuarial deficit. The most lucrative provision would close 47 percent of the deficit by eliminating cost-of-living adjustments for single beneficiaries earning more than $85,000 and couples earning more than $170,000, while using the less generous chained price index to make cost-of-living adjustments for other beneficiaries (see table 10.7).[21] A second provision would close 32 percent of the deficit by gradually raising the full retirement age to 69. Five other provisions would close 49 percent of the

TABLE 10.7. How Two Republican Bills Would Affect Social Security's 75-Year
Actuarial Deficit

Provision	Johnson (%)	Ribble (%)
Revenue Increases		
Raise taxable wage base until 90% of wages are taxable		37
Benefit Cuts		
Adjust benefits with chained price index		20
Adjust benefits with chained price index (no adjustments for affluent)	47	
Raise full retirement age to 69 (by 2030)	32	
Raise full retirement age to 69 (by 2034); then automatic increases		38
Other provisions to reduce benefits for new beneficiaries	49	25
Benefit Increases		
Higher minimum benefit for new retirees	(9)	(6)
Increase benefits for very old beneficiaries	(3)	(6)
Eliminate taxation of benefits (phased in 2045–54)	(15)	
Total of all provisions	101	108
Adjustments for interactions among provisions	(1)	(7)
Estimated share of 75-year deficit eliminated	100	101

Source: Social Security Administration 2020b (Ribble: July 13, 2016; Johnson: December 8, 2016).

Each cell shows how a provision would affect the 75-year actuarial deficit. Positive entries reduce the deficit by the given percentage; negative entries increase it. Estimates are based on the intermediate assumptions of the 2015 (Ribble) and 2016 (Johnson) Trustees Reports.

deficit by reducing benefits for new beneficiaries in various ways. Johnson's plan would also raise benefits for three groups: providing a higher minimum benefit for low-wage workers, increasing benefits for very old beneficiaries, and gradually eliminating the taxation of Social Security benefits.

The second Republican plan, introduced by Representative Reid Ribble, would close 101 percent of the long-term actuarial deficit. One provision—unique among Republican plans—would increase taxes by gradually raising the maximum taxable wage base over six years until 90 percent of wages were taxable, roughly what was taxable under the 1977 law.[22] If enacted in 2016, this provision would have raised the wage base to $346,800 in 2022. Automatic adjustments would then occur in subsequent years to keep the taxable ratio at 90 percent. Another lucrative provision would cut benefits by raising the full retirement age to 69, and then indexing the new retirement age to retirees' increasing life spans. A third provision would use the chained price index for cost-of-living adjustments. Two provisions would increase benefits, one for new beneficiaries with low-wage careers, the other for very old retirees.

Finally, Representative Paul Ryan's 2010 plan proposed reinventing Social Security with a system of voluntary individual accounts. I discuss his plan—which is not an incremental solution—in the next chapter. But it is worth noting here that his proposal would also reduce benefits for what would remain of traditional Social Security, by reducing benefits for new retirees, except for those in the lowest 30 percent of career earners, and by indexing the full retirement age for increasing longevity.

Most of these Republican plans do not mesh well with the way Republican legislators talk about Social Security (see chapter 6). Recall how legislators' 2014 rhetoric emphasized giving workers an ownership stake by establishing individual accounts. But only one of the seven plans followed that route. Recall how Republican legislators assured current retirees that their benefits were secure; but five plans would reduce cost-of-living adjustments for current retirees, two of them severely. Recall how Republican legislators said they opposed increasing the retirement age; but all seven plans would increase the full retirement age to 69, 70, or (with indexing) even higher. The only real consistency is that Republicans opposed raising taxes. Although one plan would raise the maximum taxable wage base, no plan endorsed raising the tax rate itself. But if raising taxes was unacceptable, plan designers had little choice but to cut benefits severely. Perhaps that is why so few legislators agreed to cosponsor these bills. It is awkward to endorse bills that do the opposite of what you promise on the campaign trail.

What is striking is that not a single Republican legislator has introduced a solvency bill since 2016. The best explanation is Donald Trump's election as president. Before Trump, the total number of Republican sponsors and cosponsors was roughly balanced between two factions—the partial privatizers, led by Ryan, and the benefit cutters, led by Johnson and Ribble.[23] What united these two factions was their aversion to tax increases. But Trump campaigned for office promising to protect traditional Social Security. Although he never made clear how he would protect all beneficiaries, his position made it difficult for Republicans to keep introducing benefit-cutting bills.

The Democratic plans correspond better with the way Democrats talk about Social Security. Democratic legislators promised not to cut benefits and their bill drafters did not. Legislators said they were comfortable raising taxes and their bill drafters proposed several tax increases. The one difference concerns expanding benefits. Although Democratic legislators did not talk much in 2014 about increasing Social Security benefits, such expansions are now firmly embedded in the two leading Democratic plans. These proposals reflect an evolution among Democrats in the last few years, as Senator Sanders and others have pushed legislators to think about the need for expanding social insurance, not merely making it solvent.

The real cleavage among Democratic legislators is not between those who support the Larson or Sanders plans, but rather between those who support one of these plans and those who support neither. Each of the 25 House cosponsors of the Sanders/DeFazio bill also cosponsored the Larson bill. So, although these legislators may prefer the former, they consider the latter acceptable. But 29 House Democrats did not cosponsor either 2019 bill. Moreover, these abstainers are significantly more conservative than the 205 House members who cosponsored the Larson bill.[24] Perhaps party leaders can eventually persuade the abstainers to vote for something like the Larson plan. But some of them may prove unwilling to support a plan that relies so heavily on taxation. In short, Democratic unity is far from assured for even the leading Democratic plan.

The divisions among Democrats are easy to understand: Some Democrats are simply more comfortable with large tax increases than are others. The fissures among Republicans are tougher to decipher. The real question is how much President Trump has changed the Republican Party. Did he really infuse the party with economic populism? Did he make it more of a working-class party? There are some signs that the party is changing its focus. A decade ago, Mitt Romney ran for president as a fiscal conservative, with Paul Ryan, a fiscal hawk, as his running mate. Now a Republican senator from Utah, Romney proposes expanding the safety net with an expensive child allowance plan. He is also working with Senator Tom Cotton (R-AK), a presidential aspirant, to raise the hourly minimum wage from $7.25 to $10. Meanwhile, Senator Josh Hawley (R-MO), another presidential aspirant, teamed up with Bernie Sanders to push for $1,200 per person stimulus checks, arguing, "working people and working families should be first on our to-do list, not last."[25]

It is too soon to say how the Republican quest for working-class voters might play out for Social Security. Perhaps Republican legislators will double down on their long-standing belief that ordinary workers cannot afford paying higher taxes for Social Security. Or perhaps they will abandon their affluent friends and support eliminating the maximum taxable wage base, especially now that so many affluent folks are abandoning Republican candidates. For

TABLE 10.8. Projected Median Annual Benefits by Lifetime Earnings for Two Reform Plans, 2065

Lifetime Earnings (quintile)	Current Law Scheduled Benefits (2018 $)	Larson Plan Projected Benefits		Johnson Plan Projected Benefits	
		2018 $	% Change	2018 $	% Change
Bottom	14,500	15,950	10	12,760	(12)
Second	18,900	20,034	6	16,821	(11)
Middle	23,500	24,675	5	18,800	(20)
Fourth	28,500	29,925	5	19,665	(31)
Top	33,800	35,828	6	18,928	(44)

Source: Johnson and Smith 2020, table 2.

Current law scheduled benefits refer to promised benefits, not funded benefits. Projected median annual benefits, net of any income tax, are expressed in inflation-adjusted 2018 dollars. Experts at the Urban Institute estimated all benefits with their Dynamic Simulation of Income Model, using the intermediate assumptions from the 2019 Trustees Report.

now, it seems that Republican legislators are split into three factions: the privatizers, the benefit cutters, and the working-class champions.

These divisions within the two parties are important and worth watching. But the differences *between* the parties are currently more consequential. Returning to hard data—bills introduced—the parties remain far apart. The leading Democratic plans (Larson and Sanders) seek to expand Social Security benefits. The most recent Republican plans (Johnson and Ribble) seek to reduce them.

What would Social Security look like in the long term if Congress enacted the Larson or the Johnson plan, both of which would make Social Security solvent over the entire 75-year forecasting period? First, under Larson, Social Security would grow, while under Johnson, it would shrink. In 2065, total revenues under the former would be 37 percent greater than current law, while under the latter, total revenues would be 9 percent less than current law. Second, the Larson plan would make the program more progressive on the revenue side, by increasing taxes more for upper-income workers, while the Johnson plan would make the program more progressive on the benefit side, by reducing benefits heavily for well-to-do retirees. As table 10.8 shows, under Johnson, people with high lifetime earnings would collect 44 percent less in 2065 than under current law, while those with low lifetime earnings would collect 12 percent less. That is an enormous difference. By comparison, under Larson, people in the top fifth of earners would collect 6 percent more in 2065 than under current law, while those in the bottom fifth would collect 10 percent more. Not much of a difference.[26]

The differing aims of the Larson and Johnson plans are now clear. Johnson seeks to transform Social Security, so that it provides a more level distribution of benefits, with top earners collecting not much more than those with low life-time earnings. Larson seeks to preserve what Social Security has been since 1983, with necessary revenue increases, but only modest benefit enhancements.

Reactions

How did ordinary citizens react to these 20 comprehensive solvency plans? Strictly speaking, of course, they did not. Outside Washington, no one notices the 10,000 or so bills that representatives and senators introduce every two years. Journalists do not cover them because merely introducing a bill is not a newsworthy event. Pollsters do not inquire about them because people know nothing about invisible bills. What we do know is how people reacted to sol-vency plans that *resembled* several of these plans. We know because two organ-izations administered in-depth surveys on the subject. In addition to asking about individual policy provisions, like raising the tax rate, wage base, or retire-ment age—results reported earlier in this chapter—these two organizations also asked about several comprehensive plans.

Near the end of its 2014 survey, the National Academy of Social Insurance (NASI) asked more than 2,000 respondents whether they would favor or op-pose a comprehensive plan that would close 100 percent of the long-term sol-vency gap. The plan included two provisions to increase revenues, one by rais-ing the tax rate on workers and employers from 6.2 percent to 7.2 percent over 20 years, the other by gradually eliminating the maximum taxable wage base over 10 years. The plan also included two provisions to increase benefits, one by raising the minimum Social Security benefit, the other by basing cost-of-living adjustments on the price index designed explicitly for seniors. The survey found that 76 percent of respondents preferred this plan to the status quo. The differences between Democrats and Republicans were modest—80 percent of Democrats supported the plan, as did 72 percent of Republicans—as were the differences among various income and age groups.[27]

Near the end of its 2016 survey, the Program for Public Consultation (PPC) asked more than 4,500 respondents to construct their own individual solvency packages in a multistage process. At each stage, respondents selected one of several options, then learned how much the solvency gap had declined, then selected another option, and so on, until each respondent had assembled a package that would eliminate the entire solvency gap. It was a zero-sum exercise designed to get respondents to choose options they found acceptable in a quest for solvency. The favorite provisions were on changing the maximum taxable wage base, where 59 percent of respondents chose to eliminate it, 29 percent chose to raise it gradually, and only 12 percent chose to retain the current base. Raising the tax rate was also broadly acceptable. Only one-quarter of respondents chose to retain the current tax rate, while 34 percent favored an increase to 6.6 percent, 23 percent favored an increase to 6.9 percent, and 19 percent favored an increase to 7.2 percent. Most respondents (58 percent) were willing to raise the minimum monthly benefit, even though doing so would require even larger tax increases. The only significant partisan difference was on this provision. Among Democrats, 67 percent favored raising the minimum monthly benefit, compared with 49 percent of Republicans. The other partisan differences were more about the extent of support for particular options. For example, 64 percent of Democrats, but only 54 percent of Republicans, favored abolishing the maximum taxable wage base.[28]

The PPC survey found strong support for some of the central provisions in the two Democratic bills. But the PPC survey also found qualified support for several provisions in the Republican plans. For example, the Republican plans proposed substantial increases in the retirement age. The PPC survey revealed majority support for modest, but not substantial, increases in the retirement age. Four Republican bills proposed using the less generous chained price index for cost-of-living adjustments. The PPC survey found greater support for switching to this index than for either retaining the current index or switching to the more generous price index for seniors. Several Republican bills proposed cutting benefits for future retirees in the top half of the income distribution. The PPC survey found support for cutting benefits only in the top quarter of the income distribution.[29] In short, the Republican plans contained some provisions that were potentially acceptable to citizens, but only if they were scaled back.

It is worth emphasizing that the PPC and NASI surveys were about hypothetical solvency plans. Respondents reacted to how researchers framed the questions, which in the case of PPC were vetted for fairness and accuracy by Democratic and Republican staffers on the congressional committees that handle Social Security. Once solvency reform hits the congressional agenda, however, we should expect that citizens will also respond to the ways legislators, interest groups, and the media frame the alternatives. The difference between how the NASI and PPC surveys framed an identical tax increase from 6.2 to 7.2 percent over 20 years—recall how one called it 50 cents per week in year 1, while the other called it $32 per month in year 20—is a good preview for how proponents and opponents will frame proposals when congressional action is imminent. Proponents will minimize the costs of tax increases; opponents will underline their severity.

But it is also worth recalling that many people already know a great deal about Social Security. They and their families have experienced Social Security for most of their lives. They can imagine what it would be like to pay higher taxes. They can imagine working a year or two longer. They can imagine receiving lower cost-of-living adjustments. Put differently, their current views on incremental solutions rest on experience with how the system operates. Yes, people will be open to persuasion from both sides. But shifting the public's views about incremental solutions will be more difficult than shifting their views on issues for which they have no direct experience.

Priorities

Citizens and legislators disagree about how to fix Social Security. But they also disagree about whether fixing Social Security should be a top priority. Most people believe it should be. Most legislators act as if it is not.

Identifying citizens' policy priorities is straightforward. Recall from chapter 7 how the Pew Research Center has asked people every year since 1997 which problems Congress and the president should fix in the coming year. Among 20 or so problems offered to respondents is one on "taking steps to make the Social Security System financially sound." Only four times in 25 years has fixing Social Security been lower than fifth on the list. In short, people repeatedly claim they want Congress to fix Social Security.

Identifying congressional priorities is a bit tougher. It helps to focus on what majority party leaders say and do, both because these leaders control the congressional agenda, and because they need to be responsive to their colleagues. James Curry and Frances Lee have developed a method for identifying majority leaders' priorities, first by reading the speeches that the House Speaker and the Senate majority leader made at the start of each Congress, and then by identifying any additional bills that these two leaders inserted into the symbolic slots reserved for their use (H.R. 1 through H.R. 10 for House bills, S. 1 through S. 5 for Senate bills). By this method, they identified 169 priority bills during the 11 Congresses that overlap the Pew surveys (1997–2018).[30] None of these bills included comprehensive solvency reform.[31] In short, majority party leaders have yet to make fixing Social Security a top priority.

Assessment

Why do Republican legislators have such trouble drafting politically appealing incremental solutions to the solvency problem? Why do they propose huge benefit cuts when surveys suggest that most citizens, regardless of party, oppose deep benefit cuts? Why do they shun tax increases when surveys suggest that most citizens, regardless of party, prefer raising Social Security taxes to cutting benefits? One explanation is that for two decades, Republicans have been running for office, and running for reelection, by pledging never to vote for tax increases. Perhaps when they first signed the so-called Norquist pledge, they were thinking about income taxes, not payroll taxes. Perhaps they were thinking like candidates not like future stewards of Social Security. But by taking the Norquist pledge, they have seriously constrained their options for fixing Social Security. By eliminating taxes from their choice set, Republican legislators have no broadly acceptable options for closing the solvency gap.

The other explanation for why Republican legislators shun Social Security tax increases is that they believe no-cost remedies could fix the solvency problem. Hence their fascination with market-like solutions and with the notion of privatizing Social Security. Chapter 11 explores this possibility.

Why do Democratic sponsors have such trouble moving their reform bills through the legislative labyrinth and onto the president's desk? One reason is that each chamber's majority party sets the chamber's agenda. Since 2001, Democrats have controlled both chambers of Congress only three times—the last two years of the Bush presidency, the first two years of the Obama presidency, and the first two years of the Biden presidency. There was little reason to push incremental reforms when privatization's greatest champion occupied the White House. Two years later, during the Great Recession, more urgent priorities stuffed the congressional agenda, including economic stimulus, health-care reform, and financial regulation. President Biden also began his presidency with urgent priorities stemming from the health and economic consequences of the Covid-19 pandemic.

What would a bipartisan plan look like? It is hard to know. Perhaps a proposal from the Bipartisan Policy Center (BPC), a think tank founded in 2007 by former Senate majority leaders Howard Baker, Bob Dole, Tom Daschle, and George Mitchell—two Republicans, two Democrats—would be a good place to begin. In 2016, the BPC released a plan drafted by a 19-member committee consisting of policy experts and retired politicians. The committee's plan proposed increasing revenues and cutting benefits by equivalent amounts.

The revenue changes included raising the maximum taxable wage base and raising the tax rate from 6.2 to 6.7 percent. The benefit cuts included using the less generous chained price index for inflation adjustments and increasing the full retirement age by two years, phased in over 48 years.[32] It was a share-the-pain proposal.

It is not clear how well the BPC reflects current reality on Capitol Hill. First, today's Republican Party has evolved twice since the days of Senators Baker and Dole. After they left the Senate (the former in 1985, the latter in 1996), the party continued its drift to the right, electing more and more legislators opposed to both tax increases and social spending. Then, with the election of Donald Trump in 2016, the party became more populist, at least at the top. Although it is hard to know how much the former president's support for traditional Social Security may have changed attitudes within his party, some Republican legislators who claim Trump's mantle seem more open to social spending. Second, the Democratic Party seems to be drifting leftward, as the next section shows. Ideology aside, the committee that drafted the BPC's 2016 plan had retired politicians, not active legislators, as members. Perhaps it is easier being a courageous bill drafter when you no longer need to attract voters or donors.

Presidential Candidates

The 2020 presidential campaign was unusual because five Democratic candidates released detailed plans for fixing Social Security. Senator Bernie Sanders touted the bill he had been championing in Congress since 2015; Senator Kamala Harris (D-CA) reminded everyone she was a cosponsor. Senators Amy Klobuchar (D-MN) and Elizabeth Warren (D-MA) released their own separate plans, as did former vice president Joe Biden and former mayor Pete Buttigieg. According to experts at the Urban Institute, a Washington think tank, three of the five plans would close at least three-quarters of the long-term actuarial deficit, the standard I have been using for identifying solvency bills. The Buttigieg and Warren plans would eliminate the entire 75-year deficit, the Sanders plan 82 percent, the Klobuchar plan 70 percent, and the Biden plan 26 percent (see table 10.9).[33]

All five plans would raise substantial revenue by taxing affluent workers. Four plans would eventually eliminate the maximum taxable wage base, first by taxing all wages above $250,000, and then, after the wage base gradually increased to that level (around 2035), taxing all wages. This provision would

TABLE 10.9. How Five Democratic Plans Would Affect Social Security's 75-Year Actuarial Deficit

Provision	Biden (%)	Buttigieg (%)	Klobuchar (%)	Sanders (%)	Warren (%)
Revenue Increases					
Tax wages above $250,000 (later all)		76	79	80	93
Tax wages above $400,000 (later all)	71				
Tax investment income for affluent				40	95
Increase tax rate for affluent (as needed)		86			
Benefit Increases					
Adjust benefits with price index for seniors	(14)			(14)	(14)
Increase benefits for all new retirees				(15)	(29)
Higher minimum benefit for new retirees	(8)	(39)		(8)	(39)
Provide wage credits for unpaid caregivers	(5)	(20)	(5)		(12)
Increase benefits for state and local workers	(6)				(6)
Increase benefits for various other groups	(12)		(5)	(2)	(9)
Total of all provisions	26	103	69	81	79
Adjustments for interactions		(3)	1	1	25
Estimated share of 75-year deficit eliminated	26	100	70	82	104

Source: Smith, Johnson, and Favreault 2020, table 3.

Each cell shows how a provision would affect the 75-year actuarial deficit. Positive entries reduce the deficit by the given percentage; negative entries increase it. Estimates are based on the intermediate assumptions of the 2019 Trustees Report.

raise enough revenue to close 93 percent of the long-term actuarial deficit in the Warren plan, 80 percent in the Klobuchar and Sanders plans, and 76 percent in the Buttigieg plan. Warren would raise more revenue than the others because she would simultaneously raise the tax rate for affluent workers (and their employers) from 6.2 percent to 7.4 percent. Biden proposed a similar gradual approach to eliminating the wage base, first by taxing all wages above $400,000, and then, after the wage base gradually increased to that level (around 2048), taxing all wages. His provision would close 71 percent of the long-term actuarial deficit.[34]

Three plans would raise additional revenue from affluent folks by taxing other types of income. Both Sanders and Warren would tax investment income earned by upper-income taxpayers, the former with a tax rate of 6.2 percent, the latter with a tax rate of 14.8 percent. Warren would also tax income received from limited partnerships, limited liability companies, and S-corporation shareholders, again at the 14.8 percent rate. Sanders would raise enough revenue with his provision to close 40 percent of the long-term actuarial deficit, while Warren's two provisions would close 95 percent of the deficit. Finally, the Buttigieg plan contained a provision that would, when necessary, automatically increase the tax rate for affluent workers to whatever rate would keep Social Security solvent. Some of these rate increases would be colossal, since experts estimated this provision alone would close 86 percent of the long-term deficit.

What is striking is that all five proposals avoid imposing costs on ordinary workers. Unlike the Larson plan, cosponsored by 90 percent of House Democrats, which would raise roughly half the necessary revenue by gradually raising the tax rate from 6.2 percent to 7.4 percent, all five plans avoided raising taxes on any workers earning less than $250,000. Why were House Democrats comfortable spreading the solvency costs broadly, while Democrats running for president preferred concentrating all costs on the affluent? The likely explanation is that the other four candidates feared Bernie Sanders in the primaries. His plan was first out of the gate, and no candidate wanted to appear less sympathetic to poor and middle-class voters than a candidate who almost won the 2016 nomination. Indeed, two of his four competitors (Buttigieg and Warren) proposed extracting far more revenue from the affluent than did the self-professed democratic socialist.

The other candidates also followed Sanders's lead in expanding Social Security benefits. Sanders proposed increasing the minimum benefit for Social Security recipients. Biden matched that provision; Buttigieg and Warren countered with a provision that cost five times as much. Sometimes candidates differentiated themselves from Sanders by proposing benefits that were not in his bill. For example, all four contenders proposed wage credits for unpaid caregivers, essentially allowing people to collect Social Security benefits for the years they were not in the workforce while caring for children, parents, or disabled dependents. Summing all the benefit increases in table 10.9 shows that three candidates—all but Klobuchar—assembled more expensive benefit packages than Sanders.

Most of the proposed benefit increases would correct long-standing inequities. Many women collect lower retiree benefits than men, in part because of their years as unpaid caregivers, hence the development of wage credits for caregivers. Survivors often suffer financially when losing a spouse, hence various proposals to increase survivor benefits. But at least one of the benefit changes would *create* inequities. Both Biden and Warren proposed repealing the Windfall Elimination Provision and the Government Pension Offset.[35] The former prevents state and local government workers, who already receive pensions based on their government careers, from collecting windfalls based on their short-term participation in Social Security, usually before or after their government service. This provision, enacted in 1983, was designed to remove an unintended advantage that these workers would otherwise receive because of an interaction between Social Security's progressive benefit formula, which advantages poorly paid workers, and the workers' relatively short careers in Social Security-covered employment, which makes them resemble poorly paid workers.[36] The Government Pension Offset, enacted in 1977, makes similar adjustments for spousal and survivor benefits. To be sure, these two provisions are unpopular, particularly among teachers, police officers, and firefighters, who often retire early and pursue second careers. No doubt political rewards await politicians who cater to these groups. But it is particularly odd that Biden's plan, which does the least to fix the solvency problem, does so much to service the organized.

We should recognize that these five plans were campaign documents rather than carefully crafted proposals designed to attract bipartisan support in Congress. The plans signaled what goals each candidate believed were most important. All five candidates sought to increase benefits for at least some groups. All candidates seemed to believe that the affluent should bear both the solvency costs and the costs of the new benefits. On the other hand, they disagreed about the urgency of fixing the long-term solvency problem. Although the Buttigieg and Warren plans would make Social Security solvent over the entire 75-year forecasting period, and perhaps beyond, the Sanders, Klobuchar, and Biden plans would add only 41, 26, and 5 years to the estimated date for trust fund depletion. Biden's plan, particularly, seemed designed to refute Sanders's charge that Biden had in the past, and therefore would in the future, favor cutting Social Security benefits. By promising to deliver more new benefits than Sanders himself, Biden worked to rebut that claim.

What was newsworthy about 2020 was that all the top Democratic candidates released detailed Social Security reform plans.[37] That had never happened before. To be sure, some candidates seemed more interested in delivering new benefits than in fixing the solvency problem. But every candidate made some solvency improvements, and two candidates would eliminate the long-term actuarial shortfall. What was more important than the details, however, was that the leading Democratic candidates signaled Social Security as a top priority. No presidential candidate had done that since George W. Bush advocated reinventing Social Security during the 2000 and 2004 campaigns.

Republicans in 2020 made no commitments to fix Social Security. Indeed, the party continued to be in disarray on what to do about America's largest and most popular social program. Republicans did not even write a platform in 2020. They merely reprinted their 2016 platform, including the section that opposed increasing the payroll tax and emphasized their belief in "the power of markets to create wealth and to help secure the future of our Social Security system." Meanwhile, the incumbent president, Donald Trump, signaled in 2020, as he had done in 2016, that he would do nothing to disrupt traditional Social Security. To be sure, President Trump never suggested that fixing Social Security was a top priority. And he never detailed how he would fix the solvency problem. But he made clear that he would do nothing to threaten current or future beneficiaries.

Conclusion

What would it take to enact incremental reforms in the next few years? Top on anyone's list should be realism. Surveys repeatedly show a spirit of realism among citizens when asked about fixing Social Security. Knowing that money does not grow on trees, consistent majorities from both parties favor raising taxes in order to protect valued benefits. Legislators need to be equally realistic. Yes, trimming benefits can be part of a successful plan, as Republican bill drafters often insist. But the instrument of choice should probably be the paring knife not the cleaver. And yes, increasing benefits can be part of a successful plan. But the increased benefits should probably be for groups where the two parties agree, like increasing minimum benefits for new retirees, and augmenting benefits for very old beneficiaries, rather than for groups where the parties disagree, like subsidizing government workers in states and localities that have chosen not to participate in Social Security. Fixing Social Security without raising anyone's taxes, however, seems like an impossible dream.

The next chapter shifts to proposals to reinvent the system. Unlike the current chapter, which has reached back to 1977 and 1983 for real-world examples, the next chapter opens with a more recent case, President Bush's unsuccessful plan to reinvent Social Security with voluntary personal accounts. This case provides the foundation for a discussion about the overall prospects for reinventing the system.

11

Privatization

WHEN ACCEPTING the 2000 nomination for president at the Republican National Convention, George W. Bush declared, "Social Security has been called the third rail of American politics, the one you're not supposed to touch because it might shock you. But if you don't touch it, you cannot fix it. And I intend to fix it."[1] Nine months later, he appointed the President's Commission to Strengthen Social Security, a bipartisan group tasked with drafting a plan that would create individually controlled personal retirement accounts. Although the commission issued its final report in late 2001, proposing three alternative plans, the report was overshadowed by the terrorist attacks of 9/11. It was soon forgotten.

The president returned to Social Security during the 2004 campaign, arguing that the time was ripe for action. The morning after his reelection he held a news conference, declaring, "I earned capital in the campaign, political capital, and now I intend to spend it."[2] Top on his list was Social Security. Bush formally launched his reform effort in his 2005 State of the Union address. Warning that the program faced eventual bankruptcy, he proposed a plan that would allow younger workers to divert a portion of their payroll taxes to voluntary personal retirement accounts, while preserving traditional Social Security for anyone 55 or older.[3] The president then launched a "60 stops in 60 days" national tour to convince people both of the need for action and of the desirability of personal retirement accounts. Despite immense efforts to persuade the public, his proposal attracted little support among citizens. Indeed, support for Bush and his plan declined throughout the campaign. The plan became equally unpopular on Capitol Hill, even though Republicans controlled both House and Senate. A few months later, Hurricane Katrina swept Social Security off the presidential agenda. It never returned.

This chapter explores why President Bush's plan to introduce voluntary personal accounts failed so quickly and so decisively. It then explores whether smarter tactics or a different plan would have attracted more support. It concludes by examining the prospects for reinventing Social Security before 2034.

Origins

The earliest privatization plans sought to replace traditional Social Security. For example, Peter Ferrara's 1980 book, published by the Cato Institute, proposed separating the insurance and welfare functions of Social Security. The private sector would establish and manage individual retirement accounts for workers, while the government would use general revenues to support poverty-stricken retirees, essentially reviving the old-age assistance program from the 1930s. Ferrara's book and other early studies were effective in highlighting Social Security's limitations, particularly the declining rate of return for individuals and the harmful effects on national savings of funding retirement with income transfers rather than using advance funding (see chapter 4). But these studies attracted little attention among Washington policymakers.[4]

All this changed when the 1994–96 Advisory Council on Social Security released its recommendations. At the time, the law required the secretary of health and human services to appoint an advisory council every few years to evaluate the program and recommend possible changes. This council was the first to convene after government actuaries forecast long-term solvency problems. Among its 13 members were Carolyn Weaver and Sylvester Schieber, critics of traditional Social Security; Robert Ball, a former commissioner of Social Security and the architect of its expansion; and Edward Gramlich, an economist and the council's chair. Despite their differences, council members agreed on three things: the solvency problem was serious, advance funding was desirable, and policymakers should make immediate changes to achieve long-term solvency. They disagreed, however, on how to achieve those goals. The largest faction, led by Ball, proposed retaining most of the program's pay-as-you-go character, while incorporating revenue and benefit adjustments that would create a larger trust fund, which would then be invested in the stock market. The next largest faction, led by Weaver and Schieber, proposed that half of retirement benefits would be provided by a variant of the current pay-as-you-go system and half by advance-funded, individually directed retirement accounts. The smallest faction, led by Gramlich, was a blend of the first two plans, grafting a smaller version of advance-funded individual accounts on top of a reduced pay-as-you-go system.[5] Government actuaries projected that each plan would eliminate the long-range actuarial deficit, making Social Security solvent over the 75-year forecasting period.[6]

The Advisory Council's embrace of advance funding and partial privatization transformed the Washington debate. It stimulated the creation of additional privatization proposals, not just from scholars and policy experts, but also from Democratic and Republican officials.[7] Senators Bob Kerrey (D-NE) and Alan Simpson (R-WY) drafted a bipartisan plan that would divert 2 percentage points of the payroll tax into personal retirement accounts, invest a portion of the collective trust fund in a stock index fund, and gradually reduce traditional benefits by raising the retirement age and modifying cost-of-living adjustments. Senator Daniel Patrick Moynihan (D-NY) proposed a similar diversion but with a different package of benefit cuts. Representative John Kasich (R-OH) proposed using the federal government's overall surplus to jump-start individual retirement accounts. Even President Clinton was working on a plan for individual accounts, before the prospect of impeachment made the president wary about antagonizing his Democratic base.[8]

George W. Bush was also an early advocate of privatization. During his 1978 campaign for an open congressional seat in oil-rich west Texas, he promoted individual accounts.[9] Little is known about when Bush first soured on traditional Social Security or how privatization appeared on his radar. Did Barry Goldwater's *Conscience of a Conservative*, which he read at Andover, affect his views?[10] Did he read Milton Friedman at Yale? Did his conservative oil-industry donors persuade him that dismantling Social Security was a good idea?[11] What is known is that he nearly won a district that had long been safe for Democrats. Moreover, his views on privatization did nothing to harm him. As privatization became more popular in Washington, and more popular among rich, conservative donors, Bush reminded everyone that he had long championed individual accounts. By 1997, he was dining with experts from the Cato Institute and the Hoover Institution, learning more about privatization.[12] Bush then made personal retirement accounts a centerpiece of his 2000 presidential campaign.

Soon after taking office in 2001, the president created his own bipartisan commission to draft Social Security reforms. Unlike the bipartisan Advisory Council, appointed by Clinton's secretary of health and human services, which contained champions and critics of traditional Social Security, the president appointed only members who agreed to be bound by Bush's personal preferences. Those preferences included (a) creating voluntary, individually controlled personal retirement accounts; (b) prohibiting trust fund investments in the stock market; (c) avoiding increases in the payroll tax; and (d) preserving benefits for current and near retirees.[13]

These were highly restrictive conditions. For example, they ruled out all three of the Advisory Council's solvency proposals. They also disqualified all nine proposals, introduced by Republican and Democratic legislators between 1995 and 2001, that government actuaries had scored for their effects on solvency.[14] The president's conditions also suggested that reform would do nothing to increase national savings in the near term—one of the principal goals of many reformers—because savings require benefit reductions or revenue increases, and the president's four conditions prohibited both kinds of sacrifice. Moreover, "no new taxes" was Republican dogma, certain to excite Republicans, but equally certain to repel many Democrats who believed that tax increases, especially on the wealthy, were an appropriate part of a balanced plan to restore solvency. In short, the President's Commission to Strengthen Social Security had little in common with the 1994–96 Advisory Council or with the 1983 Greenspan Commission, two groups with experience in drafting appealing solvency plans.

The President's Commission created three plans. All were supposed to meet the president's commands to create voluntary individual accounts, avoid tax increases, and avoid benefit cuts for retirees and near retirees. In fact, only one plan would make Social Security solvent over the 75-year forecasting period. This plan would achieve solvency by substantially cutting benefits for future retirees and by using debt to cover revenue shortfalls until 2054, when revenues would finally cover the diminished benefits. The other two plans would require tax increases. Model 1 quietly mentioned "additional revenues" would be needed to keep the trust fund solvent starting in the 2030s. Model 3 required both "new sources of dedicated revenue" and substantial debt to cover revenue shortfalls until 2063.[15]

The commission discovered that transitioning to individual accounts could achieve solvency only if future politicians raised taxes (models 1 and 3) or current politicians imposed substantial benefit cuts on younger workers (model 2). Apparently, "no new taxes" meant "no new taxes that current politicians would have to approve." Moreover, the benefit cuts in model 2 were camouflaged by an innocent-sounding modification of the benefit formula. The differences between the old and new formulas were relatively small for workers in their early fifties, but enormous for those in their twenties and thirties.[16] In short, the so-called "voluntary" individual accounts in model 2 were actually coercive. Young workers who chose to remain in traditional Social Security would collect much lower benefits than current law stipulated. Finally, even with benefit cuts and future tax increases, models 1 and 3 required massive government borrowing for five or six decades.

The commission revealed how hard it would be to create individual accounts and meet the president's restrictive conditions. Then the terrorist attacks of 9/11 knocked Social Security reform off the president's first-term agenda.

The 2005 Campaign

After reelection, President Bush returned to his quest for individual accounts. In February 2005, he devoted one-quarter of his State of the Union address to Social Security.[17] After first praising the program as "a great moral success of the 20th century," he declared that Social Security, "on its current path, is headed toward bankruptcy." He warned that "fixing Social Security permanently would require an open, candid review of the options," and that he would "listen to anyone who has a good idea to offer." Then he narrowed his professed openness, declaring:

> We must, however, be guided by some basic principles. We must make Social Security permanently sound, not leave that task for another day. We must not jeopardize our economic strength by increasing payroll taxes. We must ensure that lower income Americans get the help they need to have dignity and peace of mind in their retirement. We must guarantee there is no change for those now retired or nearing retirement. And we must take care that any changes in the system are gradual, so younger workers have years to prepare and plan for their future.

He argued that the best way to improve the system was to create voluntary personal retirement accounts for younger workers, describing in considerable detail how they would work and comparing them to the current retirement accounts for federal employees. The president's stated goals were two: save traditional Social Security for those 55 and older and use partial privatization to make Social Security a better deal for workers younger than 55.[18]

What happened next seemed odd at the time and still seems odd in retrospect. The president started touring the country to sell his vision for privatized Social Security without first releasing a formal plan that detailed how solvency would be achieved or who would pay the enormous transition costs. He could have championed model 2 from his 2001 commission, the only plan that met his professed principles. He could have endorsed another plan or assembled a new one. He could then have asked government actuaries to determine if his plan would achieve solvency over the 75-year forecasting period, just as the actuaries had done for 17 reform plans released between 2000 and 2004.[19] In short, he could have acknowledged that privatization would require some combination of benefit cuts, revenue increases, and government borrowing—the precise conclusions of his 2001 commission—and used his bully pulpit to convince people that swallowing painful remedies now was worth doing in order to save a valued program from eventual bankruptcy. Instead, he stuck to his principles—the ones that prohibited any sacrifices on his watch.

The campaign to privatize Social Security, therefore, took place on two tracks. President Bush launched what one presidential scholar called "the most extensive public relations campaign in the history of the presidency" to sell his vision of individual accounts.[20] Meanwhile, administration officials worked with Congress to find an acceptable way to pay the transition costs and make Social Security solvent. Bush was essentially marketing a set of appealing goals while other policymakers were struggling to design a plan that would meet those goals.

The president and other administration officials toured the country for several months, working to sell the virtues of voluntary individual accounts for younger workers, while assuring older workers and retirees that their benefits would remain safe. The president spoke to carefully curated audiences of Bush enthusiasts.[21] The advance team chose who would ask questions and what questions they would ask, often rehearsing the night before to ensure that each panelist struck the proper tone.[22] Twice former first lady Barbara Bush was one of the questioners. After claiming, "I'm here because your father and I have 17 grandchildren," she asked what could be done to secure their retirement security.[23] Her dutiful son had just the answer. It was a well-scripted national road show, but one where seldom was heard a discouraging word.

Knowing that the Senate was the greater obstacle, where a minimum of 5 Democrats would need to join what the administration hoped would be a unanimous 55 Republicans to forestall a filibuster, the president first visited states like Montana, Nebraska, and North Dakota, where moderate Democratic senators would be essential members of a winning coalition. Later, as the support of Republican senators weakened, Bush added Republican states to the mix. By the end of the campaign, he had visited 25 states, spoken and taken questions at 35 public events, delivered four radio addresses, and held one prime-time news conference.[24] It was an extraordinary commitment of presidential time to a single cause.[25]

Meanwhile, the White House and the Republican National Committee coordinated the activities of outside groups.[26] Many groups that had worked to promote the president's reelection in 2004 were enlisted to champion the plan. Some groups created advertising campaigns to promote individual accounts. Others encouraged local citizens to contact wavering legislators. Still others worked to undermine the credibility of AARP, the nation's largest organization of senior citizens, which was leading the opposition.

While the president launched the national sales campaign, White House staffers gradually released details about how individual accounts would actually work. An unnamed senior administration official briefed reporters on how workers under age 55 could redirect nearly two-thirds of their Social Security taxes—that is, 4.0 percentage points of the 6.2 percent payroll tax—into individual retirement accounts that they could then invest in stock and bond funds.[27] A few days later, Vice President Cheney acknowledged on *Fox News Sunday* that the government would need to borrow nearly a trillion dollars in the first decade, and "trillions more after that," to pay benefits for everyone 55 and older.[28] The borrowings were necessary because the full contributions of current workers would no longer be available to fund current beneficiaries. Still no one could explain how the plan would ever achieve solvency.

Legislators floated various ideas for closing the gap between revenues and benefits. Senator Lindsey Graham (R-SC) proposed raising the (then) $90,000 cap on wages subject to the Social Security tax to help pay for the transition.[29] But that proposal fizzled two weeks later as House Speaker Dennis Hastert (R-IL) and Majority Leader Tom DeLay (R-TX) declared that "subjecting more earnings to the payroll tax amounted to a tax increase and was unacceptable."[30] Others proposed raising the retirement age or modifying the benefit formula. But the need for revenue was so great that only massive reductions in benefits could eliminate the gap. Legislators were reluctant to endorse reductions sufficient to that end.

Finally, 84 days after launching his national crusade, the president endorsed a plan to reduce the funding gap.[31] The plan, developed by Robert Pozen, a member of the president's 2001 commission, proposed that, although initial retirement benefits for low-income workers would continue to be indexed for wages, initial benefits for all other workers would be totally (upper-income workers) or partially (middle-income workers) indexed for prices. Since prices typically rise more slowly than wages, the effect would be to compress retirement benefits over time, gradually reducing benefits for each new cohort of upper- and middle-income workers, until their benefits were closer to the basic level provided to low-income workers.[32] The long-standing goal that retirement benefits replace some fraction of each worker's income would be replaced by a goal of providing basic benefits for everyone. Despite the severity of the benefit cuts, the Pozen plan still did not eliminate the solvency problem. Depending on whether the benefit cuts applied to disabled workers, the plan would close between 59 and 70 percent of the 75-year solvency gap.[33] It was nearly May and the president was still marketing a plan that would not achieve solvency.

The Countercampaign

While the administration was simultaneously selling a privatization plan across the country and drafting a solvency plan in Washington, opposition leaders, including unions, AARP, and Democratic Party leaders, mounted an active defense.[34] They explained why traditional Social Security was less risky than privatized Social Security. They mobilized interest groups, policy experts, and legislators. They launched a countercampaign that was at least as large as the president's pro-privatization campaign.

Soon after Bush's reelection, the 35-million-member AARP declared its total opposition to individual accounts. A month later, it launched a national advertising campaign: "If we feel like gambling, we'll play the slots," declared one middle-aged couple in the organization's first print advertisement.[35] Just before the president's State of the Union address touting individual accounts, AARP featured the article "Why Privatization Bombed in Britain" in its monthly membership magazine. What stung the most was that AARP had been the president's essential partner in 2003 when the House passed by a single vote the Medicare Prescription Drug Act. Two years later, however, AARP was a fierce opponent of the president's plan to dismantle traditional Social Security.[36]

Opposition leaders continued to argue that easy fixes would make traditional Social Security solvent far into the future. The indomitable Robert Ball—commissioner of Social Security under Kennedy, Johnson, and Nixon, member of the 1983 Greenspan Commission, member of the 1994–96 Advisory Council, and still fighting at age 91—released his own solvency plan, which gradually increased the maximum taxable wage base, modified cost-of-living adjustments, and allowed Social Security administrators to invest

20 percent of the trust fund in the stock market. Government actuaries estimated that his plan would not only close the 75-year solvency gap, it would leave a positive balance beyond that period.[37]

Opposition leaders played an impressive ground game, too. Most legislators spend fewer days in Washington than they do in their districts, where they regularly meet constituents in open forums and organized meetings. District-based work is especially common in February and March, when an 11-day recess for Presidents' Day and a 14-day recess for Easter provide abundant opportunities for listening tours. During both breaks, legislators reported their town hall meetings were filled with angry seniors demanding that they save Social Security. After returning from the February break, Senator Rick Santorum (R-PA), a leading proponent of privatization, concluded, "The other side is better organized. They got people to all these events. They had seniors lined up to ask questions. They had staff people running up passing them notes."[38] Senator Charles Grassley (R-IA), chair of the Finance Committee, which handles all Social Security legislation in the Senate, hosted 17 town hall meetings during the February break. After the final one, he concluded dryly that the president faced "a major job of educating people."[39] Notice that Grassley considered that education was the president's job, not his.

Framing

President Bush framed the problem starkly. Social Security was "headed toward bankruptcy," according to his State of the Union address. It would go "flat bust," according to various stump speeches. The need for action was urgent. But it was difficult to convince either legislators or citizens of the urgency. At the time, Social Security's trustees—all six appointed by the president—estimated the program could pay all scheduled benefits for the next 37 years, after which it could pay 73 percent of benefits.[40] The Congressional Budget Office estimated the program could pay scheduled benefits for the next 47 years, after which it could pay 78 percent of benefits.[41] By comparison, the condition of Medicare, the other large program for seniors, was much worse. Medicare's trustees—all six appointed by the president—estimated trust fund depletion in 14 years.[42] Why was the president focused on a problem 37 or 47 years distant rather than on the more immediate problem? The mystery deepened as critics discovered the president's proposal was not really designed to restore solvency. It was a privatization plan, not a solvency plan.

The president framed his proposal as good for retirees and near retirees, so administration officials were surprised that seniors quickly became the leading critics. Why didn't they understand that nothing would change for people aged 55 and over? But actually one thing would change: rather than having their benefits funded by a continuous river of workers' contributions, which were then thought adequate for nearly four decades, their benefits would soon be partially funded by government debt. Why, exactly, was that an improvement? The government regularly faced funding crises, when legislators—usually Republican legislators—refused to raise the debt limit so that the government could pay its bills. Many recalled how House Speaker Newt Gingrich (R-GA) threatened to block raising the debt ceiling in 1995 until President Clinton accepted Gingrich's budgetary demands. Now, all of a sudden, debt was supposed to *guarantee* retiree benefits for four or five decades. Why was debt a stronger guarantee than knowing that their sons, daughters, nieces, and nephews were paying taxes that would fund their retirement? Moreover, most retirees and near retirees liked traditional Social Security. Why wouldn't they want it to continue for their children and grandchildren?

The president also framed the proposal as good for young people, allowing them to accumulate wealth in their own retirement accounts. Administration officials were perplexed that most young people were not interested in thinking about Social Security. Perhaps they should have talked with their kids. Perhaps they should have consulted with college teachers—like me—who had taught courses about retirement policy. Most people just launching careers are not interested in retirement plans. Even if they did start thinking about Social Security, young people vote at much lower rates than retirees. It is hard to build a national coalition by catering to the interests of habitual nonvoters.

In short, the president worked hard to frame his reform plan as safe for the old and lucrative for the young. But the young were not listening and the old were not convinced. Moreover, for nearly three months, the plan did nothing to avert bankruptcy, the alleged reason for reform. By the time the president issued a revised plan that closed part of the solvency gap, public opinion had turned against the whole enterprise.

Leaders of the countercampaign framed the problem very differently. First, they argued, solvency was an important problem, but not an urgent one. Policymakers had years to devise an appropriate solution. Second, privatization was risky. Rather than guaranteeing retirement income, as traditional Social Security did, it put retirees at risk of losing their savings in the stock market.

Their argument was reinforced by the bursting of the Clinton-era stock market bubble in 2000. Third, financing privatization by borrowing put both Social Security and other programs at risk, as future politicians searched for ways to trim the burgeoning deficit. Fourth, opposition leaders framed privatization in partisan terms. It was just the latest Republican attempt to weaken one of the nation's most successful programs. Finally, they claimed that privatization was designed to enrich Republicans' favorite interest group—Wall Street. These were powerful, easy-to-understand arguments.

Public Opinion

How did people react to the simultaneous campaigns for and against privatization? First, the two campaigns were relatively successful in penetrating people's often dim awareness of what policymakers were considering. Before the two campaigns were formally launched, 19 percent of respondents in a September 2004 Pew survey claimed they had heard "a lot" about a proposal that would "allow younger workers to invest a portion of their Social Security taxes in private retirement accounts." Six months later, at the height of the two campaigns, 46 percent claimed they had heard a lot about an identically described proposal.[43]

Awareness, however, differed sharply by age. Figure 11.1 shows that 34 percent of people 65 and over had heard a lot about the proposal in the initial survey.[44] Six months later, awareness in that age group had nearly doubled, to 65 percent. Awareness among people 55 to 64 more than doubled, from 27 percent initially to 63 percent. By comparison, only 4 percent of people 18 to 24 had heard a lot in the earliest poll, growing to 16 percent in March 2005. These results should have been troubling for the administration. Younger workers—the supposed beneficiaries of privatization—were not following the issue very closely, while retirees and near retirees were highly attentive.

What did people think about the president's proposal? Here the answer is complicated.[45] One problem is that the proposal itself was a moving target. It was sketchy during the president's reelection campaign, more solid at the time of his State of the Union address, but still evolving in late April as the president struggled to close the solvency gap.

The more serious problem is that most people do not have firm preferences about most policy issues. John Zaller teaches us that when people respond to pollsters' questions, they are not retrieving established preferences from memory. They answer questions on the fly, based on whatever is at the top of their

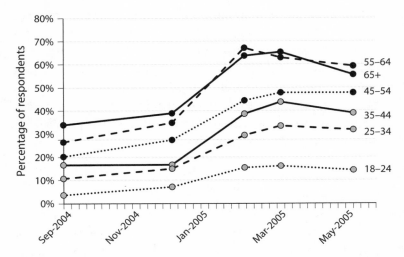

FIGURE 11.1. Respondents who have heard "a lot" about privatization, by age, 2004–5. Question: "How much, if anything, have you heard about a proposal which would allow younger workers to invest a portion of their Social Security taxes in private retirement accounts, which might include stocks or mutual funds? A lot, a little, or nothing at all?"
Source: Pew Research Center.

heads. Respondents may answer one way if they recently encountered a glowing news story about a program, and answer quite differently a month later if they happen to hear negative things about the same program. Respondents also react to the precise triggers contained in each question. For example, people are more likely to answer positively when a question mentions a program's benefits, and negatively when a question mentions its likely costs. Small variations in question wordings yield large differences in reported preferences.[46]

Pollsters asked hundreds of questions in late 2004 and early 2005 about where people stood on privatization.[47] Some pollsters asked short questions with no policy details. Others assumed that people needed some information before registering their opinions and included several details in their questions. Table 11.1 displays eight questions asked in early 2005, ranging from a bare-bones 20-word question in a January Quinnipiac survey to a detailed 98-word question in a March NBC/*Wall Street Journal* poll. Although these eight questions are just examples from a long list, they give a sense of the wide variation in prompts. The same table also displays how respondents answered each question, rank-ordered from the most supportive of privatization

TABLE 11.1. Citizens' Views on Privatization: Eight Question Wordings, 2005

Question (Source, Date)	Views on Privatization		
	For	Against	Net
A. "Thinking about Social Security contributions, do you think people under age 55 should have the right to choose between keeping all of their contributions in the current system and investing a portion of their contributions?" (Fox News, April 2005)	79	13	66
B. "Do you favor or oppose giving individuals the choice to invest a portion of their Social Security contributions in stocks or mutual funds?" (Fox News, March 2005)	60	28	32
C. "Would you support or oppose a plan in which people who chose to could invest some of their Social Security contributions in the stock market?" (ABC/WP, March 2005)	56	41	15
D. "Do you support or oppose allowing individuals to invest a portion of their Social Security taxes in the stock market?" (Quinnipiac, January 2005)	51	43	8
E. "Please tell me which of the following approaches to dealing with Social Security you would prefer: (A) Making some adjustments but leaving the Social Security system basically as is and running the risk that the system will fall short of money as more people retire and become eligible for benefits. OR, (B) Changing the Social Security system by allowing people to invest some of their Social Security taxes in private accounts—like IRA's or 401k's—and running the risk that some people will lose money in their private accounts due to drops in the stock market." (NBC/WSJ, March 2005)	40	48	−8
F. "Some people have suggested allowing individuals to invest a portion of their Social Security taxes on their own into a small number of authorized investment funds, which might allow them to make more money for their retirement, but would involve greater risk. Do you think this is a good idea or a bad idea?" (CBS/NYT, June 2005)	39	56	−17
G. "As you may know, one idea to address concerns with the Social Security system would allow people who retire in future decades to invest some of their Social Security taxes in the stock market and bonds, but would reduce the guaranteed benefits they get when they retire. Do you think this is a good idea or a bad idea?" (CNN/USA, March 2005)	33	59	−26
H. "Under the Bush plan, the federal government would have to borrow between one trillion and two trillion dollars or more over the next 10 years or so to provide Social Security to retirees in order to make up for the money going into the personal investment accounts. The money would be paid back later, over time. Would you now favor or oppose allowing some Social Security money to be invested in personal accounts and reducing benefits if the government had to borrow up to two trillion dollars in the next 10 years to pay for the new plan?" (Time, March 2005)	24	67	−43

Source: PollingReport.com 2018.

(question A), where net approval was 66 percent (79 in favor minus 13 against), to the least supportive (question H), where net approval was negative 43 percent (24 in favor minus 67 against). Depending on how pollsters framed their queries, respondents liked, hated, or were close to indifferent about privatization.

What accounts for this astonishing range in support? First, pollsters do not appear to have slanted their questions. All eight questions are reasonable ways to tap public opinion on an emerging issue. Second, the range is not a consequence of time trends. Five polls were from March, and the polls from January, April, and June are scattered about the table. The range is the consequence of different triggers in each question, some stimulating support, others opposition.

The four questions at the bottom of the table have one thing in common. They all mention the costs or risks of partial privatization. Question H informs respondents that "under the Bush plan, the federal government would have to borrow between one trillion and two trillion dollars . . . in order to make up for the money going into the personal investment accounts." Question G reminds people that the new plan "would reduce the guaranteed benefits" they would get from traditional Social Security. Question F highlights an important trade-off: the new private accounts "might allow them to make more money for their retirement, but would involve greater risk." Informing respondents about the costs of privatization—borrowing trillions, reducing guaranteed benefits, incurring losses—depresses support.

The two questions at the top of the table emphasize rights and choice, both appealing notions for Americans. Few could resist "the right to choose" (question A) or "the choice to invest" (question B). Only 13 percent of respondents opposed the first option; only 28 percent opposed the second. Indeed, net approval was positive for all four questions at the top—the only questions that mentioned nothing about costs. Once costs are included, net approval turns negative. This is true even for question E, which mentions the risks from both traditional Social Security ("running the risk that the system will fall short of money") and privatized Social Security ("running the risk that some people will lose money in their private accounts").

The point is not that people were confused about Social Security privatization. They clearly liked some aspects—the right to choose, the prospects of higher returns—and when pollsters emphasized these features, they tended to support it. They clearly disliked other aspects—losing money in the stock market, giving up guaranteed benefits, borrowing trillions—and when pollsters emphasized these features, they tended to oppose it.

Dynamic Opinion

Measuring public opinion is difficult, especially for complex issues like privatizing Social Security. Most people know nothing about how the new system would operate and are easily swayed by whatever information pollsters include in their questions. Counterintuitively, measuring *opinion change*—whether people are becoming more supportive of privatization—is the easier task. If pollsters ask the same question month after month, and each successive poll finds more support for a policy, it is reasonable to conclude that support is increasing. If the trend lines for several different questions about privatization, each asked regularly, have similar positive slopes, we can be more confident that public support is increasing.[48]

Dynamic opinion is also more consequential than static opinion. James Stimson argues that changes in public opinion are what drive politics.[49] When legislators perceive that more people support a particular policy change, whether by reading opinion surveys or talking with their constituents, they are more likely to support that change themselves. Legislators do not need to know exactly which questions best capture public opinion. All they need to know is that support is increasing across a wide range of questions.

Figure 11.2 displays the best long-term data on public support for partial privatization. The two surveys began in May 2000, early in the presidential contest and before the two candidates challenged each other's Social Security plans, and ended in June 2005, about the time that experts declared the president's proposal dead. Twelve times during this period, pollsters working for the *New York Times* and CBS News asked, "Some people have suggested allowing individuals to invest portions of their Social Security taxes on their own, which might allow them to make more money for their retirement, but would involve greater risk. Do you think allowing individuals to invest a portion of their Social Security taxes on their own is a good idea or a bad idea?" Net approval was moderately positive in seven surveys prior to 2005 (range +2 to +15) and moderately negative in the five surveys conducted in early 2005 (range 0 to −8). Eight times during the same period, pollsters working for ABC News and the *Washington Post* asked, "Would you support or oppose a plan in which people who chose to could invest some of their Social Security contributions in the stock market?" Net approval was positive in the first six polls (range +7 to +33) and negative in the last two polls (range −1 to −6). Notice that support declined in both the first question, which mentioned risk, and the second, which did not.

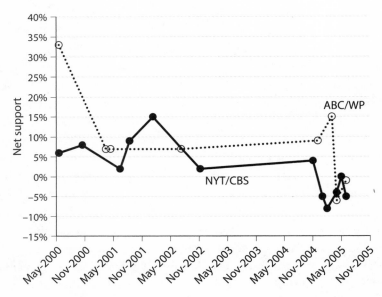

FIGURE 11.2. Net support for privatization, May 2000–June 2005. Net support is the percentage who support minus the percentage who oppose.
Source: PollingReport.com 2018.

Dynamic opinion data were more plentiful from November 2004, when the president named Social Security privatization his top domestic priority, to June 2005, when pollsters lost interest in a fading issue. Figure 11.3 displays time series responses to six questions, including the two questions featured in the previous figure, and four new questions, each asked five times. The evidence strongly supports the conclusion that public support for partial privatization declined over the seven-month period. No matter how pollsters framed their questions, they discovered dwindling support for private accounts. For five questions, the final reading was lower than the initial reading. For the sixth question (CNN/USA#2), each monthly reading was lower than the previous one except for the final reading, which revealed a surge. Even this final survey, however, showed that most respondents opposed privatization.

These two figures demonstrate how support for privatization declined over time. The decline reflects the rise of the countercampaign.[50] In the beginning, few people had heard about the risks or costs of privatization. As opponents began to mobilize, first during the 2000 and 2004 election campaigns and then during the 2005 legislative campaign, overall support diminished.

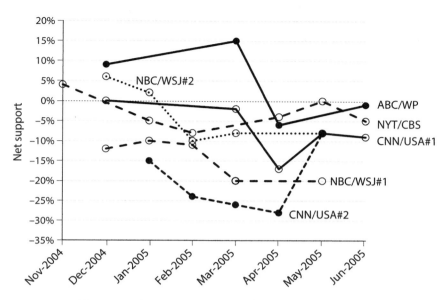

FIGURE 11.3. Net support for privatization, November 2004–June 2005. Net support is the percentage who support minus the percentage who oppose. Questions: NBC/WSJ#1: "In general, do you think that it is a good idea or a bad idea to change the Social Security system to allow workers to invest their Social Security contributions in the stock market?" CNN/USA#1: "As you may know, a proposal has been made that would allow workers to invest part of their Social Security taxes in the stock market or in bonds, while the rest of those taxes would remain in the Social Security system. Do you favor or oppose this proposal?" For ABC/WP and NYT/CBS questions, see figure 11.2. For NBC/WSJ#2 and CNN/USA#2 questions, see table 11.1, questions E and G. USA, *USA Today*; WP, *Washington Post*; WSJ, *Wall Street Journal*.

Sources: Edwards 2007; PollingReport.com 2018.

Polarization

How did Democratic and Republican respondents view privatization? In the beginning, majorities from both parties supported "a plan in which people who chose to could invest some of their Social Security contributions in the stock market" (figure 11.4).[51] Net approval in the first survey (May 2000) was 42 percent for Republicans (69 percent in favor minus 27 percent against) and 27 percent for Democrats (60 in favor minus 33 against). A year later, net approval had declined in both parties, to 32 percent for Republicans, and negative 14 percent for Democrats. After that, net approval among Democrats was steadily negative for several years, before plunging during the 2005 legislative

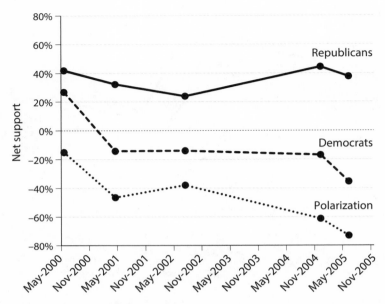

FIGURE 11.4. Net support for privatization by party, May 2000–June 2005. Net support is the percentage who support minus the percentage who oppose. Polarization is net Democratic support minus net Republican support. Democrats and Republicans include those who lean toward a party. Question: "Would you support or oppose a plan in which people who chose to could invest some of their Social Security contributions in the stock market?" (ABC News/ *Washington Post*).
Source: Roper Center.

campaign, ending at negative 35 percent. Net approval among Republicans increased during the 2004 presidential campaign, before declining again during the 2005 privatization campaign, ending at 38 percent, roughly where it began. Party polarization—the difference in net approval between Democrats and Republicans—is displayed in the bottom line. It increased from a modest 15 points in 2000 to a stunning 73 points five years later.

Support for privatization declined in all age groups. As figure 11.5 shows, net support among people 65 and over changed from mildly negative in 2000 to strongly negative in 2005.[52] Initially, the other five age groups supported a plan to allow people to "invest some of their Social Security contributions in the stock market," but by June 2005, only people younger than 35 still supported the plan. Not shown in this figure are the differential reactions of Democratic and Republican respondents. Net support among Democrats aged 65 and over dropped from negative 23 percent to negative 78 percent, and

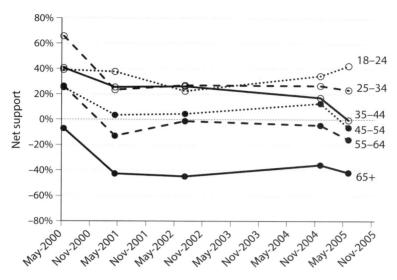

FIGURE 11.5. Net support for privatization by age, May 2000–June 2005. Net support is the percentage who support minus the percentage who oppose. The question is the same as in figure 11.4.

Source: Roper Center.

among Democrats aged 55 to 64 from negative 4 percent to negative 58 percent. Initially, the other four age groups supported privatization, but by the end, only Democrats under 25 still did. In contrast, Republicans in the five youngest age groups maintained their support for privatization across the years, while seniors started and ended roughly neutral toward privatization.

It is no secret what happened to produce partisan polarization on Social Security. In the late 1990s, advocates for partial privatization included prominent Democrats and Republicans. With little conflict among partisan elites, there was nothing to stimulate partisan conflict among citizens. That is precisely what the May 2000 survey reveals (see figure 11.4). In late 2000, however, the two presidential candidates clashed repeatedly over Bush's proposal to modify Social Security. Vice President Gore used the first and third presidential debates to pummel Bush and his proposal. Both candidates followed the debates with extensive advertising campaigns about Social Security. Daily polls from the National Annenberg Election Survey—roughly 300 interviews every day from July to November—reveal how Democratic respondents turned negative on Bush's plan within days of Gore's attack, while Republican respondents became stronger supporters.[53] Figure 11.4 merely confirms that

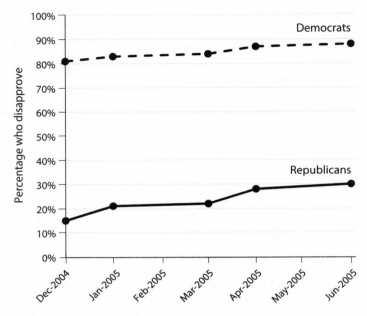

FIGURE 11.6. Disapproval of Bush's handling of Social Security by party, 2004–5. Does not include those who lean toward a party. Question: "Do you approve or disapprove of the way George W. Bush is handling Social Security?" (ABC/*Washington Post*).
Source: Roper Center.

this increased partisan gulf from the presidential campaign still existed in April 2001, six months after Election Day. The partisan divide persisted over the next several years, as Republican leaders continued to praise privatization and Democratic leaders echoed Gore's critique. Support among both Democrats and Republicans then declined during 2005, as the countercampaign, which emphasized privatization's risks, became louder and more intense.

So far, my evidence about declining support has been for generic privatization plans, not for the president's own proposal. Of course, capturing how people viewed the president's proposal is complicated by the fact that his plan was evolving throughout the legislative campaign. One survey that avoided this problem simply asked whether respondents approved or disapproved of the way the president was handling Social Security. Figure 11.6 displays disapproval rates by party.[54] Not surprisingly, most Democrats disapproved of the president on Social Security, rising from 81 percent in December 2004 to 88 percent in June 2005. More ominously, disapproval rates among

Republicans doubled, increasing from 15 percent to 30 percent. The president's own partisans, who had supported him overwhelmingly for reelection just months before, were now divided on his handling of Social Security.

Why were seniors the outliers? Why were Democratic seniors the most fiercely opposed to privatization? Why were Republican seniors roughly neutral, while other Republicans remained mildly positive? One explanation is that many seniors were cautious about modifying Social Security because their working years were behind them and they were now dependent on Social Security. Another explanation is that seniors were following the Social Security debate much more closely than younger respondents, thus making them more likely to hear arguments from the countercampaign. The evidence about awareness in figure 11.1 supports that notion. A third explanation is that many seniors were members of AARP, the organization leading the countercampaign. Members received a barrage of direct messages from the organization in the *AARP Bulletin* and the *AARP Magazine*. By delivering these messages to more than half of seniors during the privatization debate, AARP made them much more aware of the debate. By regularly exposing seniors to negative messages about privatization, AARP helped turn seniors against the president's proposal.

Legislators

Many legislators had already taken positions on privatization. After all, the issue had been on the table for nearly a decade. But legislators' early positions were often vague. Republicans could praise privatization without necessarily endorsing every bill that claimed to advance the cause. Democrats could disparage privatization without necessarily rejecting otherwise appealing solvency packages that happened to include personal accounts.

By 2005, however, legislators faced a consequential choice: Should they support or oppose the president's still-evolving plan to allow young workers to divert nearly two-thirds of their Social Security contributions to personal retirement accounts? Voting on actual bills is tougher than taking vague campaign positions because roll call votes create permanent records from which legislators can never hide.[55] Voters might punish legislators at the polls, either for dismantling a treasured program or for failing to support a better one. Campaign donors might shun legislators who violate a pledge to support or oppose privatization.

Democratic legislators faced the easier task. Democrats had claimed to be Social Security's protectors ever since President Reagan proposed deep cuts in 1981. Indeed, surveys over the intervening years discovered that people consistently rated Democrats as the better stewards for Social Security (chapter 7). So, they began with a reservoir of good feelings on this issue. Perhaps if President Bush had made a compelling case for how his plan would restore solvency, Democrats would have been tempted to support it, for the solvency problem was real. But the president's initial plan did nothing to restore solvency, and his revised plan merely reduced the solvency gap by imposing massive cuts on future beneficiaries. Perhaps if the president had galvanized young workers, while successfully assuring retirees and near retirees that they had nothing to fear, Democrats would have reconsidered their positions. But younger workers were not listening and older people were not persuaded. As public support for the president's proposal declined in early 2005, Democrats concluded that supporting traditional Social Security was the safe choice.

Republican legislators faced serious cross pressures. First, many of them had endorsed creating personal retirement accounts, so this was their first opportunity to enact what they had already promised. Second, many Republican donors, hostile to traditional Social Security, were champions of privatization. Finally, the president was their party's leader. Most Republicans recognized an obligation to support the president when they could, so that they and their party would appear competent in handling the nation's problems. Still there were strong reasons for caution. Even though Republican legislators joined Democratic legislators in quickly rejecting President Reagan's proposal to refashion Social Security, their party still suffered huge reputational losses from this and other missteps by Republican leaders. Voters trusted Democrats, not Republicans, to handle Social Security. Would enacting President Bush's plan reverse those reputational losses? Or would Republicans merely hand Democrats a larger bludgeon to use against them?

Republican legislators had powerful incentives to determine where their constituents stood on privatization and whether their constituents would reward or punish them for voting to enact the president's proposal. Early signals were mixed. As previously discussed, legislators returned to their constituencies in February to find angry seniors packing their town meetings. Opponents were organized and effective in conveying a simple message: Don't mess with Social Security. Evidence from national surveys was tougher to interpret. Yes, there were surveys showing support for privatization, but other surveys revealed substantial opposition. Legislators might take comfort in learning that Republican respondents were more supportive than Democrats were, but many Republicans still preferred traditional Social Security. That was especially true for those of retirement age. Historically, retirees and near retirees had been fierce defenders of Social Security. Moreover, they voted at far higher rates than younger people did, so their views mattered. In short, even for legislators who were themselves enthusiastic about privatization, the political terrain looked more like a minefield than a cakewalk.

By spring, it was clear that most Republican legislators did not want to vote on the president's plan. The electoral dangers were too great. No matter how legislators chose to vote, they would displease many constituents and donors. For Republican leaders, who controlled the House and Senate agendas, the solution was simple: Do not allow legislators to vote. The House Ways and Means Committee and the Senate Finance Committee never formally considered the plan, so there were no committee votes. Without committee approval, no bills reached the floor, so there were no floor votes. And that is how the president's plan to overhaul Social Security died. Quite simply, Republican legislators refused to stand up and be counted on the president's top domestic priority.

Assessment

What went wrong? Why did a plan so long in the making—conceived in a 1978 congressional race, introduced nationally in the 2000 presidential campaign, assigned to a 2001 presidential study commission, and now the domestic centerpiece of the president's second term—crash and burn so quickly? Why did a House and Senate controlled by Republicans, and stocked with legislators who had supported Social Security privatization in their own campaigns, never act? The president's plan did not falter after a long journey through the legislative labyrinth. It did not lose narrowly in a cliffhanger vote. It was not blocked by a Senate filibuster. It died near the starting gate. Moreover, the plan did not suffer from presidential inattention. The president himself visited 25 states and spoke at 35 public events, working to sell his plan to an increasingly skeptical electorate.

President Bush had an excellent track record dealing with Congress, far better than most postwar presidents.[56] His list of first-term legislative accomplishments included three large tax cuts, fast-track authority for trade deals, the Patriot Act, creating the Department of Homeland Security, prescription drug coverage for seniors, and the No Child Left Behind Act. The last two enactments were significant rewrites of two pillars of President Johnson's Great Society: Medicare and the Elementary and Secondary Education Act.

So, it was not an unreasonable quest for an experienced, accomplished president to refashion Social Security, one of the pillars of President Roosevelt's New Deal.

One problem was that the president insisted on a top-down plan, designed in the White House, with little participation from Capitol Hill. As previously discussed, the president's "basic principles" ruled out 2 of the 3 reform plans designed by his own 2001 commission, as well as 17 reform plans released between 2000 and 2004, most of them designed by legislators. The president's insistence on exclusive ownership guaranteed that the victory would be his and his alone. But by excluding legislators from the drafting table—legislators better able to judge what provisions might attract their colleagues—the president diminished the chances for victory. Legislators work harder for bills where they share ownership.

Administration officials might object to this characterization, reminding us that the president asked Congress to design a suitable way to pay for privatization. But legislators, whose terms were soon up for renewal, never understood why a term-limited president delegated to them the task of allocating costs. Why didn't the president, who in 2000 professed an eagerness to touch the third rail of American politics, realize that costs were what electrified that rail?

A second problem was that the administration adopted a partisan strategy to enact reform. Rather than beginning with a problem—say, solvency—and searching for a solution that might attract bipartisan support, the president sought to replace one of the Democrats' proudest creations with a Republican-flavored plan. With Republicans controlling both the House and Senate, the administration assumed that the principal problem was uniting all Republicans. If it could do that, it could enact reform by attracting as few as five Democratic senators. But if the administration adopted a partisan strategy, that choice practically guaranteed the Democrats would adopt a partisan strategy, too. Denied a seat at the table, they would work to undermine support for privatization across the country. Although the administration knew how to build bipartisan coalitions, as it had done for education in 2001 and Medicare in 2003, this time the president so wanted a particular outcome that he never reached out to Democrats to find common ground. That was a risky choice for overhauling a program where Democrats had the home-field advantage.[57]

A third problem was that the president believed he could build overwhelming support for privatization across the country and thereby pressure legislators to support his plan. "Going public," as political scientists call it, has a mixed record of success.[58] It is perhaps easiest for novel issues, where few people have strong opinions, and where presidents can paint on a blank canvas. When President Reagan defended his 1983 invasion of Grenada, or when the first President Bush proposed invading Kuwait in 1990, they knew that few people had views about these tiny countries. Indeed, most people would be hard-pressed to locate Grenada or Kuwait on a globe. When most citizens have strong preferences about an issue, however, as they do for Social Security, it is very difficult for a president to move the needle.

How Bush and his trusted political advisor Karl Rove came to believe that a president who was reelected by a narrow popular vote (50.7 percent) could persuade citizens to accept such massive changes in Social Security remains a mystery. Perhaps if the president were the only source of information about his reform proposal, he could have convinced voters that partial privatization would strengthen the system. But the president enjoyed no such privileged access to the electorate. Democratic leaders, unions, and AARP gave ample warning that they would oppose the president's plan.

Once the campaign and the countercampaign were fully launched, citizens reacted in predictable ways. Democrats, who had once appeared favorable toward privatization, became fierce opponents of the plan, as they heard what Democratic leaders and AARP were saying and tuned out messages from Republican sources. Republicans maintained, but did not increase, their support. Meanwhile, older people from both parties—the age group that followed the debate most closely and that participated most actively in politics—revealed little appetite for change. In short, the campaign and the countercampaign further polarized citizens and reduced overall support both for privatization and for President Bush.

Declining support for privatization among older Republicans made it electorally risky for Republican legislators to support drastic changes in Social Security. Declining support among Democrats eliminated any temptation for Democratic legislators to join the parade. Aiming to unify Republican legislators, the president unified Democrats.

The better opportunity for enacting partial privatization was in 1998 and 1999. That was a time when both Republican and Democratic legislators were promoting some variant of personal retirement accounts.[59] Although not everyone thought creating private accounts was a good idea, the issue had not yet deeply divided the parties. No one can be certain if a bipartisan deal might have been struck then, but a deal in the late 1990s was more likely than one in 2005.

The late 1990s was also a promising time for privatization because the government was running a surplus, the first since 1969. More importantly, experts predicted that the surplus would continue to grow. Many politicians—both Democrats and Republicans—proposed using the surplus to "save Social Security." To be sure, some wanted to save traditional Social Security, and some wanted to jump-start privatization, but the crucial point is that a large pile of cash suddenly appeared that could help achieve one or both of those ends. The surplus was especially important to the privatizers, who had an urgent need for revenue to pay transition costs. For example, Representative John Kasich (R-OH), chair of the House Budget Committee, proposed placing most of the surplus into individual retirement accounts for each worker, with participants choosing how to invest the funds from a government-approved list of options. In short, policymakers could have jump-started privatization, by quickly diverting annual surpluses into private accounts, without necessarily settling all the long-term solvency issues.

The 2000 presidential campaign had one unfortunate consequence for those pushing for privatization. The two candidates, George Bush and Al Gore, not only took conflicting positions on privatization during the debates, they spent millions on campaign advertisements underscoring their differences. By framing privatization in partisan terms, they pushed Democratic and Republican identifiers further apart on this issue. In less than two months, the candidates transformed modest polarization on privatizing Social Security into intense polarization.[60]

The most devastating strike against privatization occurred in 2001. Ironically, George W. Bush delivered the fatal blow. Inheriting a substantial surplus, the president decided to spend it not on Social Security, but on tax cuts. He did so knowingly. In the first presidential debate, he had promised, "I want to take one-half of the surplus and dedicate it to Social Security."[61] And his policy advisors warned him that privatization would be vastly more difficult once the surplus disappeared.[62] But ever since President Reagan campaigned and governed as a tax cutter, Republican candidates and Republican officeholders had been doing the same. The president was no exception. The primal Republican urge to cut taxes was stronger than Bush's quarter-century personal quest to reinvent Social Security.

Privatization Today

Many policymakers continue to advocate some form of privatization, although seldom using that now-toxic term. Republican platforms promise market-like solutions to Social Security's solvency problem. Republican candidates talk about eliminating mandatory contributions, giving workers an ownership stake, and allowing younger workers to control their own nest eggs. Republican donors tell candidates how much they care about replacing traditional Social Security with something resembling the private retirement system.

The one place we do not see much evidence of privatization is in the congressional hopper. Former Representative Paul Ryan (R-WI) introduced the most recent plan in 2010.[63] Ryan, arguably the leading congressional proponent of reinventing Social Security, introduced four bills that would have established voluntary individual accounts: "The Social Security Personal Savings Guarantee and Prosperity Act" in 2004, and again in 2005, and the "The Roadmap for America's Future Act" in 2008, and again in 2010. Despite his leadership positions—eight years as chair or ranking minority member of the House Budget Committee, ten months chairing the House Ways and Means Committee, and nearly four years as Speaker of the House—he was unable to attract much support for these bills. The first bill had 6 cosponsors, the second 13, the third 8, and the fourth 14. It is not clear why Republican legislators have not introduced any privatization plans since Ryan retired in 2019. Of course, other groups continue to design such plans. For example, the American Enterprise Institute released its own privatization plan in 2016.[64]

It is tempting to say that Republicans have abandoned privatization as a policy option. But Paul Ryan's 2010 plan still attracted more supporters than all the incremental plans that Republicans introduced in the past decade. His bill had 14 cosponsors, compared with 8 for the six bills that offered incremental solutions (see table 10.4). Perhaps it is not that Republican legislators have lost interest in privatization, but rather that they have lost interest in Social Security. They don't sponsor. They don't cosponsor. They don't do much to build support for either privatization or incremental solutions.

Avoiding Social Security's solvency problem today is politically costless. Everyone's benefits are secure until 2034. As the solvency cliff nears, however, the risks of inaction grow. The next chapter explores politics at the precipice.

12

Politics at the Precipice

WE SHOULD NOT BE SURPRISED if Congress does nothing to fix Social Security before 2034 when the trust fund runs dry. Although experts first identified
the long-term solvency problem nearly three decades ago, and opinion surveys
have repeatedly shown that fixing the problem is one of the public's top priorities, legislators have never voted on a proposal to fix it—not in committee, not
on the floor, not in the House, not in the Senate. Congress failed to act in the late
1990s, when some officials proposed using the growing budget surplus either to
strengthen traditional Social Security or to jump-start the creation of individual
accounts. It failed again in 2005 when President Bush proposed partial privatization. The principal reason for congressional inaction is clear: insolvency is a long-
term problem without short-term consequences.

Everything will change in 2034. Suddenly, insolvency will become an urgent problem with enormous consequences. Absent congressional action, an
estimated 83 million Social Security recipients—18 million more than
today—will face automatic benefit cuts of 21 percent.[1] Another 8 million
people filing for Social Security benefits that year will face similar reductions
from what they would otherwise collect. At the same time, the threat of insolvency will become an urgent political problem for legislators. If they cannot
find ways to block or reduce these enormous cuts, legislators will face hostile
voters at their next election.[2]

Congress has five options. One is to rerun the 1977 or 1983 playbooks,
choosing from the incremental solutions outlined in chapter 5. Another is to
adopt some variant of full or partial privatization, creating an advance-funded
defined benefit program for younger workers and using debt to fund current
and near retirees. A third is to use general funds to pay benefits, breaking the
century-old restriction that requires Social Security benefits to be funded
exclusively with Social Security taxes. A fourth is to adopt a short-term fix

designed to get legislators past the next election, perhaps using general funds or debt. A fifth is to do nothing, forcing Social Security benefits to shrink immediately.

Incremental Solutions

Twice legislators have enacted what they thought were long-term solutions to Social Security's solvency problems. That the 1977 fix lasted six years, while the 1983 fix is on track to last for more than a half century, is more a consequence of happenstance than choice. Both reforms offer practical lessons for future policymakers.

In 1977, the challenge was surging inflation. The first three automatic cost-of-living adjustments, which commenced in 1975, increased annual benefits by 8.0, 6.4, and 5.9 percent. Unfortunately, Social Security's revenue stream was not growing fast enough to support those increases. As insolvency loomed, legislators explicitly chose to protect all beneficiaries—current and future—by raising additional revenue. They increased the payroll tax rate by 25 percent, phased in over 13 years, and increased the maximum taxable wage base by 68 percent, phased in over 3 years.

When insolvency returned in 1983, legislators chose a different path. They reduced Social Security benefits by raising the retirement age, delaying cost-of-living adjustments, and taxing first upper-income beneficiaries and later middle-income beneficiaries. They also increased tax revenues by accelerating already-scheduled rate increases and eliminating the preferential rate for self-employed workers. As previously shown, benefit cuts were seven times greater than tax increases.

Why did legislators protect beneficiaries in 1977 but favor taxpayers in 1983? One explanation focuses on agenda setting. In the first instance, Democrats controlled the House, Senate, and presidency. Exclusive control gave Democrats the ability to place their own preferred options on the decision agenda. In the second instance, Democrats controlled the House, while Republicans held the Senate and presidency. Shared control allowed a wider range of alternatives to reach the decision agenda.[3]

A second explanation focuses on changing policy preferences among officeholders, particularly among Republicans. David Mayhew has shown that the vast surge of liberal legislation that began under President Johnson continued unabated under Presidents Nixon and Ford, with support not only from these presidents but also from Republican legislators.[4] These were the legislators who supported the 1977 solvency plan. President Reagan's 1980 election abruptly ended executive branch cooperation by placing a tax cutter and Social Security critic at the head of the table. Around the same time, Republicans in the House and Senate began their decades-long shift to the right, as measured by floor votes.[5] There was no way that a genuinely conservative president and a group of increasingly conservative Republican legislators would approve a solvency bill that relied exclusively on tax increases.

How policymakers decide to fix Social Security in 2034 will depend partly on whether one party controls all three institutions—House, Senate, presidency—or whether the parties share control. If there is unified Democratic control, say a 2030s version of President Obama, Speaker Nancy Pelosi (D-CA), and Senate Majority Leader Harry Reid (D-NV)—the agenda setters for the Affordable Care Act—we should expect different choices than if there is unified Republican control. Of course, if there is divided party control, we should expect choices somewhere between these two extremes, since the two parties would share control of the agenda.[6]

The interesting question is what those two extremes would look like. Can we imagine that Democrats, if they control all three institutions, would repeat what their 1977 colleagues did—namely, approve a tax-only solvency bill, thus shielding current and future beneficiaries from cuts? Can we imagine that Republicans, if they control all three institutions, would stick to their signed pledges never to raise taxes, thus closing the solvency gap exclusively with benefit reductions?

Republicans have the tougher row to hoe. Although cutting Social Security benefits is not an impossible quest, as the 1983 reforms demonstrate, Congress imposed most of the 1983 cuts on temporally distant cohorts, not current retirees. Recall that legislators raised the full retirement age from 65 to 67, but implemented the change very gradually, starting with people who were then 45 and ending with those who were then 23. The only cost that legislators imposed on current beneficiaries was a six-month delay in cost-of-living adjustments, a small price to pay for avoiding automatic benefit cuts that would have been larger. Chapter 9 outlined the political logic: impose modest cuts on current beneficiaries, because they would swiftly punish legislators for anything too painful, and impose large cuts on future beneficiaries, because future reductions would not enrage voters as much as current reductions would.

But Republicans cannot use the 1983 playbook in 2034. At that point, policymakers will require something like 1.2 percent of GDP annually to forestall 21 percent benefit cuts. They cannot raise such a colossal sum by adopting long-term solutions, like raising the retirement age, because long-term solutions produce very little immediate revenue. Moreover, short-term solutions, like delaying cost-of-living increases or reducing benefits for affluent retirees, would produce only a fraction of the revenue required to keep benefits flowing. Put differently, benefit reductions can be part of a solvency plan, but alone they cannot prevent automatic benefit cuts.

Republicans have painted themselves into a corner. Most have signed pledges that they would never vote to increase taxes. Many have promised current retirees that they would do nothing to threaten their benefits. For three decades, they have been able to keep both promises. But in 2034, the two promises will become incompatible. If Republicans stick to their pledges—no new taxes—many of their constituents will be stuck with massive benefit cuts. Moreover, these cuts will be directly traceable to legislators' actions or inactions. Finally, Republican legislators will have to choose. Will they support their tax-averse donors and constituents, who might punish them if they violate their signed pledges? Or will they support Social Security beneficiaries— often large fractions of the active voters in their districts—who might punish them for allowing large benefit cuts to take place?

Decades of procrastination are therefore particularly damaging to the Republican antitax cause. Perhaps if Republicans had used more wisely their unified control of the House, Senate, and presidency in 2005, they could have enacted gradual benefit reductions—say, slowly raising the retirement age and slowly shrinking cost-of-living adjustments.[7] Those sorts of things might have closed the long-term solvency gap without having to raise taxes. In 2034, however, gradual benefit cuts are useless. Promising to be frugal in the future is no answer when the cupboard is already bare.

Democratic legislators face no such quandaries. Although many Democrats have promised to preserve all benefits for current and future beneficiaries, they have never pledged to do so without raising taxes. Indeed, many of them have sponsored or cosponsored bills that would both raise the maximum taxable wage base and increase the tax rate. To be sure, some legislators might get cold feet in 2034, perhaps pressured by their affluent constituents to pare back the proposed tax increases. But Democrats have no signed pledges constraining their actions. For them, the only question is how to allocate costs among various types of workers, employers, and beneficiaries.

Decades of procrastination are also less damaging to the Democratic cause. If they had acted in the 1990s, say by gradually increasing both the tax rate and the wage base, they could have captured substantial revenue from the baby boomers, salted it away in the trust fund, and thereby lessened the overall burden of supporting the boomers in retirement. Additional tax increases would still be needed to deal with lengthening life spans, but those tax increases would be much less painful than those that are required to fund the boomers' retirement. In short, earlier actions by courageous politicians would have made later actions less expensive.

Despite the broad support among Democratic legislators for tax increases, they are unlikely to have enough votes to enact those increases without Republican support. Although the House is a majoritarian institution, the Senate requires a supermajority—60 out of 100 senators—to break a filibuster. Sometimes Congress uses the annual budget resolution, where simple majorities suffice, to enact tax or spending bills, thus avoiding the filibuster. But the Congressional Budget Act, as amended in 1990, explicitly prohibits using budget resolutions to change anything about Social Security. It is the *only* federal program to have such statutory protection.[8] In short, changing Social Security is necessarily a bipartisan affair, unless one party controls the House and the presidency and has a supermajority in the Senate. Such single-party dominance is rare. It has occurred for fewer than six months in the past four decades.[9]

What is essentially a statutory requirement for bipartisanship profoundly shapes the politics of Social Security. Republicans could not have enacted partial privatization in 2005 without the support of at least five Democratic senators. Democrats cannot enact a tax-only solvency package in 2034 without the support of at least some Republicans. To be sure, controlling the agenda still affects the outcome. Although Democrats may not be able to enact their most preferred plan with unified party control, at least they can begin with something closer to that ideal, and then gradually modify the plan as they work to attract Republicans. That is likely to be more satisfying for Democrats than if Republicans have the first move advantage.

This statutory requirement for bipartisanship essentially weeds out extreme proposals. For example, the 2019 Larson bill, which nearly 90 percent of House Democrats cosponsored, includes tax increases equal to 3.7 percent of taxable payrolls—almost 1 percentage point higher than necessary to close the long-term deficit—and proposes using the extra revenue to enhance various benefits (see chapter 10). Although I can imagine that some Republican legislators in 2034 might accept some tax increases in order to forestall benefit reductions, just as they did in 1977 and 1983, they are unlikely to accept a tax-only solution that is accompanied by even higher benefits. More likely, Republicans would expect some benefit reductions in exchange for their support.

One reason bipartisanship is common for most major enactments is that legislative leaders seek to enact durable laws.[10] For less durable victories, executive orders often suffice. Notice how brand-new presidents often issue a flurry of executive orders that simply reverse orders promulgated by their predecessors. But we seldom see such reversals on Capitol Hill, not just because the filibuster limits what bare majorities can accomplish, but because legislators enact most major bills with oversized majorities. In fact, James Curry and Frances Lee show that legislative leaders working in today's polarized environment are just as likely to build large bipartisan majorities as did leaders working in less polarized times.[11]

Leaders are especially likely to seek large bipartisan majorities when they must impose painful costs. If Democratic legislators somehow found a way to pass the Larson bill with a purely partisan coalition—perhaps by eliminating the filibuster as they did in 2013 for most judicial nominations—their party would then *own* the tax increases. Republicans could attack them forever for increasing taxes so much. By working to forge a bipartisan consensus, however, coalition leaders may not obtain the bill of their dreams. But they can enact a bill that binds both parties to the costs, thus protecting both sides from dagger pointing. Senator Mitch McConnell (R-KY), the top Republican leader in the Senate since 2007, has long claimed that reforming entitlement programs like Social Security is not politically feasible when a single party controls the House, Senate, and White House.[12] It is only when the parties share control of government that they can protect themselves from the partisan attacks that would otherwise follow from one party increasing taxes or cutting benefits.

Curry and Lee also demonstrate that picking off a few moderate legislators from the other party's rank and file is more difficult today than it was before the parties became so polarized. One reason is that each party is more cohesive. Another is the near disappearance of moderates. Today's party leaders, rather than negotiating with a small group of moderates from the other side, negotiate directly with the other party's leaders. These negotiations, when successful, tend to produce very large majorities, often including the bulk of each party's members.[13]

Privatization

The idea of allowing workers to divert some portion of their payroll contributions to individual investment accounts once attracted bipartisan support in Congress. It no longer does. When George W. Bush made individual accounts the centerpiece of his 2000 presidential campaign, prompting his opponent, Al Gore, to oppose the proposal, both during the debates and in a barrage of political advertisements, privatization became a partisan issue. Today, Democratic legislators regularly reject such proposals. Meanwhile, Republican legislators advocate "market solutions" to the solvency problem, although carefully avoiding the now-toxic term "privatization."

It is tough to know how committed Republican legislators are to enacting privatization (here used as a neutral descriptive term). Of course, some wealthy Republican donors are deeply committed to reinventing Social Security, so the incentives are strong for legislators to parrot support for the cause. But campaign talk is cheap talk. It does not bind legislators to work actively to advance privatization. It does not compel them to vote for privatization if given the opportunity. As we saw in 2005, when President Bush campaigned tirelessly for individual accounts, even the most conservative legislators were fair-weather friends. They spoke glowingly of giving workers control over their payroll contributions, but they did little to advance the president's plan. Even today, Republican legislators rarely introduce bills that would create the market-like solutions they regularly praise. Former representative Paul Ryan introduced the most recent privatization plan more than a decade ago.

One reason for the dearth of recent privatization proposals is that the costs of transitioning to a new system increase steeply as insolvency nears. Before President Bush proposed individual accounts in 2005, actuaries expected the trust fund would last until 2042.[14] Program designers, therefore, had a long lead time to gradually restore solvency. If such a plan had passed, Social Security finances would have turned worse for a while, as younger workers diverted their payroll contributions to individual accounts and the government borrowed to pay benefits to current and near retirees. But eventually the system would have returned to balance, as benefit cuts for temporally distant cohorts kicked in.

As 2034 nears, however, the need to borrow to jump-start privatization will increase dramatically. First, the government would no longer have a large trust fund to help subsidize benefits. That loss alone would require borrowing an additional 1.2 percent of GDP annually just to keep benefits from declining. This new borrowing would be in addition to the massive borrowing required to cover the diversion of workers' contributions to individual accounts. Second, gradual changes in the benefit formula would no longer have time to work their magic. Third, the entire boomer generation would already be collecting retirement benefits. Rather than having young boomers transition to individual accounts, as they would have under the 2005 plan, traditional Social Security would have to support all boomers until their demise. In short, delay is very costly for the privatization cause.

Privatization still offers Republican legislators one tempting treat: no new taxes. For politicians who have signed the Norquist pledge, that treat could still prove irresistible. Yes, the government would have to borrow many trillions of dollars beginning in 2034. But massive borrowing did not dissuade Republicans from supporting President Bush's 2001 tax cuts, the Bush-era wars in Iraq and Afghanistan, or President Trump's 2017 tax cuts. If Republicans did not mind borrowing for war making and tax cutting, they might not mind borrowing to avoid the political nightmare of choosing between their tax-averse supporters and their benefit-dependent constituents.

Still, the devil is in the details. Some early privatization plans proposed that the government borrow for many years to support current and near retirees, and then repay the debt as the costs of traditional Social Security declined. But as President Bush discovered in 2005, devising politically acceptable ways to reduce future benefits, and thereby repay the debt, is fiendishly difficult. What was difficult then will be even tougher in 2034 because the revenue needs will be even greater.

Also problematic is the notion that privatizers can somehow guarantee benefits for current and near retirees. AARP and other opponents will surely remind voters that Republicans have a troubled history when it comes to extending the government's borrowing authority, sometimes demanding cuts in domestic programs as the price for raising the debt limit to avoid government default. The worry is not just that Republican legislators might use future votes on debt extensions to demand reductions in Social Security benefits. Republicans might also insist that the ballooning debt—ballooning because of privatization—necessitates deep cuts in health, education, food stamps, and the like. Party reputations are sticky: it is tough to break free from them.

Finally, Republicans would face the problem of attracting Democratic support. Bipartisanship is just as much a requirement for Republicans' privatization proposals as it is for Democratic plans to increase taxes. Here the problem is that Democratic legislators have few reasons to abandon traditional Social Security. Still, if Republicans control the agenda, maintain unity among themselves, block every counterproposal, and wait until moments before the trust fund runs dry, they might attract the handful of Democrats they would need. But maintaining Republican unity to dismantle one of the government's most popular programs is far from assured. Republican legislators would face the same constituency pressures to save traditional Social Security as Democratic legislators would.

The fundamental problem for the privatizers is that traditional Social Security is popular. It enjoys broad public support among Democrats and Republicans, workers and retirees, the young and the old, the poor and the better-off. In order to replace it, the proponents of change need to make the replacement program popular, too. Only then would legislators feel comfortable voting to reinvent Social Security. President Bush understood this, as he mounted his "60 stops in 60 days" national tour. But he was unable to move the needle because the opposition enjoyed too many advantages. Democrats had been the more trusted party on Social Security for decades. AARP had direct channels for reaching and mobilizing its 35 million members. Not much has changed since then, except that Republicans no longer have a national leader with a policy fervor for individual accounts.

General Funds

A third option is to use general funds to close the solvency gap. General funds are funds derived from all government revenue sources, excepting only those derived from special purpose taxes, such as the payroll tax, which supports the Social Security and Medicare trust funds, or the gasoline tax, which supports the Highway Trust Fund.[15] General funds include revenues derived from broad-based taxes, such as corporate or personal income taxes, as well as borrowed funds that are used to close the gap between overall revenues and overall spending.

The political attraction of using general funds is that it separates voting on benefits from voting on taxes. Legislators can claim credit for delivering benefits without being blamed for imposing costs. When spending general funds, all questions about costs are deferred to the future. Indeed, given the federal government's growing propensity to borrow rather than tax—it has run large annual deficits since 2002—questions about costs are often deferred indefinitely.

There are ample precedents for using general funds to subsidize programs that have their own dedicated taxes. Congress once supported highway construction exclusively with the gasoline tax. But since legislators last raised the gasoline tax in 1993, they now supplement this dedicated tax with general funds. Since inception, Congress has funded Medicare with a combination of general funds, a dedicated payroll tax, and user premiums.

Policymakers have had good reasons for not using general funds to subsidize Social Security. Recall how President Roosevelt argued that a tight link between taxes and benefits served two important ends. It would protect Social Security from hostile actors—"no damn politician can ever scrap my Social Security program"—but it would also protect the program from unreasonable expansion. Legislators could not expand the program unless they were also willing to increase taxes. This tight link has worked for nearly a century. The program's detractors have never found a way to dismantle Social Security because workers earn their benefits by paying a dedicated tax. But neither have the program's champions been able to expand benefits since 1972 because legislators have been unwilling to increase taxes.

Using general funds in 2034, however, would offer several attractions. First, it would protect Republican legislators from having to vote to raise the payroll tax, which would violate their pledge never to raise taxes. Second, it would help Democratic legislators move the program's revenue base from the regressive payroll tax to the progressive income tax, thus making the program more equitable. The sticking point is that Social Security's revenue needs are colossal—1.2 percent of GDP. Would legislators be willing to borrow that sum, year after year, essentially taking on long-term debt to pay Social Security's monthly obligations?

Of course, the general funds alternative to massive borrowing is to increase income taxes. That alternative makes sense for many Democrats, who prefer progressive taxes. But it hardly helps Republican legislators, who oppose raising both income taxes and payroll taxes. In short, general funds are no panacea. They might help coalition leaders close a portion of the solvency gap, but only in conjunction with other revenue-raising or benefit-cutting provisions.

Stalemate

A fourth possibility is stalemate. If Democrats and Republicans cannot find common ground as the clock ticks down, program administrators would have no choice but to reduce everyone's benefits by 21 percent. That is the law. Experience suggests, however, that legislators would find a short-term fix to keep the benefits flowing. That is what they did in 1981, when they authorized the Social Security trust fund to borrow from other trust funds, thus pushing insolvency past the 1982 congressional elections, and making 1983 the year for action.[16] That is what legislators regularly do when they cannot agree about the rest of the federal budget. They adopt short-term continuing resolutions that keep funds flowing, usually at the previous year's level. But borrowing from other trust funds would not last very long in 2034, given Social Security's enormous need for immediate revenue. Moreover, experts forecast that the Medicare trust fund will be depleted long before then, leaving the retirement funds for military and civilian personnel as the only government trust funds with significant assets.[17]

If stalemate continues, the next stopgap would be using general funds to pay Social Security benefits. Although using general funds for Social Security is currently illegal, Congress could suspend that prohibition. In short, policymakers can buy as much time as they need to enact long-term changes, if majorities, or in the case of the Senate, supermajorities, agree to extend the clock. Eventually, one side or the other will conclude that actual benefit cuts are necessary to spur serious negotiations, and refuse to approve additional extensions. At that point, the first three options are back on the table.

A fifth possibility is complete policymaking breakdown. Legislators prove unable to enact either a short-term fix or a long-term solution. As the law requires, program administrators would then cut everyone's benefits by 21 percent. Next, legislators would take their cases to the people, arguing why their own plans—or their party's plan—was superior, and why citizens should reelect them and their party teammates to fix Social Security. Few legislators would welcome an accountability election like this, where swarms of ill-tempered seniors are out for revenge. And that is why legislators are likely to fix Social Security moments before it plunges over the solvency cliff.

The Finale

No one can be certain what Congress will do in 2034. We don't know what role Social Security will play in the presidential and congressional campaigns leading up to trust fund depletion, although the issue is likely to rise in importance as insolvency nears. We don't know which party will control the House, the Senate, or the presidency, and therefore whether a single party will control the agenda. We don't know whether the president or top congressional leaders will care more about enacting a specific solution—say, partial privatization—or whether they simply want to fix the solvency problem without endangering legislators' careers.

All else equal, incremental solutions are more probable than reinventing the system. First, traditional Social Security enjoys enormous public support. Retirees like it, but so do workers. Democrats like it, but so do Republicans. The poor like it, but so do better-off folks. Only the uber-wealthy seem to detest it. Although creating broad public support for some type of privatization is certainly possible, it is hard to imagine a worse time for doing so than during the weeks before Social Security plunges over the fiscal cliff. Its 83 million beneficiaries, as well as millions of soon-to-be beneficiaries, will be looking for reassurance, not fresh beginnings.

Second, many of the incremental solutions are quite popular. For example, most surveys show that large bipartisan majorities favor increasing or abolishing the maximum taxable wage base. Adopting either alternative would be quite lucrative. Abolishing the wage base would eliminate nearly three-quarters of the long-term actuarial deficit; merely restoring the wage base to where it was in the early 1980s would eliminate one-quarter. When Medicare was in crisis, legislators, desperate for revenue, first raised and later eliminated that program's maximum taxable wage base. Desperate legislators in 2034 will be tempted to do the same. To be sure, 6 percent of workers earn more than the wage base, and would therefore pay some additional taxes, but most costs would be concentrated on the richest 1 or 2 percent of workers. Although some of these affluent workers may be generous campaign donors, the ultimate political currency is votes, not dollars. The 83 million enraged Social Security beneficiaries can do more political harm than even the most irate campaign donors can.

Surveys also reveal public support for raising the tax rate, at least modestly, and perhaps substantially. Of course, most surveys have asked about raising the tax rate gradually, which is more appealing. Unfortunately, gradualism will not be an option in 2034, given the need for immediate revenue. So, it is hard to know where people would stand on substantial and immediate tax increases. Similarly, surveys show public support for gradually raising the retirement age, though not too high. Although such gradualism does little to create immediate revenue, it is the best protection against continuing increases in longevity.

Third, incremental solutions make it easier for people to calculate their own personal stakes than do novel solutions.[18] Workers can imagine how their income would decline with specific tax increases. Retirees can imagine what life would be like with particular benefit reductions. Such calculations are more difficult when policymakers consider novel solutions such as privatization. To be sure, policymakers sometimes enact novel solutions with uncertain effects. The Clean Air Act of 1990, which introduced a cap-and-trade program to curb the sulfur dioxide emissions that cause acid rain, is a good example. Stakeholders struggled to calculate how the new system would affect their own interests, while policymakers inched toward a compromise.[19] But policymakers rarely adopt novel solutions under great time pressure. Once Social Security's fiscal cliff is within sight, incremental solutions are more straightforward, not just for stakeholders calculating their personal interests, but also for legislators calculating their electoral interests.

Fourth, compromise is easier with incremental solutions than it is with novel solutions.[20] For traditional Social Security, all the basic elements—retirement ages, replacement rates, tax rates, the maximum taxable wage base, cost-of-living adjustments—are measured on interval scales. When policymakers negotiate about one of those elements—say, doubling versus quadrupling the maximum taxable wage base—all the intermediate options are obvious. For many novel solutions, however, the negotiating space is poorly defined. It is hard to find a midpoint between nominal categories, such as creating or not creating individual accounts.

How serious is the Republican pledge never to support tax increases? Can we imagine that Republican legislators would be so loyal to their tax-averse supporters that they would reject every plan to protect their benefit-dependent constituents? History suggests that elected politicians sometimes suspend their professed principles in order to resolve thorny policy problems. Although President Reagan introduced Republicans to the joy of tax cutting with his 1981 plan to reduce income taxes, the same president and the same Republican legislators raised income taxes in 1982 and 1984 when the initial cuts proved too costly.[21] In 1981, Reagan proposed reducing the statutory increases in Social Security's payroll tax, scheduled for 1985 and 1990. Days later, he abandoned that proposal. And two years later, he signed a solvency bill that not only accelerated those statutory increases but also raised taxes on self-employed workers. His successor, George H. W. Bush, made a similar switch. Although he accepted the presidential nomination with the memorable lines, "Read my lips: No new taxes," he later signed the Omnibus Budget Reconciliation Act of 1990, which did, in fact, raise taxes.

Not even the Norquist pledge has kept Republican legislators from approving tax increases. Consider Republicans' predicament after approving the massive 2001 tax cuts. The tax cuts themselves would expire after ten years because they were enacted with a budget resolution, where a simple majority suffices, rather than a tax bill, where a supermajority would be needed to avoid a filibuster. Later, Congress extended the tax cuts through 2012, but with an agreement that any further stalemate would generate not only automatic tax increases but also automatic spending cuts for all federal agencies. On New Year's Day 2013, the stakes were enormous. Inaction that day would reverse all the Bush-era tax cuts, require the sequestration of more than $100 billion from agency budgets, and thereby threaten the still-fragile economy. At that point, House Republicans caved. They voted 232 to 2 to adopt a procedure that would allow floor consideration of a bill that would make the tax cuts permanent for everyone except the wealthy. An hour later, House Republicans voted 85 to 151 to approve the bill itself. The first vote guaranteed that the nation would not plunge over the fiscal cliff and, more importantly, that Republicans would not be blamed for the economic consequences. The second vote guaranteed that most Republican House members would not be punished for violating their pledge to oppose all tax increases. But notice that 36 percent of Republicans voted explicitly to allow tax increases for affluent taxpayers, and 99 percent of Republicans voted to allow such a bill to reach the floor.[22]

New Year's Day 2013 reveals the practical limits of the Norquist pledge. Yes, Republican legislators work hard to avoid raising taxes, in part to avoid electoral and donor repercussions. But when faced with more-severe electoral repercussions, as would likely follow from sailing over the 2013 fiscal cliff, Republicans swallowed hard and accepted that politics is about trade-offs. No doubt, many legislators will come to the same conclusion just moments before skidding over the 2034 solvency cliff.

Here is where general funds—or, more accurately, debt—can play an important role. General funds would allow legislators to approve *gradual* changes in the other basic elements of a solvency package—tax rates, benefit cuts, retirement ages, and the maximum taxable wage base. Without general funds, legislators would have to approve sudden changes in these elements, thus imposing large and immediate costs on workers, employers, or beneficiaries. General funds could reduce the immediate costs, thus making them less noticeable, less traceable, and less dangerous.

Waiting until 2034 has one political advantage. It transforms policymaking from a slow, deliberative process, where partisan legislators often take extreme positions to appeal to their most attentive supporters, into a full-blown crisis, where legislators, fearing the electoral consequences of inaction, welcome compromise solutions.[23] The tragedy of 9/11 brought legislators together for bipartisan lawmaking. So, too, did the Great Recession, where bipartisan majorities approved the $700 billion Troubled Asset Relief Program. Similarly, in the early months of the Covid-19 pandemic, bipartisan majorities approved four relief bills totaling $2.9 trillion. The prospect of Social Security sailing over the fiscal cliff will be just as scary as these three crises. At that point, party leaders will negotiate a solvency package and relieved legislators will approve it.

13

Doing Better

SOCIAL SECURITY'S SOLVENCY PROBLEM deserves a moment of celebration. It deserves celebration because it is largely the consequence of two positive trends. First, retired people are living longer than ever before. Life expectancy for 65-year-old Americans, which was 13.7 years in 1940, is 20.3 years today. Moreover, it is projected to reach 24.3 years before the end of the century.[1] This increase—more than a decade of life—is an extraordinary accomplishment. Second, women have more choice than ever before in how many children they have. The decline in fertility, from 3.3 children per woman during the postwar baby boom to 1.8 children today, reflects a choice that freedom-loving people should appreciate. To be sure, both trends present financial challenges for Social Security. But is there anyone who would advocate forcibly reversing these two trends as a solution to Social Security's solvency problem?

Another reason for celebration is that the United States faces fewer demographic challenges than do most advanced countries. Figure 13.1 displays current (2020) and projected (2050) old-age to working-age ratios for nine countries.[2] The United States faces a ratio of 40 in 2050, meaning that it will then have 40 people aged 65 or older for every 100 people between 20 and 64. That is a considerable increase from its current ratio of 28. But most other OECD countries face higher ratios, including Japan (81), Korea (79), Italy (74), Germany (58), France (55), the United Kingdom (47), Canada (45), and Australia (42).[3] Indeed, only 3 of the 36 OECD countries face more favorable old-age to working-age ratios in 2050 than the United States—Mexico (29), Israel (31), and Turkey (37).

The United States faces a move favorable old-age to working-age ratio largely because fertility has declined less in the United States than it has declined in most advanced countries. Estimated fertility in the United States is 1.8 children per woman. Although this rate is shy of the rate of 2.1 children that

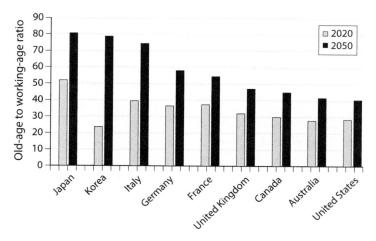

FIGURE 13.1. Old-age to working-age ratios for nine OECD countries, 2020 and 2050. The old-age to working-age ratio is the number of individuals aged 65 and over per 100 people aged between 20 and 64.
Source: OECD 2019, table 6.2.

ensures both a stable population and a stable flow of new workers, it is greater than fertility in Korea (1.1), Italy (1.3), Japan (1.4), Canada (1.5), and Germany (1.6). It is tied with Australia and the United Kingdom, and exceeded only by France (1.9) among the comparison countries.[4]

The second explanation for the more favorable old-age to working-age ratio in the United States is troubling. Many countries have achieved longer life expectancies for seniors than has the United States. Comparing life expectancies across countries requires switching from what demographers call cohort life expectancies, which I have been using throughout this book, to period life expectancies. The latter are slightly more conservative and shave about a year off American cohort estimates.[5] By the new metric, the United States has the lowest life expectancy for 65-year-olds (19.4 years) among the comparison countries. The estimates for the other countries are Japan 22.0, France 21.8, Australia 21.3, Italy 21.2, Korea 20.8, Canada 20.8, the United Kingdom 20.0, and Germany 19.6.[6] Although lower life expectancy for seniors in the United States makes it easier to solve Social Security's solvency problem, it is far from good news. Many people would welcome efforts to raise seniors' life expectancy even if the solvency problem worsened.

The third determinant of the old-age to working-age ratio is immigration. After all, the future supply of tax-paying workers depends not just on how many children American women produce, but also on how many immigrants American policymakers allow to settle in the country legally. Immigrants tend to be of working age when they arrive, so they have years to contribute to Social Security's pay-as-you-go system before collecting benefits. Although many Americans think of their country as relatively open to immigrants, and indeed the United States admitted just over a million permanent residents in 2019, these immigrants were only 0.3 percent of the nation's population, far too few to provide significant financial support for Social Security.[7] By comparison, Canada admits immigrants at triple the American rate (0.9 percent). Four other countries from the comparison group also admit immigrants at higher rates, including Australia (0.8 percent), Germany (0.7 percent), the United Kingdom (0.5 percent), and France (0.4 percent). The United States looks good on welcoming permanent immigrants only by comparison to Japan and Korea (both at 0.1 percent).[8]

These three determinants of the old-age to working-age ratio—fertility, life expectancy, and immigration—help explain the relative severity of the solvency problems for retirement systems around the world. Japan, with its low fertility, low immigration, and high life expectancy, faces significantly more difficulties than does the United States, with its higher fertility, midlevel immigration, and lower life expectancy. But these three demographic factors offer few levers for policymakers seeking to ease the financial burdens of public pensions. Providing incentives for women to have more children is both challenging and expensive. Intentionally reducing life expectancy is immoral. Admitting more immigrants is really the only demographic lever available to policymakers.[9] But many citizens and many policymakers already have strong views about immigration policy, so the politics of easing immigration restrictions is treacherous.

In short, although various demographic changes have created huge problems for people who manage public pension systems, American policymakers face less severe problems than do policymakers in most advanced countries. That does not make solving the American problem any easier. But it does suggest that the solutions should be less costly and less painful in the United States.

Retirement Age

The worldwide increase in life expectancy creates challenges for all retirement systems. It does not matter whether they are centrally managed like Social Security, employer based like traditional corporate pensions, or individually managed like IRAs. The most straightforward way to deal with increased life expectancy is simply to raise the retirement age. The argument is that as people live longer and healthier lives, they need to devote some of those extra years to working, and therefore contributing to the retirement system, rather than having all the additional years devoted to consumption in retirement. So far, most countries have not been very aggressive about raising their retirement ages. Although American legislators raised the full retirement age from 65 to 67, all other countries in the comparison group have lower ages to qualify for full benefits than the United Sates. The comparable ages are 61 in Korea, 63.3 in France, 63.9 in the United Kingdom, 64.5 in Japan, 65 in Australia and Canada, 65.5 in Germany, and 66.8 in Italy.[10]

Whether American legislators should again raise the full retirement age is complicated. Although legislators already raised the retirement age by 2 years, cohort life expectancy for seniors has increased by 6.6 years since Social Security began paying benefits in 1940. In short, the typical participant now works for 2 additional years before qualifying for full benefits, but then collects those benefits for an additional 4.6 years. Legislators have attempted to fund these lengthier retirements by raising taxes (1977), reducing average benefits (1983), and consuming the trust fund (from 2020 to 2034). But still they have not done enough to fund the increased life expectancy that has already occurred. Moreover, they have done nothing to fund the increases that are expected to occur. Recall that cohort life expectancy for seniors is forecast to increase an additional four years before the end of the century. Will working for just two additional years—from 65 to 67—be adequate when half of all retirees will be living past age 89?

If Social Security did not exist and people were saving for their own retirement, they would know instinctively that they could not save enough in two years to fund an additional 8.6 years of retirement. Arithmetic is easier when thinking about just one worker/saver/retiree. For an individual, the choice would be clear: save more during each working year, consume less during each retirement year, or work longer. Those would be the only options for the happy prospect of living a decade longer than your ancestors.

The options are fundamentally the same for legislators dealing with Social Security's longevity problem. They can require participants to contribute more during each working year, collect less during each retirement year, or work longer before qualifying for full benefits. But now the options are muddied by political questions about *who* should pay higher taxes, *who* should work longer, and *who* should collect lower benefits. With Social Security, people are not saving for their own retirement. They are participating in a vast intergenerational transfer scheme. It is much easier to insist that Congress not raise your retirement age if others would pay the cost of your lengthier retirement.

Whether legislators should raise the full retirement age is complicated by the fact that not everyone is living longer. As chapter 5 revealed, life expectancy has increased rapidly for top earners, while it has declined for those at the very bottom of the income distribution. Increasing the full retirement age once again could have the effect of forcing people with declining life expectancies to work longer to fund increasingly long retirements for better-off workers. That seems wrong. Yet *not* increasing the full retirement age simply requires that legislators raise taxes or cut benefits. One alternative is to raise the full retirement age for everyone, retain the current option for early retirement with reduced benefits, and then create ways to soften the blow for those who may not share in the longevity gains. For example, legislators could modify the benefit formula to increase benefits for people at the bottom of the earnings distribution, so that the early retirement penalties associated with the increased retirement age would not affect those with low career-average earnings.[11]

If raising the retirement age is a sensible solution to the longevity problem, why have other countries done so little to use this policy tool? First, policymakers in many countries *have* been working to raise their retirement ages. In 2019, for example, French president Emmanuel Macron proposed a vast overhaul of the country's complex system of 42 occupational pension programs, including raising the retirement age. His reward was months of nationwide strikes, school closures, and transportation shutdowns. In short, politics is a constraint everywhere, not just in the United States. Second, people in many other countries seem more tolerant of higher taxes than are Americans, and higher taxes are the principal alternative to raising the retirement age. In the most recent year with comparable data, total taxes in France were 46 percent of GDP, compared with 42 percent in Italy, 39 percent in Germany, 33 percent in Canada and the United Kingdom, 32 percent in Japan, 29 percent in Australia, and 27 percent in Korea. In the United States, federal, state, and local taxes were only 24 percent of GDP.[12] People who are already accustomed to high taxes may tolerate tax increases more readily than people who have long enjoyed low taxes.

Cost-of-Living Adjustments

It is hardly surprising that Democratic and Republican legislators disagree on whether to raise Social Security taxes. Partisan disputes about taxation are older than Social Security itself. It is surprising, however, that Democratic and

Republican legislators disagree on how to adjust benefits for inflation. After all, both parties supported the 1972 decision to index benefits for changes in the consumer price index.

The current disagreement about cost-of-living adjustments has both intellectual and partisan roots. On the intellectual side, experts disagree about how to measure inflation for older people. When Congress first voted to make cost-of-living adjustments automatic, it employed the only available metric, the Consumer Price Index for Urban Wage Earners. It still does. Later, some experts argued that this index overstates inflation because it ignores how consumers alter their buying habits—purchasing more chicken and less turkey—as relative prices change. They advocated creating something called a chained price index that adjusts for such substitutions. The Bureau of Labor Statistics now maintains such an index. Subsequently, other experts argued that the original index *understates* inflation for older people because health-care prices increase more rapidly than other prices, and because seniors purchase more health care than younger people do. A better index would use seniors' actual consumption patterns. The Bureau of Labor Statistics now maintains a special index for older people.

The Social Security actuaries estimate that using the less generous chained price index would reduce cost-of-living adjustments by about 0.3 percent annually, whereas using the more generous index for seniors would increase cost-of-living adjustments by about 0.2 percent annually. Over time, these differences would really matter for system finances. Using the less generous index would eliminate 19 percent of the 75-year actuarial deficit, while using the more generous index would increase the actuarial deficit by 13 percent.[13]

The partisan conflict over cost-of-living adjustments predates the creation of these two indexes. It first emerged in 1983, when policymakers were attempting to close the large solvency gap caused, in part, by unexpectedly high inflation. Republican policymakers, both in Congress and the White House, were looking for ways to avoid raising taxes. Reducing cost-of-living adjustments was one way to do that. The eventual bipartisan compromise was to postpone all cost-of-living adjustments for six months, while still using the original index to calculate the delayed adjustments. Once the chained price index was created in 2002, however, Republican legislators became its loudest champions, presumably because this new index would reduce the need for higher taxes. By comparison, Democratic legislators have flocked to the special index for seniors, in part because it would increase Social Security benefits. Now, when drafting solvency bills, Republican legislators regularly include the less generous index, while Democratic legislators regularly include the more generous index.

Accurate cost-of-living adjustments are important for seniors. But they are also important for taxpayers. It makes no more sense to overcompensate seniors for inflation, thus threatening the system's solvency, than it does to undercompensate them, thus threatening their financial well-being. The surprise is that most legislators seem unconcerned about getting it right. Both criticisms of the current index are persuasive. A better index should be based on what seniors consume *and* it should account for how seniors adjust their buying habits as relative prices change. That is, we need a chained price index for seniors. Why not devote the necessary resources to developing a better index for seniors? Why not commit—in advance—to using it? The reason is that the two alternative metrics serve legislators' political needs all too well. Republicans can propose reducing benefits and minimizing tax increases by using what they argue is a superior index; Democrats can propose increasing benefits with their own allegedly superior measure.

Sometimes people justify overcompensating retirees for inflation because many retirees live on limited incomes. Anything that can be done to help needy seniors is, therefore, worth doing. The problem with this argument is that across-the-board policies are inefficient methods for helping the needy. If everyone is overcompensated for inflation by 0.3 percent, those in the bottom fifth of retiree households would receive, on average, an unjustified $31 annually, while those in the top fifth would receive, on average, an unjustified $74.[14] Why pay so much to affluent retirees if the aim is to help needy retirees? If policymakers seek to target the needy, they should target the needy. Italy offers one sensible policy. It employs progressive indexation by adjusting lower pensions more generously than higher pensions.[15]

Trade-Offs

Social Security is a self-supporting system. By law, Social Security taxes cannot be used to fund other programs; other revenues cannot be used to support Social Security. This type of closed financial system should make it easier for both citizens and policymakers to recognize the inherent trade-offs between raising Social Security taxes and cutting Social Security benefits. In fact, ordinary citizens seem to recognize the trade-offs more readily than members of Congress do.

The most impressive opinion surveys that I have found about fixing Social Security were designed and administered by the Program for Public

Consultation (PPC) at the University of Maryland (see chapter 10). These are the surveys where researchers first taught respondents how Social Security works and shared with them arguments for and against various solvency options. Then, near the end of the surveys, researchers asked respondents to design their own individual solvency packages in a multistage process where each respondent first selected a most-preferred option, then learned how much the solvency gap would decline, then selected another option, and so on, until each respondent had assembled a package that would eliminate the entire 75-year solvency gap. What is striking is that majorities of respondents ended up supporting most of the major solvency options—at least in moderation—including raising the retirement age, increasing the tax rate, raising the maximum taxable wage base, and using the less generous index for making cost-of-living adjustments. To be sure, respondents were willing to raise the retirement age only modestly, whereas eliminating the maximum taxable wage base was a real crowd pleaser. But respondents were open-minded. They were willing to impose some costs on most Social Security participants, including themselves. Moreover, Democratic and Republican respondents made roughly similar choices.

It is tougher to find such open-mindedness among legislators. On the campaign trail, some legislators oppose all tax increases; others oppose all benefit cuts. Still others oppose virtually every solvency option. Recall Representative Martha Roby's proud declaration: "I oppose raising the retirement age; I oppose cutting benefits; I oppose increasing payroll taxes" (chapter 6). In short, most legislators do little on the campaign trail to educate citizens about the trade-offs inherent in all the leading solvency plans. They do little to suggest that any sort of middle ground exists between their absolutist positions.

Once they reach Washington, most Republican legislators refuse to endorse bills that would modify either taxes or benefits. Recall from chapter 10 that only six Republican legislators introduced incremental plans between 2010 and 2020, and none more recently than 2016. Although one House bill attracted six cosponsors, and one Senate bill attracted two, the other four bills failed to attract a single cosponsor. One reason for the dearth of cosponsors is that these six bills would slash benefits. By avoiding tax increases—only one bill proposed raising any new revenue—bill drafters had little choice but to cut benefits deeply. All six bills would raise the full retirement age, in one case higher than 70. Five bills would reduce cost-of-living adjustments, including one that would eliminate cost-of-living adjustments for upper-income beneficiaries. And five bills would reduce benefits for new retirees.

Representative Paul Ryan's 2010 plan to reinvent Social Security with a system of individual accounts was a bit more popular, attracting 14 Republican cosponsors. But notice that his bill is now more than a decade old. Moreover, Ryan left the House several years ago, as did 11 of his cosponsors. No one has designed a successor plan or asked the actuaries to update their scoring of Ryan's original plan.

Democratic legislators are more willing to bite the bullet and specify exactly how they would allocate the costs of fixing Social Security. For example, Representative John Larson has proposed gradually raising the tax rate from 6.2 to 7.4 percent of taxable wages, while eventually eliminating the maximum taxable wage base. Nearly 90 percent of House Democrats have cosponsored Larson's bill, which would not only close the 75-year actuarial deficit, but also provide funds for increasing Social Security benefits.

What is striking is how quickly House Democrats converged on a single plan for restoring solvency. Although only 2 representatives cosponsored Larson's first plan in 2014, 205 House Democrats cosponsored the fourth iteration in 2019. Also noteworthy is that his plan imposes solvency costs on taxpayers, not beneficiaries. Increasing the tax rate provides roughly half the revenue; targeting affluent workers by eliminating the maximum taxable wage base provides the other half. The retirement age would remain unchanged. And rather than reducing retirement benefits, the plan increases benefits for retirees with low-wage careers and introduces a more generous cost-of-living adjustment for all beneficiaries. The Larson plan is right out of the 1977 playbook, where policymakers protected all beneficiaries from both inflation and insolvency, while imposing all costs on workers and their employers. No doubt, Democratic cosponsors have concluded that endorsing gradual tax increases to save Social Security is not electorally risky. So far, I have not seen any evidence that their endorsements have been used against them.

It is striking how timid Republican legislators have been. By promising never to raise taxes, Republican bill drafters must cut benefits. That is the essence of trade-offs. But the benefit cuts that would be necessary to fix Social Security are so enormous that few legislators want to endorse benefit-cutting solvency bills. The fear of electoral retribution forces most Republican legislators to remain mute.

The greatest impediment to solvency reform, then, is not public opinion. Citizens clearly want action. And they seem open to solvency packages that include raising the retirement age, increasing the tax rate, raising the maximum taxable wage base, and reducing benefits. Moreover, the differences among

Democratic and Republican citizens are small. The principal impediment is that Republican bill drafters have not designed solvency bills that appeal to other Republican legislators. That is the minimum that is required before negotiations can begin among Democratic and Republican leaders.

Encouraging Action

Waiting until 2034 to fix Social Security will seriously restrict legislators' options. If they act earlier, legislators can implement changes gradually—slowly raising the retirement age, slowly scaling back benefits, slowly increasing the tax rate, slowly extending the maximum taxable wage base, slowly introducing individual investment accounts—so that workers, employers, and retirees can anticipate and accommodate these changes. If legislators wait until the trust fund disappears, all slow and gradual options disappear. At that point, large and immediate changes are all that remain to restore solvency.

Unfortunately, waiting until 2034 to fix Social Security is the most likely outcome. Legislators waited until the last moment to fix the 1977 and 1983 solvency problems. Moreover, legislators have done nothing to address Social Security's problems since 1994 when the actuaries first sounded the alarm. They did nothing in 1999 when President Clinton and others proposed using the budget surplus to save traditional Social Security. They did nothing in 2005 when President Bush pushed for partial privatization.

What can be done to increase the chances for earlier action? One thing we need is a broader collection of plans. From 1995 to 2005, plans emerged from every direction. There were Democratic plans, Republican plans, bipartisan plans, think-tank plans, and commission plans. Today few policymakers are developing, updating, or introducing solvency bills. Old plans are not very helpful because they include now-impossible actions, such as raising the tax rate in 2005, introducing individual accounts in 2006, or reducing cost-of-living adjustments beginning in 2007.

Many Republican legislators say they want market-like reforms for Social Security. But the most recent congressional plan fitting that description was introduced by Representative Ryan in 2010. If that is what Republicans have in mind today, someone should either update Ryan's plan and submit it to the actuaries for scoring or draft a new plan. Of course, outside groups can also design privatization plans. But legislators still need to sponsor these plans for the actuaries to devote their scarce resources to estimating their effects over the 75-year forecasting period.[16] Moreover, bill drafters need to attract cosponsors to demonstrate the breadth of support for reinventing Social Security. It is not enough to endorse the *notion* of market-like reforms. Legislators need to attach their names to bills that detail the incidence of costs and benefits.

Most Republican legislators continue to insist that Social Security can be fixed without raising anyone's taxes. But when legislators draft tax-free solvency plans, their bills attract few cosponsors. Bill drafters need to design bills that other Republicans find appealing. If they cannot attract cosponsors for their tax-free solutions, they should admit that tax-free solutions are not politically feasible.

It is not that we need dozens of plans before Congress can begin work. But we do need a *diversity* of plans. Since House Democrats have converged on a single plan to restore solvency, they can switch from drafting and endorsing plans to educating the public and persuading uncommitted legislators to join their parade. In contrast, Republicans need to draft either a single consensus plan, like the Democrats, or several plans that appeal to the various Republican factions, including those who seek to reinvent Social Security and those who prefer incremental solutions. If Republicans do not develop their own plans, they have little role left in policymaking other than to criticize Democrats for their proposed tax increases. To be sure, there is nothing to stop Republican legislators from doing this for the next decade. After all, Democrats proposed no alternative to President's Bush's 2005 privatization proposal, just as Republicans proposed no alternative to President Obama's 2009 health-care plan. But once the precipice nears, their own constituents will demand solutions, not critiques. So, why not develop some proposals now?

Strictly speaking, one can legislate based on a single bill. House Democrats could attempt to enact something like the Larson bill by first working to attract Republican support in the House. Finding no Republicans willing to support the original version, they could gradually modify it to make it more appealing. The only problem is that most Republican legislators insist that tax-free reform is possible, so endorsing a Democratic bill, even one that scales back the tax increases in the Larson bill, remains politically risky for legislators who have signed the Norquist pledge—no tax increases ever. By arguing that Republicans need to rally around a Republican bill first, I am suggesting that they need to work through the trade-offs between tax increases and benefit cuts themselves, in the privacy of the Republican caucus, rather than expecting them to endorse some version of a Democratic bill that rests so firmly on tax increases.

It might help if advocacy groups pressured every Republican legislator to sponsor or cosponsor at least one Social Security solvency bill. When Republicans last controlled the House, and therefore controlled the Social Security subcommittee of the House Ways and Means Committee, both the chair, Sam Johnson (R-TX), and the ranking minority member, John Larson (D-CT), sponsored separate solvency bills. But once Democrats took control of the House, only the new chair, John Larson, sponsored a solvency bill. So, the most recent Republican solvency bill was drafted in 2016 by a now-deceased representative. Perhaps AARP and other advocacy groups could pressure the current ranking minority member Tom Reed (R-NY) to draft a bill and work to attract sponsors. After all, AARP has roughly 80,000 members in Reed's upstate district who could reinforce the group's message about the urgency for action and the need for a broadly supported plan.

It also might help if outside groups drafted new plans or updated previous ones. Peter Diamond and Peter Orszag's superb book-length analysis of Social Security, which includes a detailed solvency plan, is now 17 years old.[17] The Bipartisan Policy Center—the think tank founded by four former Senate majority leaders—last released a bipartisan solvency plan six years ago. It is odd that so many groups created solvency plans when insolvency was temporally distant, but now that it nears, the plans are less plentiful.

Finally, the actuaries could do more to quantify the costs of delay. Of course, the actuaries are neutral, nonpartisan experts. They should do nothing to threaten their reputations for impartiality. But given their existing models, they could estimate the effects of each solvency provision not only if it were implemented today, but also if it were implemented in each successive year from 2022 to 2034. The actuaries are in the best position to quantify the costs of delay. Perhaps the chairs and ranking minority members of the House Ways and Means and Senate Finance Committees could encourage the actuaries to create sequential estimates like these.

Presidents

Does it make sense for presidents to create their own solvency plans? Presidential proposals were once a great way to galvanize legislators into action. Think Franklin Roosevelt and the New Deal or Lyndon Johnson and the Great Society. Today, presidential proposals are a good way to polarize legislators into inaction. President Reagan and the second President Bush helped to polarize legislators on Social Security. Presidents Clinton and Obama did the same for health care.

Citizens are now remarkably unpolarized on Social Security. It would be helpful to keep them that way. Although legislators are divided on what to do about Social Security's solvency problem—the principal fault line is taxes—they mostly agree on the need to fix it. In any event, legislators are less polarized on Social Security than they are in many other policy areas, such as health care or climate change.

If we take reinventing Social Security off the table for a moment, fixing Social Security is essentially a budgetary problem. And Congress is quite good at solving budgetary conflicts. Legislators begin with the status quo alternative and ask what changes they should make at the margin. If one faction favors X and another favors 3X, they often compromise near 2X. To be sure, compromise often emerges as the clock ticks down and the prospect of no X becomes more likely. But there is little evidence that presidents are essential for brokering budgetary compromises, whether between Democrats and Republicans or between representatives and senators.

In 1981, legislators were working toward fixing Social Security, but doing so quietly and out of the limelight. Then, as chapter 2 recounted, President Reagan intervened, proposing massive changes in Social Security. The net result was to derail the committee-level negotiations and to polarize legislators—and, to a lesser extent, citizens—along party lines. It took nearly two years to get things back on track and pass the 1983 solvency reform. George W. Bush, first as a candidate in 2000 and then as president in 2005, reignited the partisan splits by advocating a presidentially designed reinvention of Social Security.

In short, presidents do not seem essential for fixing Social Security. Indeed, they do not seem much interested in drafting solvency plans. Recall that President Bush's initial 2005 proposal was all about creating individual accounts. It did nothing to fix the long-term solvency problem. Only under congressional pressure did the president revise his plan to close part of the solvency gap.

President Biden's 2020 plan is no different. Indeed, it is more a benefit-raising plan than a solvency plan. Yes, it proposes increasing taxes on the affluent by using the principal revenue raiser in the Larson plan. Both Biden and Larson would begin applying the payroll tax to earnings over $400,000, and would eventually tax all earnings after the maximum taxable wage base increased to that level. As table 10.9 showed, this provision would eliminate 71 percent of the 75-year actuarial deficit. But Biden's plan would use *most* of the new revenue to expand benefits. It would increase the minimum benefit for low-wage workers, give earnings credits to unpaid caregivers, employ a more generous cost-of-living index, and repeal the windfall elimination provision that prevents state and local government workers from being overcompensated for their short-term participation in Social Security. Unlike Larson's plan, which would eliminate the 75-year actuarial deficit, Biden's plan would close only a quarter of the shortfall and extend solvency by only five years.[18]

It is a mystery why 90 percent of House Democrats endorsed the Larson plan, which would eliminate the long-term deficit, while the party's eventual nominee for president would close only 26 percent of the solvency gap. Indeed, only two candidates running for president—Buttigieg and Warren—designed plans to eliminate the entire 75-year deficit. In short, there is nothing about running for president that suddenly gives politicians the wisdom and courage to deal with long-term problems like Social Security. House Democrats have displayed more political courage than most of their party's presidential contenders.

Moreover, even presidents who display little personal interest in drafting solvency plans inhibit legislators from developing their own. Before Donald Trump became president, Republican legislators regularly introduced plans that would achieve solvency, usually by reducing future benefits. But since 2016, when Trump promised to protect traditional Social Security, Republicans have not introduced a single solvency plan. It is too risky. Before Joe Biden became president, Democratic legislators had converged on a single plan that would achieve solvency by raising the tax rate and eventually eliminating the maximum taxable wage base. But seven months into the 117th Congress, Democrats have not introduced a single solvency plan—not even Representative Larson, the author of the 2019 plan that attracted 90 percent of House Democrats as cosponsors.[19] The likely reason is that previous Democratic solvency bills would violate Biden's promise not to raise taxes on people earning less than $400,000.[20]

If we don't need presidents to create their own solvency plans, we also don't need outside assemblies such as the Greenspan Commission to design bipartisan fixes. The principal function of the Greenspan Commission was to tiptoe through the political minefield that President Reagan created with his 1981 plan to cut Social Security benefits. But it was the presidentially induced conflict that made a commission seem necessary at the time, not something inherent in Social Security.

Presidents still have important roles to play. First, they can work to place Social Security solvency on the congressional agenda. Presidents do not need to submit detailed proposals to hold legislators' feet to the fire. They can use their bully pulpit to make Social Security a more urgent issue. Second, presidents can help negotiate compromises among congressional leaders. Legislators seek to pass bills that presidents will sign, which gives presidents a natural role to play. Finally, presidents can help their fellow partisans accept seemingly toxic options. Just as President Nixon's 1972 trip to China helped make engaging with that country tolerable for China-phobic Republicans, so too could a Republican president endorsing tax increases for Social Security make that option tolerable for tax-phobic Republicans. Similarly, a Democratic president could make raising the retirement age or using a less generous cost-of-living index more acceptable for Democrats afraid to cut benefits.

Citizens

What can citizens do to encourage legislators to fix Social Security now rather than waiting until insolvency nears? First, individuals can pressure their representatives and senators directly. Mail works nicely—digital or snail—because legislators have staffers who read, summarize, and respond to whatever their constituents write. Don't just tell legislators that you care about the program. Ask them what bills they have sponsored or cosponsored to fix Social Security. Most Democrats can answer that question with ease. Most Republicans cannot. Better yet, ask your family, friends, and colleagues to write. Politics is about numbers, so don't be a loner. Best of all, whenever legislators hold town hall meetings, show up with as many friends as you can muster. Communicate with legislators on their home turf. And when legislators' initial responses are vague and inadequate—after all, most of them have *not* sponsored or cosponsored solvency plans—show up again, month after month, until they produce better answers.

Once legislators endorse specific bills, tell them what you like and dislike about their solvency plans. Trust me: legislators would rather know where you stand in advance of congressional action than learn your views on Election Day. But first assure them that you understand the trade-offs involved. If you think increasing taxes is a bad idea, tell them why you think raising the retirement age is a better one. If you think raising the retirement age is a bad idea, tell them why you think paying higher taxes is a better one. Avoid mimicking people—some of them serving in Congress—who pretend there are cost-free solutions. If there were, Congress would have fixed Social Security decades ago.

Citizens can also encourage interest groups, like AARP, to push legislators to tackle Social Security's solvency problem. Interest groups are great at protecting their turf when action is imminent. AARP worked closely with President Bush to enact the Medicare Prescription Drug Act in 2003. And it pulled out all the stops to defeat his plan for partial privatization two years later. But what has AARP done to persuade legislators—and particularly Republican legislators—to sponsor or cosponsor solvency plans? Nothing that I can see. Perhaps the reason is that AARP's leaders fear the kinds of plans that Republicans might sponsor, say plans for partial privatization or plans with draconian benefit cuts. But getting Republicans to design solvency plans that can appeal to Republican cosponsors is an important beginning. If Democrats are the only ones sponsoring and cosponsoring reform plans, it makes solvency reform seem like a partisan issue. Yet recent polls show that Republican respondents are even more likely than Democrats to believe fixing Social Security should be a top priority (figure 7.9).

Citizens, social movements, and interest groups have long records of forcing issues on the congressional agenda. The Townsend movement agitated for retirement security in the 1930s, and both parties responded. The civil rights movement pushed both parties to address institutionalized racial discrimination in the 1960s, and they did. The environmental movement forced both parties to address air and water pollution in the 1970s. In all three cases, citizens were angry about current policies and pushed legislators to chart new directions. Citizens are sure to be angry in 2034 if legislators fail to fix Social Security. But if citizens would only get angry sooner, they could push legislators to address the solvency problem before it gets worse.

Journalists could do more, too. Reporters like to focus on presidents and presidential candidates. In 17 presidential debates during the last six general elections, journalists asked five questions about Social Security—one each in 2000, 2004, 2008, 2012, and 2016.[21] That's a good record. They fell short only in 2020. But journalists have an uneven record covering legislators, especially at the local level.[22] And they are especially weak covering temporally distant problems, like Social Security, at both the national and local levels.

Since I have been critical about Republican legislators for not sponsoring or cosponsoring solvency bills, it is worth exploring how journalists cover what legislators are doing to fix Social Security. So, I searched electronically for national and local coverage that mentioned both Representative Tom Reed and Social Security. Reed, the ranking Republican on the Social Security subcommittee, has the institutional responsibility for drafting a Republican solvency plan. Moreover, according to press accounts, he holds regular conference calls with regional media, as well as frequent town hall meetings. In short, he is important and accessible. Here are excerpts from three typical articles about Reed and Social Security.

> Meanwhile, by calling for the reform of both Social Security and Medicare, Reed is making himself a target in the upcoming general election because it's considered controversial anytime a politician calls for changing the programs, especially in a district where many constituents rely on the programs' services. Reed said that many in Congress won't discuss the two programs because they are too concerned about how it might impact their re-election bids, but he feels the issue is too important to ignore and wants to work toward a solution. (June 2018)[23]

> Speaking at a town hall on the topic of the solvency of the federal Social Security program, Representative Tom Reed said there is a good chance reforms make it to President Donald Trump's desk for approval in September. (July 2019)[24]

> But he defended a staunchly Republican position to neither decrease benefits nor increase taxes going to support the program. (September 2019)[25]

Put differently, Reed is politically courageous, action is imminent, and the plan will include neither tax increases nor benefit cuts.

But notice that nowhere—not in local coverage, not in national coverage—can I discover how the ranking Republican tasked with drafting legislation to fix Social Security would accomplish that Herculean task.[26] The top Democrat (Larson) has a plan. The previous top Republican (Johnson) had a plan. So, one surprise is that Reed does not have a plan. Or at least not a plan that the self-described courageous leader can share with his constituents. Another surprise is that citizens at the town hall meetings did not ask how he proposed to fix Social Security—remember he was forecasting that reforms would reach the president's desk in less than three months. The third surprise is that journalists did not demand details. How exactly would he fix Social Security without raising taxes or cutting benefits? A well-informed journalist might also have asked Reed what he meant by promising "equal treatment for public servants" (July 2019)—a phrase that sounds suspiciously like Biden's proposal to provide extra Social Security benefits for state and local workers—and how he planned to pay for those extra benefits. It is not just that local journalists did not ask hard questions. Why weren't national journalists pressing for answers from Reed and his Republican colleagues on the Social Security subcommittee?

Finally, challengers could do more. Why aren't Democratic candidates for Congress pressing Republican candidates to reveal their plans to fix Social Security? Why do they allow Republican incumbents to pretend to be courageous, when those legislators consistently avoid taking courageous positions?

Once Social Security reaches the decision agenda, many citizens will be watching attentively as legislators decide how to allocate the costs of solvency reform. At that point, some legislators will be quivering in their boots. But there is no reason to postpone the quivering for another decade. Citizens, activists, advocacy groups, challengers, and journalists can press legislators to specify how they would fix Social Security today. And then they can press legislators to settle their differences and restore solvency to the nation's premier retirement program. It should not take four decades to fix a problem first discovered in 1994.

NOTES

Chapter 1

1. The closing date for this book—the last opportunity for updates or additions—was July 29, 2021. As of that date, Social Security's actuaries had not released their 2021 projections. Therefore, all projections throughout this book are for the combined Old-Age and Survivors Insurance (OASI) and Disability Insurance (DI) Trust Funds (collectively OASDI), using the intermediate assumptions, as published in April 2020 (Board of Trustees 2020). The one exception is the year of insolvency, which the actuaries revised, six months later, from 2035 to 2034, to reflect the effects of the pandemic and the recession (Goss and Glenn 2020).

2. Board of Trustees 1994, 2009.

3. These estimates of life expectancy for 65-year-olds are the mean cohort life expectancies for men and women at that age under the actuaries' intermediate assumptions (Board of Trustees 2020, table V.A5).

4. Of course, declines in mortality are not inevitable. They can plateau or reverse.

5. Board of Trustees 2020, table V.A1 and p. 83.

6. For fertility prior to 1946, see Carter et al. (2006, data series Ab52). For postwar fertility, see Social Security Administration (2020d, table V.A1). See Munnell, Chen, and Sanzenbacher (2018) for an excellent discussion of trends in fertility.

7. Board of Trustees 2020, table IV.B3.

8. Under the 1977 law, the OASDI tax rates in 1990 would have been 6.2% for employed workers and 9.3% for self-employed workers. Under the 1983 law, the tax rates in 1990 were 6.2% and 12.4%, respectively (Svahn and Ross 1983, table A).

9. These calculations are based on 2019 data (Social Security Administration 2021a, tables 4.A3 and 4.B2).

10. Social Security Administration 2021a, tables 4.A1 to 4.A3.

11. Chen, Munnell, and Sanzenbacher 2018.

12. For data supporting the points in this and the next two paragraphs, see Bureau of Labor Statistics (2020, tables 2CW, 2PIW, and 2SLGW). These data exclude federal, military, and agricultural workers.

13. These differences reflect whether workers have access to employer-sponsored plans and whether workers choose to participate if they do have access.

14. The estimated costs, at the time of enactment, are from *Congress and the Nation* (2006, 89, 105, 496). The comparison is with actual GDP from 2002 to 2011, which totaled $136 trillion (Social Security Administration, 2020d, table VI.G6).

15. *Congress and the Nation* 2006, 234, 283; Crawford 2014. The comparison is with actual GDP from 2001 to 2014, which totaled $197 trillion (Social Security Administration 2020d, table VI.G6).

16. Health-care expenditures include all health-related spending, whether for personal care or public health, and whether paid by households, private organizations, or federal, state, and local governments.

17. Several critics have challenged Social Security's actuaries for their failure to incorporate more realistic demographic and economic assumptions. Most of their recommendations would affect long-term forecasts more than near-term forecasts (Kashin, King, and Soneji 2015; Technical Panel on Assumptions and Methods 2015).

18. Patashnik 2000.

19. The relative importance of legislation is a judgment call. My assessment is based on reading the Congressional Research Service's synopses of all 58 laws that affected Social Security from 1935 to 2018 (Breslauer and Morton 2019).

20. Although one party could control the House and the presidency and have a supermajority in the Senate, such single-party dominance is rare, having occurred for fewer than six months in the past four decades.

21. Kingdon 1984.

Chapter 2

1. On the politics of self-maintaining systems, see Patashnik (2008).

2. Arnold 1990.

3. Derthick 1979.

4. Committee on Economic Security 1937, table 30.

5. Committee on Economic Security 1937, 146–48.

6. In 1935, there were 110,000 pensioners from the private sector and 49,000 pensioners from the federal government. Although data for retirees from state and local governments are not available for 1935, I estimate there were about 69,000 pensioners, given that five years later state and local pensioners were 140% of federal pensioners. See Carter et al. 2006, data series Bf848, Bf722, Bf329, Bf328, and Aa139.

7. Schieber and Shoven 1999, 22.

8. The 1934 data show $32 million split among 206,000 beneficiaries (Carter et al. 2006, data series Bf626 and Bf621). Average monthly pensions ranged from $0.69 in North Dakota to $26.08 in Massachusetts (Parker 1935, 322). For comparison, the average monthly wage for manufacturing workers in 1934 was $79 (Carter et al. 2006, data series Ba4362).

9. Amenta 2006.

10. Béland 2005, 74.

11. Schieber and Shoven 1999, 30.

12. Witte 1963, 18.

13. Witte 1963, 74.

14. The political scientist Luther Gulick wrote a memo summarizing the 1941 meeting (Gulick 1941).

15. Jacobs 2010, 108–10.

16. Witte 1963, 93–97; Derthick 1979, 219–22.

17. Witte 1963, 93.

18. Witte 1963, 78–79, 95.

19. Carter et al. 2006, data series Bf621 and Bf626. The national program provided large matching grants to encourage the original 28 states to expand their programs and to prompt other states to create comparable programs. By late 1938, all 48 states had established old-age assistance programs and were receiving matching grants (Social Security Board 1940, 15).

20. Carter et al. 2006, data series Bf395 and Bf621.

21. Derthick 1979, 430.

22. The comparison is for 1938 (Carter et al. 2006, data series Bf493, Bf622, Bf624, and Bf621).

23. Carter et al. 2006, data series Bf493, Bf621, Bf622, Bf624, Ea585, and Ca10.

24. Social Security Administration 1935.

25. On the initial scheme for increasing rates every three years, see Witte (1963, 150).

26. DeWitt, Béland, and Berkowitz 2008, 80.

27. Witte 1963, 152.

28. They projected that by 1980 the reserve fund would be 19 times annual contributions and 12 times annual benefits (DeWitt, Béland, and Berkowitz 2008, 80).

29. Witte 1955; 1963, 93–94, 154–57, 204.

30. Witte 1963, 153. Although some people argue that Southern legislators removed agricultural and domestic workers from the bill for racial reasons, the proximate cause was that lower-level Treasury officials charged with designing a nationwide system for collecting taxes objected based on administrative feasibility. Whether they objected in anticipation of, or in response to, pressure from Southern legislators is not known. But most other countries, including Britain and Canada, excluded agricultural and domestic workers from their initial social insurance programs, on the same administrative grounds. See Davies and Derthick 1997; Béland 2005.

31. Wendt 1938, 10.

32. On political equilibrium, see Heclo (1998). On the incentives for policymakers to preserve, redesign, or dismantle programs, see Patashnik (2008).

33. Gulick 1941.

34. Landon: The Social Security Act "assumes that Americans are irresponsible. It assumes that old-age pensions are necessary because Americans lack the foresight to provide for their old age. I refuse to accept any such judgment of my fellow citizens" (DeWitt, Béland, and Berkowitz 2008, 94–97, quote at 94).

35. In 1964, Senator Barry Goldwater (R-AZ), Republican candidate for president, suggested that Social Security should be voluntary. President Johnson's landslide victory buried that idea, too.

36. Derthick 1979, 232. See also Patashnik 2000; DeWitt, Béland, and Berkowitz 2008, 103–24.

37. DeWitt, Béland, and Berkowitz 2008, 115–24.

38. DeWitt 2007, 53.

39. DeWitt 2007, 58. See also Leff 1988; Zelizer 1997.

40. DeWitt 2007, 52.

41. Quoted in DeWitt 2007, 57.

42. Roosevelt objected to other portions of the 1944 tax bill, too. The House override vote was 299 to 95, the Senate, 72 to 14 (Congressional Quarterly, Inc. 1949).

43. Legislators enacted increases in 1950, 1952, 1954, 1958, 1965, 1967, 1969, 1971, 1972, and twice in 1973 (Derthick 1979, 430–32).

44. The cumulative increase for the 11 benefit adjustments listed in the text was 393%. Between 1940 (when benefits began) and 1974, the consumer price index increased 252% (Carter et al. 2006, data series Cc6).

45. Campbell 2003, fig. 2.6. See also chapter 8 of this book.

46. DeWitt, Béland, and Berkowitz 2008, 527.

47. Derthick 1979, 82.

48. Legislators also inserted an intermediate rate (2.25% in 1957) to smooth the transition from 2.0% in 1954 to 2.5% in 1959 (Social Security Administration 2021a, table 2.A3).

49. Derthick 1979, 223.

50. The average was 0.20 percentage points for the eight old-age insurance steps between 1960 and 1974 and 0.08 percentage points for the four disability insurance steps (Social Security Administration 2021a, table 2.A3).

51. The 1950 Social Security Amendments set tax rates until 1970, the 1954 Amendments until 1975, the 1961 Amendments until 1968, the 1965 Amendments until 1973, and the 1967 Amendments until 1987 (Congressional Quarterly, Inc. 1950, 1954, 1961, 1965, 1967).

52. Arnold 1990, 1998b.

53. Carter et al. 2006, data series Ca6.

54. For a complete list of the various extensions to Social Security's coverage from 1935 to 1998, see Social Security Administration (2021a, table 2.A1).

55. The 75% combined OASDI tax rate for self-employed workers held from 1951 to 1972, before dropping to 72% (1973), 71% (1974), 70% (1978), and 69% (1979). The calculations are mine from data in Social Security Administration (2021a, table 2.A3).

56. Jacobs 2010, 108–10.

57. The ratio of tax-paying workers to benefit-collecting retirees was 42:1 in 1945, 17:1 in 1950, 9:1 in 1955, 5:1 in 1960, and 4:1 in 1965. The current ratio is 2.8 to 1 (Board of Trustees 2020, table IV.B3).

58. On the indexation of benefits as a conservative idea, see Altman and Marmor (2009, 165).

59. The cumulative increase was based on annual increases of 20%, 7%, and 4% (Derthick 1979, 432). On inflation, see Carter et al. (2006, data series Cc6).

60. In addition, no one had imagined that the designers of the automatic indexing scheme in 1972 could have made such an expensive mistake in constructing the index. Although the automatic index treated current retirees fairly, it overcompensated future retirees by including both wage and price inflation.

61. This is a cumulative increase based on individual-year adjustments of 8.0%, 6.4%, and 5.9% in 1975, 1976, and 1977. The next five automatic adjustments were 6.5%, 9.9%, 14.3%, 11.2%, and 7.4% (Board of Trustees 2020, table V.C1).

62. In 1975, 1976, and 1977, the unemployment rate was 8.5%, 7.7%, and 7.0%. Real wage growth was −2.5%, +2.5%, and +1.6% (Schieber and Shoven 1999, 174, 184).

63. Board of Trustees 2020, table VI.A1.

64. Derthick 1979, 381–411.

65. Congressional Quarterly, Inc. 1977.

66. Snee and Ross 1978, table 4.

67. Derthick 1979, 285; Altman 2005, 155; Li 2019a, 3–4.

68. Policymakers also fixed an error in the 1972 law that overcompensated new retirees for inflation.

69. Congressional Quarterly, Inc. 1977, 184–87-H, 204–5-H.

70. Congressional Quarterly, Inc. 1977, 87–91-S.

71. Board of Trustees 1980.

72. Light 1995, 46.

73. For details of the president's proposal, see Svahn and Ross (1983, 47).

74. All three quotations are from Schieber and Shoven (1999, 188).

75. Light 1995, 111.

76. For a complete account of the Social Security Amendments of 1983, see Congressional Quarterly, Inc. (1983), Svahn and Ross (1983), and Light (1995).

77. The taxes paid on Social Security benefits are credited to the Social Security trust fund.

78. Svahn and Ross 1983, 15; Light 1995, 197–200.

79. These estimates are based on actuarial estimates prepared for the House Ways and Means and the Senate Finance Committees (Svahn and Ross 1983; Gregory et al. 2010).

80. The advantaged groups included surviving, divorced, and disabled spouses; aged disabled widows and widowers; and people choosing to delay retirement past their full retirement age (Svahn and Ross 1983).

81. Arnold 2015.

82. Congressional Quarterly, Inc. 1978.

83. Light 1995, 177.

84. Wallach 2019.

85. Safire 2007.

86. For vote totals by party on Social Security legislation, see DeWitt, Béland, and Berkowitz (2008, 527).

87. Jacobs 2011, 175–76.

Chapter 3

1. On how self-interest affects public opinion, see Sears and Funk (1990), Campbell (2003), Kumlin (2007), and Jacobs and Mettler (2018).

2. On the difference between privately oriented and publicly oriented evaluations, see Barry (1965, 12–13).

3. Zaller 1992.

4. McKinley and Frase 1970; Puckett 2009.

5. McKinley and Frase 1970, 356–66, 447–59; Puckett 2009, 59–61.

6. Puckett 2009, 60–61.

7. Social Security Administration 2021a, table 4.B3.

8. The federally subsidized, state-administered old-age assistance program, created by the Social Security Act of 1935, was replaced in 1974 by a federally funded, federally administered program, known as the Supplemental Security Income program (SSI), which provides cash support for nearly 9 million blind, disabled, or aged people who have minimal income. Although the Social Security Administration administers this program, general revenues fund it.

9. Derthick 1979, 273.

10. This section is based on an exhaustive search of the online archive of opinion surveys held by the Roper Center for Public Opinion Research at Cornell University, between 1935 and 1945, for questions that mentioned pensions, old-age insurance, Social Security, or the elderly. Although other surveys asked questions that mentioned Social Security, only three Gallup and two other surveys asked about approval. The rest of this chapter is also based on the Roper Center archive, which contains more than 9,000 questions that mentioned Social Security between 1935 and 2020. For complete details on surveys cited in this book, enter the all-caps source code in each endnote into the "Keyword" section of the iPOLL database at https://ropercenter .cornell.edu/ipoll/.

11. Gallup was inconsistent about reporting nonresponses, so I report results for respondents favoring as a fraction of those who expressed an opinion (USGALLUP.36-053.Q3; USGALLUP. NV2236.R05; USGALLUP.37-65.Q05; all Roper Center).

12. USGALLUP.011236.R01, Roper Center. On four subsequent occasions, Gallup asked whether a respondent "believed in government old-age pensions," without the qualifier "needy." Respondents were strongly supportive, with 91%, 94%, 90%, and 93% supporting pensions. Again, Gallup was inconsistent about reporting nonresponses, so the results are for respondents favoring as a fraction of those who expressed an opinion (USGALLUP.38-130.QAB02A; USGALLUP.022639. RA01A; USGALLUP.112639.RA02A; USGALLUP.080841.RK01A; all Roper Center).

13. USNORC.430211.Q15AB; USNORC.440226.R17; both Roper Center.

14. USGALLUP.012338.R10; USNORC.440226.R18; USGALLUP.434T.QT05BA; USGALLUP.434T.QT05BC; USGALLUP.434T.QT50BD; USGALLUP.434T.QT05BB; all Roper Center.

15. USROPER.RCOM52-060.Q14A, Roper Center.

16. Pollsters seldom repeat questions when agreement is so strong (Baggette, Shapiro, and Jacobs 1995, 420–21).

17. The data for figure 3.5 are from four survey organizations. Michigan's Survey Research Center conducted 2 surveys and Gallup conducted 3 between 1961 and 1976; Trendex conducted 16 from 1978 to 1982; the General Social Survey conducted 22 from 1984 to 2018 (Shapiro and Smith 1985; General Social Survey 2019). In years when an organization conducted multiple surveys, I use the mean.

18. Stimson 1998, 2015.

19. The correlation (r) between public mood and the liberal alternative (i.e., the bottom line in figure 3.5) is 0.004. Annual measures of public mood between 1961 and 2018 are from Stimson (2019).

20. For additional work on public attitudes toward Social Security, see Cook and Barrett (1992); Baggette, Shapiro, and Jacobs (1995); Jacobs and Shapiro (1998); and Cook and Moskowitz (2014).

21. USGALLUP.012338.R08; USGALLUP.012338.R09; USROPER.38-01.Q05; USGALLUP.080941.RK02; all Roper Center.

22. USROPER.780648.Q32; USCBSNYT.012090.R36; USYANK.788161.Q09D; all Roper Center.

23. Although interviewers also asked about state income taxes, I ignored these responses because nine states do not tax wages, including several large states like Texas and Florida. The

numbers quoted in the text, therefore, are the percentage of respondents naming a tax as a fraction of those naming one of the four taxes (Campbell and Morgan 2005, 195).

24. Again, I ignored those who chose state income taxes and adjusted the percentages accordingly (USASFOX.040815.R43, Roper Center).

25. Internal Revenue Service 1940, 35.

26. Joint Committee on Taxation 2019, table 7.

27. Williamson 2017, 52–59, 83, 252 (quote at 58).

28. Himelfarb 1995.

Chapter 4

1. See, for example, Friedman (1962), Ferrara (1980), and Tanner (2004).

2. See, for example, Graetz and Mashaw (1999); Marmor, Mashaw, and Pakutka (2014); and Altman (2018).

3. Schieber 2012.

4. Employee Benefits Security Administration 2021, table E7.

5. Employee Benefits Security Administration 2021, table E7.

6. The total market capitalization of the S&P 500 Index was $31.7 trillion on December 31, 2020.

7. On how the federal government shaped private sector pensions, see Congressional Budget Office (1987), Hacker (2002), Patashnik (2008), and Schieber (2012).

8. In 1975, there were 27 million active participants in private sector defined benefit plans, compared with 11 million in defined contribution plans. By 1984, active participants were roughly equal (30 million each). In 2018, there were 13 million in defined benefit plans and 83 million in defined contribution plans (Employee Benefits Security Administration 2021, table E7).

9. Most union workers have access to defined benefit plans, where employers pay most costs, whereas most nonunion workers have access only to defined contribution plans, where workers pay most costs. Among private sector workers, 64% of union workers have access to defined benefit plans, compared with 11% of nonunion workers (Bureau of Labor Statistics 2020, table 2PIW).

10. Internal Revenue Service 2020, table 1.

11. Among all households, 6% have IRA assets only, 27% have employer-sponsored plans only, 30% have both, and 37% have neither (Investment Company Institute 2019, 3). See Chen and Munnell (2017) for similar data from a different source.

12. Internal Revenue Service 2020, table 1.

13. By a different accounting, one that considers when retirees make taxable withdrawals, the present value of these subsidies was $145 billion in 2019. For both estimates, see Department of the Treasury (2020, tables 2b and 4, lines 141–45).

14. Employee Benefits Security Administration, 2021, table E13.

15. For introductions to the privatization debate, see Arnold, Graetz, and Munnell (1998); Aaron and Shoven (1999); and Diamond (1999).

16. See, for example, Ferrara (1980) and Beach (1998).

17. Geanakoplos, Mitchell, and Zeldes 1998; Diamond 1999, 17.

18. The real internal rate of return controls for expected inflation. Other measures include the payback period, the lifetime transfer, and the benefit/tax ratio (Leimer 1995).

19. The collective real internal rate of return for all cohorts born prior to 1876 was 75% (Leimer 1994, 14).

20. The 1939 benefit formula awarded benefits based on 40% of the first $50 in average monthly wages and 10% of the next $200, with the total increased by 1% for each tax-paying year. So, the 1940 retiree would have received $20.00 plus $5.00 plus $0.75, and the 1947 retiree $20.00 plus $5.00 plus $2.50. By comparison, the worker and his employer would have paid $24 annually in taxes (2% of $1,200), or $72 for the three-year worker and $240 for the ten-year worker. The 1939 formula was more generous than the 1935 formula, which it replaced (Munnell 1977, tables A5 and A12). Life expectancy in 1940 is from Board of Trustees (2020, table V.A5).

21. Aaron and Shoven 1999, 23–24.

22. Diamond and Orszag 2005, 4.

23. On the legacy debt, see Geanakoplos, Mitchell, and Zeldes (1998, 144–48); Diamond and Orszag (2005, 4–7); and Leimer (2016).

24. See, for example, Feldstein (1974) and Munnell (1977).

25. Diamond 1999, 58–66.

26. The adjustment is for long-term changes in wages, not prices. On alternative ways to estimate replacement rates, see Biggs and Springstead (2008) and Goss et al. (2014).

27. Social Security Administration 2021a, tables 2.A21 and 2.A22.

28. Pechman, Aaron, and Taussig 1968, 33–34; Munnell 1977, 5–8; Derthick 1979, 213–27.

29. Ferrara 1980, 351–97.

30. Among workers in private industry, 64% have access to defined contribution plans and 47% participate in those plans, for a take-up rate of 74% (Bureau of Labor Statistics 2020, table 2PIW). These results differ slightly from those reported in table 4.2, which include both defined benefit and defined contribution plans, where the take-up rate is 76%.

31. Vanguard 2019, fig. 114.

32. McLean and Elkind 2004, 401. It was not just Enron. Among the 20 largest defined contribution plans in 2001, the average share of plan assets in the company's own stock was 44%. At Proctor & Gamble, it was 93%; General Electric, 68%; BellSouth, 66%; and Exxon-Mobil, 64%. Only 4 of the 20 firms reported less than 20% of plan assets in company stock (Poterba 2003, 399).

33. Vanguard 2019, fig. 71.

34. See Nesbitt 1995; Agnew, Balduzzi, and Sundén 2003; Benartzi and Thaler 2007; Tang et al. 2010; Clark, Lusardi, and Mitchell 2015; Bekaert et al. 2017.

35. Finkelstein and Poterba 2004; Hu and Scott 2007; Pashchenko 2013.

36. On alternative ways to pay benefits from individual accounts, see Apfel and Graetz (2005, 45–142).

37. Aaron and Shoven 1999, 60–68.

38. The S&P 500 Index closed at 677 on March 9, 2009, compared with 1,273 on March 10, 2008, and 1,146 on March 10, 2010.

39. Aaron and Shoven 1999, 99–104; Diamond and Orszag 2005, 214–16.

40. Aaron and Shoven 1999, 104–8; Diamond 1999.

41. For example, a bill introduced by Paul Ryan in 2010 would index the full retirement age (FRA) to maintain a constant ratio of expected retirement years (life expectancy at FRA) to potential work years (FRA minus 20). See Social Security Administration 2020a, provision C1.3.

42. Eaton 1989; Patashnik 2000, 88–90; Breslauer and Morton 2019, 67.

Chapter 5

1. Board of Trustees 2020.

2. Social Security reached milestones as follows. Benefits first exceeded tax revenue in 2010. Benefits first exceeded total revenue (tax revenue plus interest) in 2021 (see figure 1.1). Trust fund redemptions began that year and will end in 2034.

3. The Office of the Chief Actuary publishes other measures that capture the program's sustainability, especially near the end of the 75-year period. One helpful measure of sustainability requires that the trust fund remain positive throughout the projection period and that the trust fund be stable or rising as a percentage of the annual cost of the program in the 75th year (Goss 2010, 118).

4. The Congressional Budget Office (CBO) also estimates Social Security's revenues and benefits as part of its long-term budget projections. Although the CBO does not regularly evaluate Social Security solvency plans, it could. In addition, experts at the Urban Institute, a Washington think tank, have developed a model for forecasting Social Security's revenues and benefits and for evaluating solvency plans (see chapter 10).

5. This is a made-up example. The actual difference would depend on the details of each bill.

6. Congress later postponed some of these increases, so they took place later than originally scheduled.

7. My counts are for the combined OASI and DI taxes, not including changes in how the combined rate was apportioned between the programs (Social Security Administration 2021a, table 2.A3). The 1977 plan added six rate increases. The 1983 plan accelerated several of those increases and inserted an additional step to smooth out the changes (Snee and Ross 1978; Svahn and Ross 1983).

8. Notice that this rate increase—from a combined worker/employer rate of 12.4% to one of 15.8%—is higher than the one quoted in the previous section (to 15.6%). One reason is that this calculation assumes implementation in 2021, not 2020, thus removing one balanced year (2020) and adding one unbalanced year (2096). A second is that the actuaries evaluate solvency proposals by requiring that the trust fund maintain a 1-year reserve throughout the 75-year estimation period (Board of Trustees 2020, 5).

9. These four examples are from Social Security Administration (2020a, provisions E1.1, E1.9, E1.4, and E1.10). These estimates—as well as estimates for other similarly numbered provisions throughout this book—are based on the intermediate assumptions in the 2020 Trustees Report (Board of Trustees 2020). The actuaries update these estimates annually, using the same numbering scheme, so that readers can quickly research for subsequent years how effective each provision would be in closing the actuarial deficit.

10. Social Security Administration 2020a, provisions E2.1, E2.2, E2.3, E3.1, and E3.2.

11. These two provisions were part of the Affordable Care Act.

12. Social Security Administration 2020a, provision F6.

13. Social Security Administration 2020a, provisions F3 and F4.

14. Social Security Administration 2020a, provision F1.

15. Li 2019c.

16. Diamond and Orszag 2005, 88–90.

17. Technically, it is the year for which administrators calculate a worker's *primary insurance amount*. This is a foundational number used to calculate retirement, spousal, family, and survivor benefits.

18. Diamond and Orszag 2005, 21.

19. Board of Trustees 2020, table V.C3.

20. Social Security Administration 2020a, provisions C2.5 and C1.2.

21. The comparisons are for people born in 1930 and 1960 (National Academies of Sciences 2015, 52). See also Isaacs and Choudhury (2017), for a discussion of other studies on life expectancy by income, and Case and Deaton (2020), for a discussion of recent declines in life expectancy among middle-aged Whites without college degrees.

22. National Academies of Sciences 2015, 65–140.

23. The current index is the Consumer Price Index for Urban Wage Earners. The proposed index is the Chained Consumer Price Index for All Urban Consumers. The Bureau of Labor Statistics maintains both indexes. On the differences between various price indexes, see Burdick and Fisher (2007) and Whittaker (2015).

24. Social Security Administration 2020a, provisions A3 and A2.

25. Social Security Administration 2020a, provisions B1.2 and B4.1.

26. Burdick and Fisher 2007; Whittaker 2015.

27. Social Security Administration 2020a, provision A6.

Chapter 6

1. There were no clear patterns in the 1940 and 1944 platforms. All but one of the 38 Democratic and Republican platforms between 1948 and 2020 discussed Social Security. Only the 1992 Democratic platform did not (Woolley and Peters 2020a).

2. The 1996 claim was partly an effort to boost the presidential candidacy of Senator Bob Dole (R-KS), who played a central role in the 1983 compromise, both as member of the Greenspan Commission and as chair of the Senate Finance Committee.

3. The 2016 Republican Platform (Woolley and Peters 2020a).

4. The 2016 Democratic Party Platform (Woolley and Peters 2020a).

5. The 2020 Democratic Party Platform (Woolley and Peters 2020a).

6. The 1980 Republican Platform (Woolley and Peters 2020a).

7. *New York Times* 1980, B18.

8. Trump 2020.

9. The 1999 State of the Union Address (Woolley and Peters 2020b).

10. AARP staff performed what the organization called "extensive research" on all major-party candidates for the House and Senate in 2014. The staff found relevant statements on Social Security for (a) 367 of 392 House members seeking reelection, (b) 27 of 28 senators seeking reelection, and (c) 278 candidates who were either challenging incumbents or running for open seats (AARP 2014).

11. AARP presented opposing candidates' statements in parallel columns. For some candidates, the flyers stated, "AARP did extensive research but was unable to find any public statement on this issue by July 11, 2014." The organization published up to 100 words from each candidate and included hyperlinks to the original sources (AARP 2014).

12. I downloaded the 471 four-page flyers—435 House contests, 36 Senate contests—from the AARP website (www.aarop.org/yourvote) on October 31, 2014. Since the flyers are no longer publicly available, I posted them on my website (https://scholar.princeton.edu/arnold/social-security), so that other scholars can use them. Although my analysis is based on Social Security statements from 367 House incumbents running for reelection, I posted the complete collection of flyers.

13. Martha Roby (AL 2). This and subsequent citations to the AARP collection refer to the name of the House member running for reelection and the state and district number for the flyer that contains the member's statement (AARP 2014).

14. See, for example, Rob Bishop (UT 1), Dave Reichert (WA 8), Kevin Yoder (KS 3).

15. John Boehner (OH 8), Kevin Cramer (ND 1), Scott Garrett (NJ 5), Andy Harris (MD 1), Mark Meadows (NC 11), Luke Messer (IN 6), John Shimkus (IL 15).

16. John Boehner (OH 8).

17. Mark Meadows (NC 11), John Shimkus (IL 15).

18. Ron DeSantis (FL 6), Trent Franks (AZ 8), Thomas Massie (KY 4).

19. Jim Costa (CA 16), Jared Huffman (CA 2).

20. Joaquin Castro (TX 20), Mike Doyle (PA 14), Bill Foster (IL 11), Jim Langevin (RI 2), Kyrsten Sinema (AZ 9).

21. Dan Benishek (MI 1) and Chuck Fleischman (TN 3).

22. John Fleming (LA 4).

23. Campbell and Morgan 2005; Teles and Derthick 2009.

24. Derthick 1979, 17–37, 158–82.

25. Pechman, Aaron, and Taussig 1968; Britain 1972.

26. Teles and Derthick 2009.

27. Ferrara 1980.

28. Derthick 1979, 110–31.

29. Derthick 1979, 132, 349.

30. Day 2017.

31. Information on AARP's lobbyists and lobbying expenditures is from OpenSecrets.org.

32. Information on NFIB's lobbyists is from OpenSecrets.org.

33. National Federation of Independent Business 2021.

34. Total expenditures are from the 2017 IRS Form 990 for each organization (available from GuideStar.org).

35. On its website (2021), Americans for Tax Reform claims 86% of House Republicans and 88% of Senate Republicans have signed the pledge. The most recent published list of signatories (2014) lists 93% of House Republicans and 87% of Senate Republicans as signatories.

36. According to its 2017 IRS Form 990 (available from GuideStar.org), ATR spent $1.6 million on its pledge campaign, out of a total budget of $6.1 million. Lobbying expenses that year were $660,000 (OpenSecrets.org).

37. Crosson, Furnas, and Lorenz 2020.

38. Derthick 1979, 89–109.

39. Derthick 1979, 102.

40. For a chronological list of advisory councils, see Social Security Administration 2001.

41. On the appointment of the 13 members, see Laursen (2012, 322–26).

42. Arnold 1998a; Schieber and Shoven 1999.

43. Arnold 1998a; Teles and Derthick 2009.

44. Congress eventually replaced the advisory councils with a permanent bipartisan Social Security Advisory Board, which has a narrower mission.

45. For an excellent guide to recent literature on party polarization, see McCarty (2019).

46. McCarty 2019, 119–20; Bonica 2014.

47. Hertel-Fernandez, Skocpol, and Sclar 2018; Mayer 2017.

Chapter 7

1. Zaller 1992.

2. Egan and Mullin 2017.

3. The GSS surveys in figure 7.1 also appear in the longer time series in figure 3.6.

4. ANES asked the question nine times from 1984 to 2002, but only three times since (2004, 2012, 2016). See American National Election Studies 2018, 374.

5. The rest of the 1984 figure would include big cities (21 points), space (18), education (16), foreign aid (14), law enforcement (9), drug rehabilitation (8), parks (7), bridges/highways (4), drug addiction (3), mass transit (2), and crime (2). The GSS did not ask questions on childcare, science, or alternative energy in 1984.

6. The R^2 for the linear trend line is .82 for defense, .79 for assistance to Blacks, .78 for welfare, .71 for the environment, .35 for health, and .06 for Social Security.

7. For simplicity, figure 7.5 includes full-time workers (52% of respondents), part-time workers (12%), and retirees (13%), but excludes those who are unemployed (3%), temporarily not working (2%), keeping house (13%), in school (4%), or doing something else (2%). Other than clutter, nothing distinctive emerges by including the omitted categories.

8. For workers, the net preference for spending more on Social Security averaged 50 points from 1984 to 2018. For retirees, it averaged 45 points.

9. During the entire period, the General Social Survey asked six versions of the family income question (1984–85; 1986–90; 1991–96; 1998–2004; 2006–14; 2016–18). Within each period, I sorted respondents by income category and then assigned cut points that best divided respondents into the first three deciles, the middle three deciles, the next three deciles, and the top decile. In all years, the so-called top decile was drawn exclusively from the top income category within the GSS coding scheme, so it was impossible to focus on smaller segments within the well-off group.

10. Median household wealth was $7.5 million (Page, Bartels, and Seawright 2013, 53).

11. Among the wealthy, the net preference for spending was positive in only three policy areas (infrastructure, science, education) and negative in nine others (job programs, environmental protection, homeland security, health care, food stamps, Social Security, defense, foreign aid, farm subsidies). Among the general population, the net preference was positive for eight, negative for one, and not asked for three others (Page, Bartels, and Seawright 2013, 56).

12. Worth noting is that we have only one study with a small sample to examine the views of the very wealthy, whereas 22 surveys with large national samples support the broader conclusion. The study of Chicago wealth holders interviewed 83 respondents; the 22 national surveys interviewed 49,235.

13. I estimated two logistic regression models, one for 1984 to 2018 (n = 48,882) and one for 2018 (n = 2,248). The dependent variable was coded 1 for respondents who supported more spending on Social Security and 0 otherwise. The other variables were exact chronological age and five dummy variables for working, Republican, and three of the four income groups. I found nothing in the multivariate analysis to challenge the bivariate findings in figures 7.2, 7.5, 7.6, and 7.7.

14. These results are from the published accounts of the 25 annual surveys. Although the number of issues varied year to year, with a median of 21, and a range of 12 to 23, Social Security always made the list. See Pew Research Center (2020) for the results from 1997 to 2020 and Pew Research Center (2021) for the 2021 results.

15. There is a slight decline for those 70 and over (to 75%), perhaps because the oldest retirees are less worried about solvency than the youngest ones. All results in this paragraph are from the 2018 survey because Pew does not release full data sets immediately (Pew Research Center 2018).

16. The results for the five income groups are roughly linear, with 77% of those earning less than $20K, 65% of those earning between $20K and $40K, 72% of those earning between $40K and $75K, 62% of those earning between $75K and $150K, and 60% of those earning over $150K identifying Social Security as a top priority. Party polarization in the 2018 survey was zero—68% of Democrats and 68% of Republicans identified Social Security as a top priority.

17. The Opinion Research Corporation conducted all five polls (USORC.54SEP.R13M; USORC.55SEP.R23; USORC.56OCT.R19; USORC.57MAR.R11; USORC.57SEP.R15; all Roper Center).

18. I searched the Roper Center's archive and found 24 questions mentioning Social Security and these five presidents. None asked respondents to evaluate presidential performance.

19. *Time*/Yankelovich conducted the survey in October 1980 (USYANK.808605.Q11AD, Roper Center).

20. During this period, 14 Harris polls asked respondents to rate him, while 8 ABC polls asked whether they approved of how he was dealing with the financial problems of Social Security. I have combined (a) excellent and pretty good from the first set with approved from the second, and (b) fair and poor from the first set with disapproved from the second. All polls are available from the Roper Center.

21. Gordon Black/*USA Today* conducted the survey in September 1987 (USGBUSA.873039. Q43, Roper Center).

22. ABC News conducted the three surveys between October 28 and November 1 (USABC.103100.R07; USABC.2000ELETRACKO29.Q020D; USABC.2000ELETRACKO30. Q020D; all Roper Center).

23. In 12 ABC News/*Washington Post* polls between May 31, 2001, and April 15, 2004, approval averaged 45% and disapproval averaged 43% (USABCWP.060401.R02H; USAB-CWP.080101.R02G; USABCWP.091001.R02G; USABCWP.012802.R02F; USABCWP.071802A. R14H; USABCWP.092702.R03D; USABCWP.121702.R02E; USABCWP.050103.R02D; USAB-CWP.091403.R002D; USABCWP.110203.R002D; USABCWP.030804.R02D; USAB-CWP.041904.R02D; all Roper Center).

24. In six ABC News/*Washington Post* polls between December 16, 2004, and August 25, 2005, approval averaged 36% and disapproval averaged 57% (USABCWP.122004.R02D;

USABCWP.011705.R02C; USABCWP.031405.R02A; USABCWP.042505A.R02A; USAB-CWP.060705.R02A; USABCWP.083005.R02D; all Roper Center).

25. USABCWP.042505A.R02A.

26. In the June ABC/*Washington Post* poll, 29% chose Clinton, 26% Bush, and 25% Perot (USABCWP.060892.R23O, Roper Center).

27. USABC.5514.Q010D, Roper Center.

28. Egan 2013.

29. ABC/*Washington Post* and *Time*/CNN/Yankelovich conducted the seven polls between March 1995 and January 1999 (USABCWP.5598.Q011D; USABCWP.072395.R11D; USABCWP.95SP28.R07D; USWASHP.5852.Q006D; USYANKP.050997.R04D; USY-ANKP.041098.R05B; USYANKP.012299.R09A; all Roper Center).

30. The Associated Press, NBC/*Wall Street Journal*, and CNN conducted the six polls between June and September 2008 (USAP.062808.R20E; USNBCWSJ.08AUG.R22I; USORC.082708.R22H; USORC.090308.R13G; USAP.091908.R19E; USORC.090808A.R10F; all Roper Center).

31. ABC/*Washington Post* and the Associated Press conducted the two polls in October 2008 (USABCWP.20081076.Q009E; USAP.102108.R06C; both Roper Center).

32. Politico, Pew, and ABC/*Washington Post* conducted the three polls in late 2010 and early 2011 (USTARR.10BATT6.R22BB; USPSRA.111110.R60F; USABCWP.20111121.Q004C; all Roper Center).

33. Politico conducted the two polls in May and August 2011 (USTARR.11BATT1.R17B; USTARR.11BATT2.R40B; both Roper Center).

34. The question is from NBC/*Wall Street Journal*, the pollster that most regularly asks a question on this subject. Other pollsters use variants of this question.

35. I searched the Roper Center's archive for any question mentioning Social Security and Democrats/Democratic between January 1, 1945, and December 31, 2018, and then examined the results for questions like the NBC/*Wall Street Journal* question (search conducted July 11, 2019). I did not include questions that focused on the parties dealing with specific aspects of Social Security. Figure 7.10 contains the results from 62 polls, including 29 from NBC/*Wall Street Journal*, 16 from CBS/*New York Times*, 6 from the Associated Press, 5 from ABC/*Washington Post*, and 1 each from Harris, Kaiser, *Los Angeles Times*, *Los Angeles Times*/Bloomberg, *Washington Post*, and the Winston Group. (A subsequent search of the archive on November 18, 2020, found no additional surveys on this subject.)

36. On the Democratic advantage on Social Security, see Egan (2013, 153–55).

37. The Democratic advantage nearly disappeared in late 1994 and late 2010, just before Republicans recaptured control of the House. These polls may reflect overall dissatisfaction with Democrats, rather than anything specific about Social Security.

38. Egan 2013.

39. A search of the Roper Center archive found 121 questions that mentioned AARP between January 1, 2000, and May 1, 2020. Although some surveys were sponsored by AARP, though administered by established firms, the results from the sponsored surveys did not diverge from the findings in the independent surveys.

40. Roper conducted the survey in December 2004 for AARP (USAARP.05SOCSEC.R13; USAARP.05SOCSEC.R15; USAARP.05SOCSEC.R12; all Roper Center).

41. Gallup conducted the poll in December 2003 (USGALLUP.03DEC05.R33, Roper Center).

42. Gallup conducted the poll in December 2003 (USGALLUP.03DEC05.R34, Roper Center).

43. Tesler 2015, 808.

44. See figures 7.2, 7.10, and 11.4.

Chapter 8

1. Median ages for beneficiaries are calculated with data from December 2019 (Social Security Administration 2021a, tables 5.A1.1–5.A1.8).

2. Social Security Administration 2021a, table 5.A1.2.

3. The percentage distribution of children by age in table 8.1 is calculated from 2019 data and then used to estimate the numerical distribution for 2021 data.

4. The small blips at ages 18 and 19 are for the adult children of deceased, disabled, and retired participants who are still attending school during their final 14 months of benefit eligibility. The odd blips for nonbeneficiaries in their early seventies reflect problems comparing December 2018 administrative records by age with July 2018 population projections by age.

5. The unisex percentages in the text are the mean for women and men. In 2018, women began collecting benefits at ages 62 (37%), 63 (8%), 64 (8%), 65 (12%), 66 (17%), 67 to 69 (10%), and 70 or later (8%). The corresponding percentages for men are 33, 7, 7, 13, 23, 12, and 5 (Social Security Administration 2019a, table 6.B5). Since those who collect disability benefits automatically switch to retirement benefits at their full retirement age, I have removed disabled beneficiaries from these calculations. To do otherwise would make the full retirement age seem more popular than it is (Munnell and Chen 2015).

6. Board of Trustees 2020, table V.A5.

7. A longitudinal study, which followed the 1996 cohort of disability awardees for ten years, found that, although 28% of disabled workers returned to work at least part-time and earned at least $1,000 during the decade, only 4% worked regularly enough to leave the disability rolls (Liu and Stapleton 2011).

8. Among the 877,000 workers who exited the disability rolls in 2018, 58% transitioned to retirement benefits at age 66 (then the full retirement age), 28% died, and 13% failed to meet medical standards, forcing them off the disability roll even if they did not find a job (Social Security Administration 2019a, table 6.F2).

9. For consistency, I define adults as 18 or older, even though the voting age was 21 in most states until 1971.

10. The peaks at each end ($< \$3,600$ and $> \$32,100$) are meaningless. They are an incidental consequence of officials creating too few categories to capture the distribution at the two tails.

11. The example is for someone who was born on January 1, 1953, and retired on January 1, 2019. (The full retirement age was 66 for someone born on that date.) I constructed a 45-year earnings profile for this hypothetical worker by first multiplying each year's federal minimum wage by 2080 (i.e., 40 hours $\times$ 52 weeks) from 1974 to 2018, then entering annual earnings into the online benefit calculator (Social Security Administration 2019b), and finally asking for a benefit calculation in 2019 dollars. The benefit calculator automatically chooses the 35 best years

(inflation adjusted), which means, in this case, it selected those years when the real minimum wage was highest.

12. The estimate for a maximum-taxable-wage earner was made by the Office of the Chief Actuary (Social Security Administration 2019d, table C). Although nearly 6% of workers earn at least the maximum taxable limit in a typical year, few accomplish this feat in each of 35 years.

13. For an excellent study that compares the accuracy of individual-level data from the *Current Population Survey* (CPS), the *Health and Retirement Study* (HRS), the *Panel Survey of Income Dynamics* (PSID), the *Survey of Consumer Finances* (SCF), and the *Survey of Income and Program Participation* (SIPP) with aggregate data from the Internal Revenue Service and the Social Security Administration, see Chen, Munnell, and Sanzenbacher (2018).

14. In 2016, there were 3.3 million workers aged 72 or older, with median earnings of $10,584, compared with a 2018 total population in that age group of 28.9 million (Social Security Administration 2019a, tables 4.B5 and 4.B6; Census Bureau 2019a).

15. In 2018, there were 2.3 million SSI beneficiaries aged 65 or older, compared with a 2018 total population in that age group of 52.4 million (Social Security Administration 2019a, table 7. A1; Census Bureau 2019a).

16. Chen, Munnell, and Sanzenbacher (2018) performed these calculations for four of the five federal surveys on income and assets (HRS, PSID, SCF, and SIPP). All four surveys indicated that retirees in the lowest three quintiles were withdrawing a bit too much (between 4% and 16% too much, with a mean of 8%), whereas retirees in the highest quintile were withdrawing, on average, 78% of what an appropriate annuity would pay. My calculations are from the authors' online spreadsheets. Note that the quintiles in their study are for net worth, not net income.

17. Arnold 1990, 44–51.

18. About 70% of tax filers (individuals, couples, etc.) in 2016 paid taxes on at least some Social Security benefits. Nearly everyone with adjusted gross incomes above $25K paid taxes on some portion of their benefits, with those between $25K and $40K paying taxes on 24% of benefits, those between $40K and $75K paying taxes on 64% of benefits, and those above $75K paying taxes on 84% of benefits. The calculations are mine, based on Internal Revenue Service (2018, table 1.4, cols. 69–72).

19. The actuaries estimated the deficit reductions for the first two provisions (Social Security Administration 2020a, provisions E1.1 and E2.1). My estimate for the third is based on 47% of E1.1 (because raising the tax rate to 7.0% raises 47% as much revenue as raising it to 7.9%) and 45% of E2.1 (calculated from the distributional data in my table 10.6), the latter increased by 13% because of the higher tax rate.

20. The counts and percentages are for 2018, the most recent year with accurate tax data (Social Security Administration 2021a, tables 4.B2 and 4.B4).

21. Li 2019a, 7.

22. Social Security Administration 2020c.

23. For previous research on age and turnout, see Wolfinger and Rosenstone (1980, 37–60); Rosenstone and Hansen (1993, 136–41); Campbell (2003, 38–92); Schlozman, Verba, and Brady (2012, 199–231); Leighley and Nagler (2014, 72–76).

24. The x axis in figure 8.5 ends at age 79 because the Census Bureau no longer releases voting data by exact age higher than 79. The box in figure 8.5 contains grouped data (from the same source) for older respondents.

25. Audit studies, which compare citizens' reported voting with official records, show that senior citizens are less likely to lie about voting than other age groups, so the actual difference between turnout for the young and turnout for the old is probably greater (Campbell 2003, 28).

26. The effects of age on turnout during presidential elections resemble those for midterm elections. In general, voter turnout is highest in presidential years, next highest in midterm years, and lowest in congressional primaries. Since senators and House members face threats in all three venues, I focus on the middle category.

27. On life-cycle, period, and cohort effects, see Prior (2019, 108–11).

28. Turnout in each cohort's first election, highlighted with black circles, was 17% (1960s), 20% (1970s), 11% (1980s), and 18% (1990s).

29. ANES collected information about campaign contributions for all 17 presidential years from 1952 to 2016, but for only 10 midterm years from 1962 to 2002. Campbell (2003, 31) analyzed both time series through 2000, but found no major differences between contributions by age in midterm and presidential years.

30. Campbell 2003, 28–33; Schlozman, Verba, and Brady 2012, 212–13.

31. Campbell 2003.

32. On how new policies first create new beneficiaries and then affect politics itself, see the literature on policy feedback (Pierson 1994; Mettler 2005; Campbell 2012; Jacobs and Mettler 2018).

33. Williamson 2017, 58–59.

34. Hughes 2017.

Chapter 9

1. Although a 21% tax increase in 2034 would prevent a 21% benefit cut that year, a larger increase would be required to achieve long-term solvency. For example, a 27% tax increase would be required in 2021 to achieve solvency over the next 75 years (Social Security Administration 2020a, provision E1.1).

2. Kingdon 1989, 265–74.

3. Mayhew 1974; Arnold 1990.

4. Ambar 2017, 83.

5. This entire section draws from Arnold (1990). Indeed, most arguments in this chapter have roots in that book, which is a theoretical analysis of how legislators make policy decisions.

6. The mean is 22.6, the standard deviation 4.9, and the median 23.0.

7. The excluded groups—unemployed workers, college students, full-time homemakers— are small, temporary, or both.

8. Social Security Administration, 2020a, provision E2.1.

9. The comparison is not perfect because households differ in their composition. A $200,000 household with two adults earning $100,000 each is below the Social Security wage base for both workers, while a similar household with one worker is well above the wage base. The $200K level screens out some people who should be in, and screens in some people who should be out, but the errors should cancel out (unless household composition varies widely by district).

10. The mean of the overall distribution is 6.3, the standard deviation 4.8, and the median 4.7.

11. The 80 high-income districts are from the right tail of figure 9.2. In Pennsylvania, one cannot match 2016 income data by congressional district with election returns from 2018 because the state redrew the districts just prior to the election. For the 18 Pennsylvania districts, I coded party according to the representatives elected in 2016. Three of these districts, which elected Republicans in 2016, were among the 80 high-income districts.

12. Given that I am comparing households (contributors) to individuals (beneficiaries), I first calculate the ratio of high-income households to total households, then calculate the ratio of adult beneficiaries to adult residents, and finally calculate the ratio of the former to the latter. In 15 districts, the final ratio is greater than 1.0 (ranging from 1.03 to 1.82, with a median of 1.32). The 15 districts are California 12 (San Francisco), 14 (SF Peninsula), 15 (East Bay), 17 (San Jose), 18 (Silicon Valley), 19 (San Jose), 33 (Los Angeles), 45 (Orange County); Connecticut 4 (Stamford); New Jersey 7 (Somerset); New York 10 (Manhattan), 12 (Manhattan); and Virginia 8 (Alexandria), 10 (Loudon), and 11 (Fairfax).

13. Stimson 2015, xv–xx.

14. Mayhew 1974, 126–27.

15. These arguments are from Arnold (1990, 47–51).

16. Tax Policy Center 2018, table T18-0140.

17. Mayhew 1974, 69–73.

Chapter 10

1. Although I searched for surveys between 2012 and 2019, I found no surveys that asked appropriate questions about incremental solutions after 2016.

2. Program for Public Consultation 2013a, b; 2016a, b.

3. Tucker, Reno, and Bethell 2012; Walker, Reno, and Bethell 2014.

4. The sources for table 10.1 include six surveys from the Roper Center: USASFOX.042513. R34; USCNBC.12ECON4.R21E; USGREEN.13DCJAN.R052; USNBCWSJ.120214.R21N; USSELZER.121212B.R02G; USTARR.12BATT6.R32.

5. Worth noting is that people did not react differently if they received lots of information and arguments about raising the retirement age or if they heard nothing.

6. The sources for table 10.2 include two surveys from the Roper Center: USGREEN.13DCJAN.R048; USMARIST.120913M.R07.

7. The five income categories with percentage opposing were $30K or less (10%), $30K to $50K (7%), $50K to $75K (8%), $75K to $100K (7%), and $100K or more (10%). See Tucker, Reno, and Bethell 2012, 19.

8. The proposal was for raising the payroll tax from 6.2% to 7.2 % over 20 years. The five income categories with percentage opposing were $30K or less (13%), $30K to $50K (8%), $50K to $75K (11%), $75K to $100K (10%), and $100K or more (11%). See Tucker, Reno, and Bethell 2012, 19.

9. The first question is from Walker, Reno, and Bethell (2014, Q43). The second is from Program for Public Consultation (PPC) (2016a, Q22c). The reductions in the Social Security shortfall differ slightly (49% vs. 52%) because the actuaries were estimating them in different years. NASI used a slightly different question in 2012 (Tucker, Reno, and Bethell 2012, Q31). PPC used an identical question in 2013 (PPC 2013a, Q22c).

10. The careful reader will notice an error in how PPC calculated the tax increase. Those earning $32,000 a year would actually see their monthly payroll tax go up by $27, from $165 to $192, not by $32. The organization's first two questions, which asked about "a median full-time worker earning about $39,000 a year," calculated the tax increases correctly for raising the rate to 6.6% and 6.9%. The third question, however, mentions a "person earning $32,000 a year," but calculated the tax increase for a worker earning $39,000. Presumably, PPC intended to use $39,000 in all three questions. The error occurs in both the 2013 and 2016 surveys.

11. These results are for the NASI 2014 and PPC 2016 surveys only. The results in table 10.3 are the mean of the NASI 2012 and 2014 surveys and the PPC 2013 and 2016 surveys.

12. The surveys cited are USMARIST.031213M.R14, USGALLUP.081315.R37, and USAARP.081415.R06K (Roper Center), and Walker, Reno, and Bethell (2014, 13).

13. Researchers asked the two questions in random order (Walker, Reno, and Bethell 2014, 11, 12, 47).

14. Between 2010 and 2020, legislators submitted 81 plans to the Chief Actuary for scoring. I read the 81 actuarial reports to identify which plans met my standard of reducing the 75-year actuarial deficit by at least 75%. In addition to these 20 plans, 9 plans would have reduced the long-term deficit by 50% to 74%. Most other plans were narrow (e.g., altering benefits for government workers) or involved calculating the effects of some other bill (say immigration reform) on Social Security's revenues and benefits (Social Security Administration 2020b).

15. All eight precursors also met my standard of closing at least three-quarters of the 75-year actuarial deficit.

16. I exclude from these counts cosponsorships by nonvoting delegates.

17. Exactly 1 of the 263 cosponsors in table 10.4 crossed party lines. Representative Jim Cooper (D-TN) cosponsored Ribble's bill, as did 5 Republicans.

18. The actuaries scored the 2019 Larson bill twice, first in January, using assumptions from the 2018 Trustees Report, and again in September, using assumptions from the 2019 Report. Tables 10.4 and 10.5 use the first scoring so that it compares directly with the Sanders bill.

19. For each provision, the actuaries estimate how much it would change the projected long-range actuarial balance, expressed as a percentage of taxable payroll. The percentages reported in table 10.5 are those estimates divided by the long-range actuarial imbalance, which was −2.84% of taxable payroll in the 2018 Trustees Report.

20. Larson would provide some benefit credits for the newly taxed wages. Sanders would not.

21. My method for constructing this table was the same as for table 10.5, except that the denominator was −2.68% for the Ribble plan and −2.66% for the Johnson plan, which were based on the 2015 and 2016 Trustees Reports.

22. Ribble would provide some benefit credits for the newly taxed wages.

23. Privatizers (1 sponsor and 15 cosponsors); benefit cutters (6 sponsors and 8 cosponsors).

24. Using NOMINATE, a standard measure of ideology based on floor votes, where smaller scores are more liberal, the mean scores for these three groups are as follows: cosponsored the Sanders/DeFazio bill, −0.46; cosponsored the Larson bill, −0.39; and cosponsored neither, −0.23. These comparisons include the two lead sponsors and exclude the House Speaker and the majority leader, who rarely cosponsor bills (Lewis et al. 2021).

25. Solender 2020.

26. All estimates in this paragraph are from Johnson and Smith (2020).

27. Walker, Reno, and Bethell 2014, 16, 52.

28. Program for Public Consultation 2016a, Q 37, Q 38, and Q 39a.

29. Program for Public Consultation 2016a, Q 36, Q 41, and Q 35.

30. Republican leaders, who controlled 15 chambers during these 11 Congresses, identified 115 priority bills, while Democratic leaders, who controlled 7 chambers, identified 54 priority bills (Curry and Lee 2020, table A.1).

31. Of the 169 priority bills, 5 concerned Social Security, including President Bush's 2001 and 2005 plans to introduce individual accounts. But as chapter 11 will show, Bush's proposals had more to do with reinventing Social Security than with restoring solvency. The other 3 bills were these. In 1999, Republican leaders proposed repealing the Social Security earnings test for beneficiaries who continued to work past their full retirement ages. The same year Republican leaders proposed putting Social Security surpluses into a symbolic "lockbox" until after Congress enacted Social Security reform. In 2011, Republican leaders proposed changing various entitlement programs, including Social Security, as part of a fiscal grand bargain. Congress enacted only the first bill.

32. Social Security Administration 2020b.

33. The Social Security actuaries scored the Sanders bill according to the intermediate assumptions in the 2018 Trustees Report, while the Urban Institute experts scored the same plan using their own model and using the intermediate assumptions of the 2019 Trustees Report (Smith, Johnson, and Favreault 2020). The similarity of the results—compare tables 10.5 and 10.9—suggests that the Urban Institute model closely resembles the actuaries' model. My method for constructing table 10.9 was the same as for tables 10.5 and 10.7, except that the denominator was −2.78%, based on the 2019 Trustees Report.

34. Buttigieg would provide some benefit credits for the newly taxed wages. The other four would not.

35. For primers on these two provisions, see Li (2019b, c).

36. There are some genuine inequities within the Windfall Elimination Provision and its cousin the Government Pension Offset. But these inequities could be fixed easily and inexpensively, as several reformers have proposed. For example, Representative Kevin Brady (R-TX), former chair of the Ways and Means Committee, repeatedly introduced a bill that would replace the Windfall Elimination Provision with a more straightforward adjustment. The actuaries estimate that the net effect of Brady's bill on the long-term actuarial deficit would be less than 0.005% of taxable payroll—about one-thirtieth the cost of what Biden and Warren propose (Social Security Administration 2020b).

37. So, too, did some of the less successful candidates, including Senator Michael Bennet (D-CO) and Representative Tulsi Gabbard (D-HA).

Chapter 11

1. Bush 2000.

2. Bush 2004.

3. Bush 2005a.

4. Ferrara 1980; Weaver 1982.

5. Arnold 1998a; Schieber and Shoven 1999, 263–89; Laursen 2012, 321–39.

6. Advisory Council 1997, 165.

7. Arnold 1998a.

8. Birnbaum 2005b.

9. Stevenson 2005.

10. Romano and Lardner 1999.

11. Dreyfuss 1999.

12. Hook 2005; Teles and Derthick 2009, 275.

13. US President 2001.

14. Social Security Administration 2020b.

15. President's Commission 2001, 14–23.

16. The best way to grasp the magnitude of the benefit cuts is to ask how large a tax increase would be required to forestall them. The answer is a tax of 2.07% of taxable payrolls. Put differently, preserving wage indexing for all retirees would require immediately increasing the combined payroll tax from 12.4% to 14.47% of taxable earnings (Social Security Administration 2002, 4).

17. For other accounts of the 2005 privatization campaign, see Hiltzik (2005), Edwards (2007), Galston (2007), Ross (2007), Teles and Derthick (2009), Campbell and King (2010), and Béland and Waddan (2012). I also read contemporaneous journalistic accounts in the *New York Times*, *Washington Post*, and *CQ Weekly*.

18. Bush 2005a.

19. Social Security Administration, 2020b.

20. Edwards 2007, 252.

21. Crawford 2005.

22. VandeHei and Baker 2005.

23. Bush 2005b.

24. The counts are mine from the transcripts of all presidential events about Social Security between February 3 and July 22, 2005 (Bush 2005c).

25. In addition to the president's efforts, 31 administration officials visited 127 cities and participated in 61 town hall meetings with members of Congress (Social Security Information Center 2005).

26. Edwards 2007, 234–42.

27. Rosenbaum and Toner 2005; Bush 2005d.

28. Lee 2005.

29. Stolberg and Hulse 2005.

30. Stevenson and Toner 2005.

31. VandeHei and Fletcher 2005.

32. Furman 2005; Diamond and Orszag 2005, xvi–xxi.

33. Furman 2005.

34. Wayne 2005.

35. *Economist* 2005.

36. On the resource advantages of AARP, see Birnbaum (2005a).

37. Social Security Administration 2005.

38. Stolberg and Toner 2005.

39. Stolberg and Toner 2005.

40. Board of Trustees 2004.

41. Congressional Budget Office 2005.

42. Boards of Trustees 2004.

43. Pew Research Center for the People and the Press (USPSRA.200409EAR.Q37; USPSRA.032405.R09; both Roper Center).

44. The five surveys in figure 11.1 are from the Pew Research Center for the People and the Press (USPSRA.200409EAR.Q37; USPSRA.011305A.R31; USPSRA.030205.R11; USPSRA.032405.R09; USPSRA.051905.R21; all Roper Center).

45. For other interpretations of opinion change on Social Security privatization, see Edwards (2007, 255–64) and Campbell and King (2010).

46. Zaller 1992.

47. In the 12 months beginning November 1, 2004, pollsters represented in the Roper Center archive asked 988 questions that mentioned Social Security (search conducted November 16, 2018). Although not every question asked for the respondent's position on the president's privatization proposal, many did.

48. Stimson 2015.

49. Stimson 2015.

50. Zaller (1992) shows how attitudes change with two-sided information flows.

51. The five surveys in figure 11.4 are from ABC News/*Washington Post* (USABCWP.051500.R12; USABCWP.042301.R27; USABCWP.071702A.R57; USABCWP.122104.R15; USABCWP.060705.R11; all Roper Center).

52. Figure 11.5 uses the same data source as figure 11.4.

53. Johnston, Hagen, and Jamieson 2004, 164.

54. The five surveys in figure 11.6 are from ABC News/*Washington Post* (USABCWP.122004.R02D; USABCWP.011705.R02C; USABCWP.031405.R02A; USABCWP.042505A.R02A; USABCWP.060705.R02A; all Roper Center). The source did not report information on party leaners.

55. Kingdon 1989; Arnold 1990.

56. David Mayhew (2005, 2018) identified 26 important legislative enactments between 2001 and 2004, 6 of them of historic importance. The number of historic laws was the highest for any first-term postwar president (Truman to Bush). Important enactments were also above average for this comparison group.

57. Ross 2007; Egan 2013.

58. Edwards 2003; Canes-Wrone 2006; Lee 2009.

59. Teles and Derthick 2009, 263.

60. Johnston, Hagen, and Jamieson 2004, 144–73.

61. Debate on October 3, 2000 (Commission on Presidential Debates 2021).

62. Teles and Derthick 2009, 176.

63. Although Representative Thaddeus McCotter designed a similar plan in 2011, it was not, according to the actuaries' report, a fully specified plan.

64. Biggs et al. 2016.

Chapter 12

1. Board of Trustees 2020, table IV.B3.

2. For my early thoughts on politics at the precipice, see Arnold (2015).

3. On the effects of agenda control, see Cox and McCubbins (2005).

4. Mayhew 2005, 80–91.

5. McCarty 2019, 43.

6. Arnold 2016, 309–10.

7. Of course, Republicans could not have done this alone. They would have needed the support of some Democratic senators to avoid a filibuster.

8. The protection includes "Old-Age, Survivors, and Disability Insurance" but explicitly excludes "Medicare or other programs established as part of that act" (Heniff 2016, 5).

9. The Democrats controlled the House and the presidency and had a supermajority in the Senate between the seating of Al Franken (D-MN) on July 7, 2009, and the death of Ted Kennedy (D-MA) on August 25, 2009, and again between the seating of Kennedy's appointed successor, Paul Kirk (D-MA), on September 25, 2009, and the seating of his elected successor, Scott Brown (R-MA), on February 4, 2010. Although the supermajority totaled 182 days, the effective supermajority was shorter, given Kennedy's declining health.

10. Arnold 1990, 118.

11. Curry and Lee 2020, 19–51. See also Mayhew 2005 and 2011.

12. Curry and Lee 2020, 83.

13. Curry and Lee 2020, 118–21.

14. Board of Trustees 2004, 2.

15. On the politics of trust funds, see Patashnik (2000).

16. Light 1995, 126–30.

17. Congressional Budget Office 2020; Government Accountability Office 2020.

18. Braybrooke and Lindblom 1963, 81–110.

19. Patashnik 2008.

20. Wildavsky 1964.

21. Arnold 1990, 210.

22. CQ Roll Call Staff 2013; Arnold 2017.

23. Wallach 2020.

Chapter 13

1. These estimates of life expectancy for 65-year-olds are the mean cohort life expectancies for men and women at that age under the actuaries' intermediate assumptions (Board of Trustees 2020, table V.A5).

2. Until recently, this measure was called the old-age dependency ratio (OECD 2017, table 5.5; OECD 2019, table 6.2).

3. Moreover, most OECD countries face greater increases in the old-age to working-age ratio. The projected ratio for the United States is 43% higher than the current ratio, compared with Korea (229% higher), Italy (85%), Germany (57%), Japan (56%), Australia and Canada (50%),

France (49%), and the United Kingdom (47%). OECD refers to the Organisation for Economic Co-operation and Development, an international organization that, among other things, collects and distributes comparable data about its member countries.

4. OECD 2019, table 6.1.

5. Compare tables V.A4 and V.A5 in Board of Trustees (2020).

6. These estimates of life expectancy for 65-year-olds are the mean period life expectancies for men and women at that age. All estimates are from 2018, except for Japan, which is from 2017 (OECD 2020a).

7. Although permanent migration to the United States in 2019 was down from its most recent peak (2016), it was roughly equal to the mean from 2010 to 2018 (OECD 2020b).

8. Italy tied the United States at 0.3 percent. What counts as a permanent immigrant is defined by the receiving country. For Australia, Canada, and the United States, it consists of immigrants who receive the right of permanent residence. For the other six countries, it refers to immigrants who are granted a residence permit that is indefinitely renewable, although renewal is sometimes subject to conditions, such as holding a job (OECD 2020b).

9. On the effects of immigration on Social Security's finances, see Brown et al. (2018).

10. For countries that have different full retirement ages for men and women (Italy, Japan, United Kingdom), the reported ages are the mean of the separate ages (OECD 2019, table 4.4).

11. On applying mortality adjustments to proposals to raise the retirement age, see Reznik et al. (2019).

12. The data are for 2018 (OECD 2020c, table 3.1).

13. Social Security Administration 2020a, provisions A3 and A6.

14. The calculations are for the lowest and highest income quintiles in figure 8.4.

15. Diamond 2018, 677.

16. Although the actuaries have occasionally scored proposals submitted by nongovernmental organizations, Stephen Goss, the chief actuary, has ranked his office's priorities as (a) the administration, (b) the House Ways and Means Committee and the Senate Finance Committee, (c) other legislators, and (d) outside organizations (Goss 2020).

17. Diamond and Orszag 2005.

18. Smith, Johnson, and Favreault 2020.

19. Previously, Larson introduced his plan in the first three months of each new Congress (March 17, 2015; April 5, 2017; January 30, 2019). The lack of any solvency bills in the 117th Congress—Republican or Democratic—is as of July 29, 2021 (Social Security Administration 2020b).

20. The 2019 Larson bill would violate Biden's campaign promise by gradually increasing the tax rate for all workers from 6.2% to 7.4%. The 2019 Sanders bill would violate Biden's promise by increasing taxes for workers earning more than $250,000.

21. Four journalist/moderators framed their questions directly (October 3, 2000; October 13, 2004; October 3, 2012; October 19, 2016). The fifth (October 7, 2008) chose a Social Security question from 80 questions submitted by audience members (Commission on Presidential Debates 2021).

22. Arnold 2004.

23. WRFA 2018.

24. Pudney 2019.

25. Golden 2019.

26. OnTheIssues.org, a group that seeks to provide nonpartisan information for voters culled from newspapers, speeches, press releases, and the internet, found Reed's positions on 22 out of 24 policy issues, all except for drugs and Social Security (https://www.ontheissues.org/NY /Tom_Reed.htm, searched on April 12, 2021).

REFERENCES

Aaron, Henry J., and John B. Shoven. 1999. *Should the United States Privatize Social Security?* Cambridge, MA: MIT Press.

AARP. 2014. "Social Security: AARP Four-Page Flyers from 2014 Election Season." AARP Voters' Guides. Available to download from R. Douglas Arnold's website. https://scholar .princeton.edu/arnold/social-security.

Advisory Council on Social Security. 1997. *Report of the 1994–1996 Advisory Council*. Vol. 1, *Findings and Recommendations*. Washington, DC: Government Publishing Office.

Agnew, Julie, Pierluigi Balduzzi, and Annika Sundén. 2003. "Portfolio Choice and Trading in a Large 401(k) Plan." *American Economic Review* 93 (1): 193–215.

Altman, Nancy. 2005. *The Battle for Social Security: From FDR's Vision to Bush's Gamble*. Hoboken, NJ: Wiley.

———. 2018. *The Truth about Social Security*. Washington, DC: Strong Arm.

Altman, Nancy, and Ted Marmor. 2009. "Social Security from the Great Society to 1980." In *Conservatism and American Political Development*, edited by Brian J. Glenn and Steven M. Teles, 154–87. Oxford: Oxford University Press.

Ambar, Saladin. 2017. *American Cicero: Mario Cuomo and the Defense of American Liberalism*. New York: Oxford University Press.

Amenta, Edwin. 2006. *When Movements Matter: The Townsend Plan and the Rise of Social Security*. Princeton, NJ: Princeton University Press.

American National Election Studies. 2018. "Time Series Cumulative Data File, 1948–2016." American National Election Studies. https://electionstudies.org/data-center/.

Apfel, Kenneth S., and Michael J. Graetz. 2005. *Uncharted Waters: Paying Benefits from Individual Accounts in Federal Retirement Policy*. Washington, DC: Brookings Institution Press.

Arnold, R. Douglas. 1990. *The Logic of Congressional Action*. New Haven, CT: Yale University Press.

———. 1998a. "The Political Feasibility of Social Security Reform." In *Framing the Social Security Debate: Values, Politics, and Economics*, edited by R. Douglas Arnold, Michael J. Graetz, and Alicia H. Munnell, 389–417. Washington, DC: Brookings Institution Press.

———. 1998b. "The Politics of Reforming Social Security." *Political Science Quarterly* 113 (2): 213–40.

———. 2004. *Congress, the Press, and Political Accountability*. Princeton, NJ: Princeton University Press

———. 2015. "Politics at the Precipice: Fixing Social Security in 2033." *Forum* 13 (1): 3–18.

———. 2016. "Explaining Legislative Achievements." In *Congress and Policy Making in the 21st Century*, edited by Jeffrey A. Jenkins and Eric M. Patashnik, 301–23. New York: Cambridge University Press.

———. 2017. "The Electoral Connection, Age 40." In *Governing in a Polarized Age: Elections, Parties, and Political Representation in America*, edited by Alan S. Gerber and Eric Schickler, 15–34. New York: Cambridge University Press.

Arnold, R. Douglas, Michael J. Graetz, and Alicia H. Munnell, eds. 1998. *Framing the Social Security Debate: Values, Politics, and Economics.* Washington, DC: Brookings Institution Press.

Baggette, Jennifer, Robert Y. Shapiro, and Lawrence R. Jacobs. 1995. "Poll Trends: Social Security—an Update." *Public Opinion Quarterly* 59 (3): 420–42.

Barry, Brian. 1965. *Political Argument.* London: Routledge and Kegan Paul.

Beach, William W. 1998. *Social Security's Rate of Return.* Washington, DC: Heritage Foundation.

Bekaert, Geert, Kenton Hoyem, Wei-Yin Hu, and Enrichetta Ravina. 2017. "Who Is Internationally Diversified? Evidence from the 401(k) Plans of 296 Firms." *Journal of Financial Economics* 124 (1): 86–112.

Béland, Daniel. 2005. *Social Security: History and Politics from the New Deal to the Privatization Debate.* Lawrence: University Press of Kansas.

Béland, Daniel, and Alex Waddan. 2012. *The Politics of Policy Change: Welfare, Medicare, and Social Security Reform in the United States.* Washington, DC: Georgetown University Press.

Benartzi, Shlomo, and Richard H. Thaler. 2007. "Heuristics and Biases in Retirement Savings Behavior." *Journal of Economic Perspectives* 21 (3): 81–104.

Biggs, Andrew G., James C. Capretta, Robert Doar, Ron Haskins, and Yuval Levin. 2016. *Increasing the Effectiveness and Sustainability of the Nation's Entitlement Programs.* Washington, DC: American Enterprise Institute.

Biggs, Andrew G., and Glenn R. Springstead. 2008. "Alternate Measures of Replacement Rates for Social Security Benefits and Retirement Income." *Social Security Bulletin* 68 (2): 1–19.

Birnbaum, Jeffrey H. 2005a. "AARP Leads with Wallet in Fight over Social Security." *Washington Post*, March 30, 2005.

———. 2005b. "Private Account Concept Grew from Obscure Roots." *Washington Post*, February 22, 2005.

Board of Trustees. 1980. *The 1980 Annual Report of the Board of Trustees of the Federal Old-Age and Survivors Insurance and Disability Insurance Trust Funds.* Washington, DC: Government Publishing Office.

———. 1994. *The 1994 Annual Report of the Board of Trustees of the Federal Old-Age and Survivors Insurance and Disability Insurance Trust Funds.* Washington, DC: Government Publishing Office.

———. 2004. *The 2004 Annual Report of the Board of Trustees of the Federal Old-Age and Survivors Insurance and Disability Insurance Trust Funds.* Washington, DC: Government Publishing Office.

———. 2009. *The 2009 Annual Report of the Board of Trustees of the Federal Old-Age and Survivors Insurance and Disability Insurance Trust Funds.* Washington, DC: Government Publishing Office.

———. 2020. *The 2020 Annual Report of the Board of Trustees of the Federal Old-Age and Survivors Insurance and Disability Insurance Trust Funds*. Washington, DC: Government Publishing Office.

Boards of Trustees. 2004. *The 2004 Annual Report of the Boards of Trustees of the Federal Hospital Insurance and Federal Supplementary Medical Insurance Trust Funds*. Washington, DC: Government Publishing Office.

Bonica, Adam. 2014. "Mapping the Ideological Marketplace." *American Journal of Political Science* 58 (2): 367–86.

Braybrooke, David, and Charles E. Lindblom. 1963. *A Strategy of Decision*. New York: Free Press.

Breslauer, Tamar B., and William R. Morton. 2019. *Social Security: Major Decisions in the House Since 1935*. Washington, DC: Library of Congress, Congressional Research Service.

Britain, John A. 1972. *The Payroll Tax for Social Security*. Washington, DC: Brookings Institution.

Brown, Theresa Cardinal, Jeffrey Mason, Kenneth Megan, and Cristobal Ramón. 2018. *Immigration's Effect on the Social Security System*. Washington, DC: Bipartisan Policy Center.

Burdick, Clark, and Lynn Fisher. 2007. "Social Security Cost-of-Living Adjustments and the Consumer Price Index." *Social Security Bulletin* 67 (3): 73–88.

Bureau of Labor Statistics. 2020. *National Compensation Survey: Employee Benefits in the United States, March 2020*. Bulletin 2793. Washington, DC: Department of Labor.

Bush, George W. 2000. "Address Accepting the Presidential Nomination at the Republican National Convention in Philadelphia." August 3, 2000. In *The American Presidency Project*, edited by John T. Woolley and Gerhard Peters. Santa Barbara: University of California. https://www.presidency.ucsb.edu/documents/app-categories/elections-and-transitions/convention-speeches.

———. 2004. "President Holds Press Conference." White House Archives, George W. Bush. November 4, 2004. https://georgewbush-whitehouse.archives.gov/news/releases/2004/11/20041104-5.html.

———. 2005a. "Address before a Joint Session of the Congress on the State of the Union." February 2, 2005. In *The American Presidency Project*, edited by John T. Woolley and Gerhard Peters. Santa Barbara, CA: University of California. https://www.presidency.ucsb.edu/documents/app-categories/spoken-addresses-and-remarks/presidential/state-the-union-addresses.

———. 2005b. "President Discusses Strengthening Social Security in Pensacola, Florida." Social Security Online. March 18, 2005. https://www.ssa.gov/history/gwbushstmts5.html#03182005.

———. 2005c. Presidential statements about Social Security, 1st and 2nd quarters. Social Security Online. https://www.ssa.gov/history/gwbushstmts5.html and https://www.ssa.gov/history/gwbushstmts5b.html.

———. 2005d. "Strengthening Social Security for the 21st Century." February, 2005. http://purl.access.gpo.gov/GPO/LPS71114.

Campbell, Andrea Louise. 2003. *How Policies Make Citizens: Senior Political Activism and the American Welfare State*. Princeton, NJ: Princeton University Press.

———. 2012. "Policy Makes Mass Politics." *Annual Review of Political Science* 15:333–51.

Campbell, Andrea Louise, and Ryan King. 2010. "Social Security: Political Resilience in the Face of Conservative Strides." In *The New Politics of Old Age Policy*, 2nd ed, edited by Robert B. Hudson, 233–53. Baltimore: Johns Hopkins University Press.

Campbell, Andrea Louise, and Kimberly J. Morgan. 2005. "Financing the Welfare State: Elite Politics and the Decline of the Social Insurance Model in America." *Studies in American Political Development* 19 (Fall): 173–95.

Canes-Wrone, Brandice. 2006. *Who Leads Whom? Presidents, Policy, and the Public*. Chicago: University of Chicago Press.

Carter, Susan B., Scott Sigmund Gartner, Michael R. Haines, Alan L. Olmstead, Richard Sutch, and Gavin Wright, eds. 2006. *Historical Statistics of the United States*. Millennial Edition Online. New York: Cambridge University Press.

Case, Anne, and Angus Deaton. 2020. *Deaths of Despair and the Future of Capitalism*. Princeton, NJ: Princeton University Press.

Census Bureau. 1939. *Vital Statistics of the United States, 1937*. Table III, "Enumerated Population by Age, Race, and Sex on April 1, 1930." Washington, DC: Department of Commerce.

———. 1943. *Vital Statistics of the United States, 1940*. Table III, "Enumerated Population by Age, Race, and Sex on April 1, 1940." Washington, DC: Department of Commerce.

———. 1954. *Vital Statistics of the United States, 1950*. Table 2.21, "Total Population Residing in Continental United States, by Age, Race, and Sex, 1940–1950." Washington, DC: Department of Commerce.

———. 1991. *Population by Age Groups, Race, and Sex for 1960 to 1997*. Washington, DC: Department of Commerce.

———. 2001. *Census 2000*. Table 1, "Total Population by Age, Race, and Hispanic or Latino Origin, 2000." Washington, DC: Department of Commerce.

———. 2010. *National Intercensal Tables: 2000–2010*. "Intercensal Estimates of the Resident Population by Sex and Age: April 1, 2000 to July 1, 2010." Washington, DC: Department of Commerce.

———. 2011. *Current Population Survey, Annual Social and Economic Supplement*. Table 1, "Population by Age and Sex, 2010." Washington, DC: Department of Commerce.

———. 2015a. *Current Population Survey. Voting & Registration Series Historical 1972–2012*. Washington, DC: Department of Commerce. Custom DVD by Unicon Research Corporation, July 24, 2015.

———. 2015b. *National Population Projections*. Table 9, "Projections of the Population by Sex and Age, 2015 to 2060." Washington, DC: Department of Commerce.

———. 2015c. *Voting and Registration in the Election of November 2014*. Report P20–577, table 1. Washington, DC: Department of Commerce.

———. 2017. *Voting and Registration in the Election of November 2016*. Report P20–580, table 1. Washington, DC: Department of Commerce.

———. 2018. *My Congressional District*. Based on the 2016 American Community Survey. Washington, DC: Department of Commerce. Accessed June 18, 2018. https://www.census.gov/mycd/.

———. 2019a. *National Population by Characteristics*. "Annual Estimates of the Resident Population by Single Year of Age and Sex: April 1, 2010 to July 1, 2018." Washington, DC: Department of Commerce.

———. 2019b. *Voting and Registration in the Election of November 2018*. Report P20–583, table 1. Washington, DC: Department of Commerce.

Centers for Medicare and Medicaid Services. 2018. "Ratio of HI Taxable Payroll to GDP." Centers for Medicare & Medicaid Services. Accessed January 11, 2019. https://www.cms.gov/Research-Statistics-Data-and-Systems/Statistics-Trends-and-Reports/ReportsTrustFunds/Downloads/TR2018-Tables-Figures.zip.

———. 2020. *National Health Expenditures Summary, Including Share of GDP, CY 1960–2018*. Baltimore: Centers for Medicare & Medicaid Services.

Chen, Anqi, and Alicia H. Munnell. 2017. "Who Contributes to Individual Retirement Accounts?" Issue in Brief #17-8. Chestnut Hill, MA: Center for Retirement Research.

Chen, Anqi, Alicia H. Munnell, and Geoffrey T. Sanzenbacher. 2018. "How Much Income Do Retirees Actually Have: Evaluating the Evidence from Five National Datasets." Working Paper 2018-14. Chestnut Hill, MA: Center for Retirement Research.

Clark, Robert, Annamaria Lusardi, and Olivia S. Mitchell. 2015. "Financial Knowledge and 401(k) Investment Performance." *Journal of Pension Economics and Finance* 14 (4): 1–24.

Commission on Presidential Debates. 2021. "Debate Transcripts." Commission on Presidential Debates. https://www.debates.org/voter-education/debate-transcripts/.

Committee on Economic Security. 1937. *Social Security in America: The Factual Background of the Social Security Act as Summarized from Staff Reports*. Washington, DC: Social Security Board.

Congress and the Nation 2001–2004: Politics and Policy in the 107th and 108th Congresses. 2006. Washington, DC: CQ Press.

Congressional Budget Office. 1987. *Tax Policy for Pensions and Other Retirement Saving*. Washington, DC: Congress of the United States.

———. 2005. *Updated Long-Term Projections for Social Security*. March 3, 2005. Washington, DC: Congress of the United States.

———. 2020. *The Outlook for Major Federal Trust Funds: 2020 to 2030*. September 2020. Washington, DC: Congress of the United States.

Cook, Fay Lomax, and Edith J. Barrett. 1992. *Support for the American Welfare State: The Views of Congress and the Public*. New York: Columbia University Press.

Cook, Fay Lomax, and Rachel L. Moskowitz. 2014. "The Great Divide: Elite and Mass Opinion about Social Security." In *The New Politics of Old Age Policy*, 3rd ed., edited by Robert B. Hudson, 69–96. Baltimore: Johns Hopkins University Press.

Cox, Gary W., and Mathew D. McCubbins. 2005. *Setting the Agenda*. New York: Cambridge University Press.

Congressional Quarterly, Inc. 1949. "Appendix: Description of Key Votes, 1919–1944." In *CQ Almanac*. Washington, DC: Congressional Quarterly.

———. 1950. "Social Security Act." In *CQ Almanac*, 165–77. Washington, DC: Congressional Quarterly.

———. 1954. "Social Security Extension." In *CQ Almanac*, 188–94. Washington, DC: Congressional Quarterly.

———. 1961. "Social Security Benefits and Taxes Increased." In *CQ Almanac*, 257–61. Washington, DC: Congressional Quarterly.

———. 1965. "Social Security Medicare Program Enacted." In *CQ Almanac*, 236–45. Washington, DC: Congressional Quarterly.

———. 1967. "Social Security Aid Raised." In *CQ Almanac*, 892–916. Washington, DC: Congressional Quarterly.

———. 1977. "Congress Clears Social Security Tax Increase." In *CQ Almanac*, 161–72. Washington, DC: Congressional Quarterly.

———. 1978. "Social Security Tax Rollback." In *CQ Almanac*, 257. Washington, DC: Congressional Quarterly.

———. 1983. "Social Security Rescue Plan Swiftly Approved." In *CQ Almanac*, 219–26. Washington, DC: Congressional Quarterly.

CQ Roll Call Staff. 2013. "Congress Narrowly Averts Fiscal Cliff." *CQ Weekly*, January 7, 2013.

Crawford, Craig. 2005. "Winning the 'Debate.'" *CQ Weekly*, March 14, 2005.

Crawford, Neta C. 2014. *U.S. Costs of Wars through 2014: $4.4 Trillion and Counting*. Providence, RI: Watson Institute for International and Public Affairs at Brown University.

Crosson, Jesse M., Alexander C. Furnas, and Geoffrey M. Lorenz. 2020. "Polarized Pluralism: Organizational Preferences and Biases in the American Pressure System." *American Political Science Review* 114 (4): 1117–37.

Curry, James M., and Frances E. Lee. 2020. *The Limits of Party: Congress and Lawmaking in a Polarized Era*. Chicago: University of Chicago Press.

Davies, Gareth, and Martha Derthick. 1997. "Race and Social Welfare Policy: The Social Security Act of 1935." *Political Science Quarterly* 112 (2): 217–35.

Day, Christine L. 2017. *AARP: America's Largest Interest Group and Its Impact*. Santa Barbara, CA: Praeger.

Department of the Treasury. 2020. "Tax Expenditures." Office of Tax Analysis. February 26, 2020. https://home.treasury.gov/system/files/131/Tax-Expenditures-2021.pdf.

Derthick, Martha. 1979. *Policymaking for Social Security*. Washington, DC: Brookings Institution.

DeWitt, Larry W. 2007. "Financing Social Security, 1939–1949: A Reexamination of the Financing Policies of this Period." *Social Security Bulletin* 67 (4): 51–69.

DeWitt, Larry W., Daniel Béland, and Edward D. Berkowitz. 2008. *Social Security: A Documentary History*. Washington, DC: CQ Press.

Diamond, Peter A., ed. 1999. *Issues in Privatizing Social Security: Report of an Expert Panel of the National Academy of Social Insurance*. Cambridge, MA: MIT Press.

———. 2018. "The Future of Social Security." *Economic Inquiry* 56 (2): 661–81.

Diamond, Peter A., and Peter R. Orszag. 2005. *Saving Social Security: A Balanced Approach*. Rev. ed. Washington, DC: Brookings Institution.

Dreyfuss, Robert. 1999. "George W.'s Compassion." *American Prospect*, September/October 1999.

Eaton, William J. 1989. "Moynihan Urges Social Security Tax Cut, Return to Pay-as-You-Go Benefits." *Los Angeles Times*, December 30, 1989.

Economist. 2005. "The AARP: Still the Biggest Bruiser?" February 3, 2005.

Edwards, George C., III. 2003. *On Deaf Ears: The Limits of the Bully Pulpit*. New Haven, CT: Yale University Press.

———. 2007. *Governing by Campaigning: The Politics of the Bush Presidency*. New York: Pearson.

Egan, Patrick J. 2013. *Partisan Priorities: How Issue Ownership Drives and Distorts American Politics*. New York: Cambridge University Press.

Egan, Patrick J., and Megan Mullin. 2017. "Climate Change: US Public Opinion." *Annual Review of Political Science* 20:209–27.

Employee Benefits Security Administration. 2021. *Private Pension Plan Bulletin Historical Tables and Graphs, 1975–2018.* Washington, DC: Department of Labor.

Feldstein, Martin. 1974. "Social Security, Induced Retirement, and Aggregate Capital Accumulation." *Journal of Political Economy* 82 (5): 905–26.

Ferrara, Peter J. 1980. *Social Security: The Inherent Contradiction.* San Francisco: Cato Institute.

Finkelstein, Amy, and James Poterba. 2004. "Adverse Selection in Insurance Markets." *Journal of Political Economy* 112 (1): 183–208.

Friedman, Milton. 1962. *Capitalism and Freedom.* Chicago: University of Chicago Press.

Furman, Jason. 2005. *How Would the President's New Social Security Proposals Affect Middle-Class Workers and Social Security Solvency?* Washington, DC: Center on Budget and Policy Priorities.

Galston, William A. 2007. *Why President Bush's 2005 Social Security Initiative Failed, and What It Means for the Future of the Program.* New York: Brademas Center for the Study of Congress.

Geanakoplos, John, Olivia S. Mitchell, and Stephen P. Zeldes. 1998. "Would a Privatized Social Security System Really Pay a Higher Rate of Return?" In *Framing the Social Security Debate: Values, Politics, and Economics,* edited by R. Douglas Arnold, Michael J. Graetz, and Alicia H. Munnell, 137–57. Washington, DC: Brookings Institution Press.

General Social Survey. 2019. "General Social Survey, 1984 to 2018." Electronic data set. NORC at the University of Chicago. Accessed June 7, 2019. Available from the GSS Data Explorer website. https://gssdataexplorer.norc.org/.

Golden, Vaughn. 2019. "Tom Reed Brings National Social Security Reform Discussion to Ithaca." *Ithaca Voice.* September 4, 2019.

Goss, Stephen C. 2010. "The Future Financial Status of the Social Security Program." *Social Security Bulletin* 70 (3): 111–25.

——. 2020. Letter to Senator Chuck Grassley, chair of the Senate Finance Committee, and Representative Kevin Brady, ranking minority member of the House Ways and Means Committee. October 23, 2020. Social Security Administration, Office of the Chief Actuary. https://www.ssa.gov/oact/solvency/LetterGrassleyBrady_20201023.pdf.

Goss, Stephen C., Michael Clingman, Alice Wade, and Karen P. Glenn. 2014. "Replacement Rates for Retirees: What Makes Sense for Planning and Evaluation?" Actuarial Note #155. Baltimore: Social Security Administration, Office of the Chief Actuary.

Goss, Stephen C., and Karen P. Glenn. 2020. "Updated Baseline for Actuarial Status of the OASI and DI Trust Funds, Reflecting Pandemic and Recession Effects." November 24, 2020. Baltimore: Social Security Administration, Office of the Chief Actuary. https://www.ssa.gov/oact/solvency/UpdatedBaseline_20201124.pdf.

Government Accountability Office. 2020. "Federal Trust Funds and Other Dedicated Funds." Government Accountability Office, January 16, 2020. https://www.gao.gov/products/gao-20-156.

Graetz, Michael J., and Jerry L. Mashaw. 1999. *True Security: Rethinking American Social Insurance.* New Haven, CT: Yale University Press.

Gregory, Janice, Thomas Bethell, Virginia Reno, and Benjamin Veghte. 2010. "Strengthening Social Security for the Long Run." Social Security Brief. Washington, DC: National Academy of Social Insurance.

Gulick, Luther. 1941. "Memorandum on Conference with FDR Concerning Social Security Taxation, Summer 1941." Hyde Park, NY: FDR Presidential Library. Reproduced by Larry Dewitt. "Luther Gulick Memorandum Re: Famous FDR Quote." Research Note #23. 2005. Baltimore: Social Security Administration, Office of the Historian.

Hacker, Jacob S. 2002. *The Divided Welfare State*. New York: Cambridge University Press.

Heclo, Hugh. 1998. "A Political Science Perspective on Social Security Reform." In *Framing the Social Security Debate: Values, Politics, and Economics*, edited by R. Douglas Arnold, Michael J. Graetz, and Alicia H. Munnell, 65–93. Washington, DC: Brookings Institution Press.

Heniff, Bill, Jr. 2016. *The Budget Reconciliation Process: The Senate's "Byrd Rule."* Washington, DC: Library of Congress, Congressional Research Service.

Hertel-Fernandez, Alexander, Theda Skocpol, and Jason Sclar. 2018. "When Political Mega-donors Join Forces: How the Koch Network and the Democracy Alliance Influence Organized U.S. Politics on the Right and Left." *Studies in American Political Development* 32 (2): 127–65.

Hiltzik, Michael A. 2005. *The Plot against Social Security*. New York: Harper Collins.

Himelfarb, Richard. 1995. *Catastrophic Politics: The Rise and Fall of the Medicare Catastrophic Coverage Act of 1988*. University Park: Pennsylvania State University Press.

Hook, Janet. 2005. "They Invested Years in Private Accounts." *Los Angeles Times*, January 30, 2005.

Hu, Wei-Yin, and Jason S. Scott. 2007. "Behavioral Obstacles in the Annuity Market." *Financial Analysts Journal* 63 (6): 71–82.

Hughes, Adam. 2017. *Five Facts about U.S. Political Donations*. Washington, DC: Pew Research Center.

Internal Revenue Service. 1940. *Statistics of Income for 1937*. Washington, DC: Government Printing Office.

———. 2018. *Statistics of Income 2016: Individual Income Tax Returns*. Washington, DC: Statistics of Income Division.

———. 2020. *Accumulation and Distribution of Individual Retirement Arrangements, Tax Year 2018*. Washington, DC: Statistics of Income Division.

Investment Company Institute. 2019. *The Role of IRAs in US Households' Saving for Retirement*. Washington, DC: Investment Company Institute.

———. 2021. *Report: The US Retirement Market, Fourth Quarter 2020*. Washington, DC: Investment Company Institute.

Isaacs, Katelin P., and Sharmila Choudhury. 2017. *The Growing Gap in Life Expectancy by Income*. Washington, DC: Library of Congress, Congressional Research Service.

Jacobs, Alan M. 2010. "Policymaking as Political Constraint: Institutional Development in the U.S. Social Security Program." In *Explaining Institutional Change*, edited by James Mahoney and Kathleen Thelen, 94–131. New York: Cambridge University Press.

———. 2011. *Governing for the Long Term: Democracy and the Politics of Investment*. New York: Cambridge University Press.

Jacobs, Lawrence R., and Suzanne Mettler. 2018. "When and How New Policy Creates New Politics: Examining the Feedback Effects of the Affordable Care Act on Public Opinion." *Perspectives on Politics* 16 (2): 345–63.

Jacobs, Lawrence R., and Robert Y. Shapiro. 1998. "Myths and Misunderstandings about Public Opinion toward Social Security." In *Framing the Social Security Debate: Values, Politics, and*

Economics, edited by R. Douglas Arnold, Michael J. Graetz, and Alicia H. Munnell, 355–88. Washington, DC: Brookings Institution Press.

Johnson, Richard W., and Karen E. Smith. 2020. *Comparing Democratic and Republican Approaches to Fixing Social Security: An Analysis of the Larson and Johnson Bills*. Washington, DC: Urban Institute.

Johnston, Richard, Michael G. Hagen, and Kathleen Hall Jamieson. 2004. *The 2000 Presidential Election and the Foundations of Party Politics*. New York: Cambridge University Press.

Joint Committee on Taxation. 2019. "Overview of the Federal Tax System as in Effect for 2019." JCX-9-19. Washington, DC: United States Congress. https://www.jct.gov/publications/2019/jcx-9-19/.

Kashin, Konstantin, Gary King, and Samir Soneji. 2015. "Systematic Bias and Nontransparency in U.S. Social Security Administration Forecasts." *Journal of Economic Perspectives* 29 (2): 239–58.

Kingdon, John W. 1984. *Agendas, Alternatives, and Public Policies*. Boston: Little, Brown.

———. 1989. *Congressmen's Voting Decisions*. 3rd ed. Ann Arbor: University of Michigan Press.

Kumlin, Staffan. 2007. "The Welfare State: Values, Policy Preferences, and Performance Evaluations." In *The Oxford Handbook of Political Behavior*, edited by Russell J. Dalton and Hans-Dieter Klingemann, 362–82. Oxford: Oxford University Press.

Laursen, Eric. 2012. *The People's Pension: The Struggle to Defend Social Security since Reagan*. Oakland, CA: AK Press.

Lee, Christopher. 2005. "Cheney: Social Security Plan to Cost Trillions." *Washington Post*, February 7, 2005.

Lee, Frances E. 2009. *Beyond Ideology*. Chicago: University of Chicago Press.

Leff, Mark H. 1988. "Speculating in Social Security Futures: The Perils of Payroll Tax Financing, 1939–1950." In *Social Security: The First Half-Century*, edited by Gerald D. Nash, Noel H. Pugach, and Richard F. Tomasson, 243–78. Albuquerque: University of New Mexico Press.

Leighley, Jan E., and Jonathan Nagler. 2014. *Who Votes Now?* Princeton, NJ: Princeton University Press.

Leimer, Dean R. 1994. "Cohort-Specific Measures of Lifetime Net Social Security Transfers." Working Paper No. 59. Washington, DC: Social Security Administration, Office of Research and Statistics.

———. 1995. "A Guide to Social Security Money's Worth Issues." *Social Security Bulletin* 58 (2): 3–20.

———. 2016. "The Legacy Debt Associated with Past Social Security Transfers." *Social Security Bulletin* 76 (3): 1–15.

Lewis, Jeffrey B., Keith Poole, Howard Rosenthal, Adam Boche, Aaron Rudkin, and Luke Sonnet. 2021. *Voteview: Congressional Roll-Call Votes Database*. UCLA Department of Political Science and Social Science Computing. Accessed January 28, 2021. https://voteview.com/.

Li, Zhe. 2019a. *Social Security: Raising or Eliminating the Taxable Earnings Base*. Washington, DC: Library of Congress, Congressional Research Service.

———. 2019b. *Social Security: The Government Pension Offset*. Washington, DC: Library of Congress, Congressional Research Service.

———. 2019c. *Social Security: The Windfall Elimination Provision*. Washington, DC: Library of Congress, Congressional Research Service.

Light, Paul. 1995. *Still Artful Work: The Continuing Politics of Social Security Reform.* 2nd ed. New York: McGraw Hill.

Liu, Su, and David C. Stapleton. 2011. "Longitudinal Statistics on Work Activity and Use of Employment Supports for New Social Security Disability Insurance Beneficiaries." *Social Security Bulletin* 71 (3): 35–59.

Marmor, Theodore R., Jerry L. Mashaw, and John Pakutka. 2014. *Social Insurance: America's Neglected Heritage and Contested Future.* Los Angeles: Sage.

Martin, Joyce A., Brady E. Hamilton, Michelle J. K. Osterman, and Anne K. Driscoll. 2019. "Births: Final Data for 2018." *National Vital Statistics Reports* 68 (13).

Mayer, Jane. 2017. *Dark Money: The Hidden History of the Billionaires behind the Rise of the Radical Right.* New York: Anchor Books.

Mayhew, David R. 1974. *Congress: The Electoral Connection.* New Haven, CT: Yale University Press.

———. 2005. *Divided We Govern: Party Control, Lawmaking, and Investigations, 1946–2002.* New Haven, CT: Yale University Press.

———. 2011. *Partisan Balance: Why Political Parties Don't Kill the U.S. Constitutional System.* Princeton, NJ: Princeton University Press.

———. 2018. "Lists of Important Enactments by Congress, 1991–2014." David Mayhew's website. Accessed December 30, 2018. https://campuspress.yale.edu/davidmayhew/files/2016/06/datasets-laws-1991-2014-arnold-20f8cyy.pdf.

McCarty, Nolan. 2019. *Polarization: What Everyone Needs to Know.* New York: Oxford University Press.

McKinley, Charles, and Robert W. Frase. 1970. *Launching Social Security: A Capture-and-Record Account, 1935–1937.* Madison: University of Wisconsin Press.

McLean, Bethany, and Peter Elkind. 2004. *The Smartest Guys in the Room: The Amazing Rise and Scandalous Fall of Enron.* New York: Penguin Group.

Mettler, Suzanne. 2005. *Soldiers to Citizens.* New York: Oxford University Press.

Munnell, Alicia H. 1977. *The Future of Social Security.* Washington, DC: Brookings Institution.

Munnell, Alicia H., and Anqi Chen. 2015. "Trends in Social Security Claiming." Issue in Brief #15-8. Chestnut Hill, MA: Center for Retirement Research.

Munnell, Alicia H., Anqi Chen, and Geoffrey T. Sanzenbacher. 2018. "Is the Drop in Fertility Temporary or Permanent?" Issue in Brief #18-14. Chestnut Hill, MA: Center for Retirement Research.

National Academies of Sciences, Engineering, and Medicine. 2015. *The Growing Gap in Life Expectancy by Income.* Washington, DC: National Academies.

National Federation of Independent Business. 2021. "NFIB Members Serving in Congress." National Federation of Independent Business. Accessed March 12, 2021. https://www.nfib.com/advocacy/members-in-congress/.

Nesbitt, Stephen L. 1995. "Buy High, Sell Low: Timing Errors in Mutual Fund Allocations." *Journal of Portfolio Management* 22 (1): 57–60.

New York Times. 1980. "Debate Transcript: Rivals for Presidency Discuss Views about Social Security." October 29, 1980.

OECD (Organisation for Economic Co-operation and Development). 2017. *Pensions at a Glance, 2017.* Paris: OECD.

———. 2019. *Pensions at a Glance, 2019.* Paris: OECD.

———. 2020a. "Life Expectancy at Age 65." OECD. Accessed December 5, 2020. https://data
.oecd.org/healthstat/life-expectancy-at-65.htm.

———. 2020b. "Permanent Migration by Country, 2010–2019." OECD. Accessed December 5,
2020. https://www1.compareyourcountry.org/migration/en/0//datatable/.

———. 2020c. *Revenue Statistics 2020*. Paris: OECD.

Office of Management and Budget. 2020. *Fiscal Year 2020 Historical Tables: Budget of the United
States Government*. Washington, DC: Government Publishing Office.

Page, Benjamin I., Larry M. Bartels, and Jason Seawright. 2013. "Democracy and the Policy
Preferences of Wealthy Americans." *Perspectives on Politics* 11 (1): 51–73.

Parker, Florence E. 1935. "Experience under State Old-Age Pension Acts in 1935." *Monthly Labor
Review* 41 (2): 303–26.

Pashchenko, Svetlana. 2013. "Accounting for Non-annuitization." *Journal of Public Economics*
98:53–67.

Patashnik, Eric M. 2000. *Putting Trust in the US Budget: Federal Trust Funds and the Politics of
Commitment*. New York: Cambridge University Press.

———. 2008. *Reforms at Risk: What Happens after Major Policy Changes Are Enacted*. Princeton,
NJ: Princeton University Press.

Pechman, Joseph A., Henry J. Aaron, and Michael K. Taussig. 1968. *Social Security: Perspectives
for Reform*. Washington, DC: Brookings Institution.

Pew Research Center. 2018. "January 2018 Political Survey." Electronic data set. Pew Research
Center. Accessed July 6, 2019. https://www.people-press.org/datasets/.

———. 2020. "As Economic Concerns Recede, Environmental Protection Rises on the Public's
Policy Agenda." Pew Research Center. February 13, 2020. https://www.pewresearch.org
/politics/2020/02/13/as-economic-concerns-recede-environmental-protection-rises-on
-the-publics-policy-agenda/.

———. 2021. "Economy and Covid-19 Top the Public's Policy Agenda for 2021." Pew Research
Center. January 28, 2021. https://www.pewresearch.org/politics/2021/01/28/economy-and
-covid-19-top-the-publics-policy-agenda-for-2021/.

Pierson, Paul. 1994. *Dismantling the Welfare State: Reagan, Thatcher, and the Politics of Retrench-
ment*. New York: Cambridge University Press.

PollingReport.com. 2018. "Social Security." PollingReport.com. Accessed November 16, 2018.
https://www.pollingreport.com/social.htm.

Poterba, James M. 2003. "Employer Stock and 401(k) Plans." *American Economic Review* 93 (2):
398–404.

President's Commission to Strengthen Social Security. 2001. *Strengthening Social Security and
Creating Personal Wealth for All Americans*. Washington, DC: President's Commission.

Prior, Markus. 2019. *Hooked: How Politics Captures People's Interest*. New York: Cambridge
University Press.

Program for Public Consultation. 2013a. *Is It Really a Third Rail? How the American People Would
Reform Social Security: Questionnaire and Frequencies*. College Park: University of Maryland.
http://www.publicconsultation.org/wp-content/uploads/2016/03/ss_quaire.pdf.

———. 2013b. *Is It Really a Third Rail? How the American People Would Reform Social Security:
Report*. College Park: University of Maryland. http://www.publicconsultation.org/wp
-content/uploads/2016/03/ss_report-1.pdf.

———. 2016a. *Americans on Fixing Social Security: Questionnaire and Frequencies*. College Park: University of Maryland. http://www.publicconsultation.org/wp-content/uploads/2016/10 /SS2016_Quaire.pdf.

———. 2016b. *Americans on Fixing Social Security: Report*. College Park: University of Maryland. http://www.publicconsultation.org/wp-content/uploads/reports/Social_Security _Report_NATL_Oct2016.pdf.

Puckett, Carolyn. 2009. "The Story of the Social Security Number." *Social Security Bulletin* 69 (2): 55–74.

Pudney, Thomas Giery. 2019. "Tom Reed Talks Social Security, Trump, and Racist Rhetoric at Elmira Town Hall." *Star-Gazette*, July 30, 2019.

Reznik, Gayle L., Kenneth A. Couch, Christopher R. Tamborini, and Howard M. Iams. 2019. "Longevity-Related Options for Social Security." *Journal of Policy Analysis and Management* 38 (1): 210–38.

Romano, Lois, and George Lardner, Jr. 1999. "Young Bush, a Political Natural, Revs Up." *Washington Post*, July 29, 1999.

Rosenbaum, David E., and Robin Toner. 2005. "Introducing Private Investments to the Safety Net." *New York Times*, February 3, 2005.

Rosenstone, Steven J., and John Mark Hansen. 1993. *Mobilization, Participation, and Democracy in America*. New York: Macmillan.

Ross, Fiona. 2007. "Policy Histories and Partisan Leadership in Presidential Studies: The Case of Social Security." In *The Polarized Presidency of George W. Bush*, edited by George C. Edwards III and Desmond King, 419–46. Oxford: Oxford University Press.

Safire, William. 2007. "On Language: Third Rail." *New York Times*, February 18, 2007.

Schieber, Sylvester J. 2012. *The Predictable Surprise: The Unraveling of the U.S. Retirement System*. Oxford: Oxford University Press.

Schieber, Sylvester J., and John B. Shoven. 1999. *The Real Deal: The History and Future of Social Security*. New Haven, CT: Yale University Press.

Schlozman, Kay Lehman, Sidney Verba, and Henry E. Brady. 2012. *The Unheavenly Chorus*. Princeton, NJ: Princeton University Press.

Sears, David O., and Carolyn L. Funk. 1990. "Self-Interest in Americans' Political Opinions." In *Beyond Self-Interest*, edited by Jane J. Mansbridge, 147–70. Chicago: University of Chicago Press.

Shapiro, Robert Y., and Tom W. Smith. 1985. "The Polls: Social Security." *Public Opinion Quarterly* 49 (4): 561–72.

Smith, Karen E., Richard W. Johnson, and Melissa M. Favreault. 2020. *Five Democratic Approaches to Social Security Reform: Estimated Impact of Plans from the 2020 Presidential Campaign*. Washington, DC: Urban Institute.

Snee, John, and Mary Ross. 1978. "Social Security Amendments of 1977: Legislative History and Summary of Provisions." *Social Security Bulletin* 41 (3): 3–20.

Social Security Administration. 1935. "Congressional Vote Totals by Party." Baltimore: Office of the Historian.

———. 2001. "Listing of Social Security Advisory Councils and Commissions." Research Note #13. Baltimore: Office of the Historian.

———. 2002. "Estimates of Financial Effects for Three Models Developed by the President's Commission to Strengthen Social Security." Baltimore: Office of the Chief Actuary.

———. 2005. "Estimated OASDI Financial Effects for a Proposal with Six Provisions That Would Improve Social Security Financing." Baltimore: Office of the Chief Actuary.

———. 2018. "Congressional Statistics, 2017." Washington, DC: Office of Retirement and Disability Policy.

———. 2019a. *Annual Statistical Supplement to the Social Security Bulletin, 2019*. Washington, DC: Office of Retirement and Disability Policy.

———. 2019b. "Benefits Planner: Online Calculator." Social Security Administration. Accessed July 29, 2019. https://www.ssa.gov/planners/retire/AnypiaApplet.html.

———. 2019c. "Internal Real Rates of Return under the OASDI Program for Hypothetical Workers." Actuarial Note #2018.5. Baltimore: Office of the Chief Actuary.

———. 2019d. "Replacement Rates for Hypothetical Retired Workers." Actuarial Note #2019.9. Baltimore: Office of the Chief Actuary.

———. 2020a. "Estimates of Individual Changes Modifying Social Security." Office of the Chief Actuary. https://www.ssa.gov/OACT/solvency/provisions/index.html.

———. 2020b. "Estimates of Proposals to Change the Social Security Program." Office of the Chief Actuary. https://www.ssa.gov/OACT/solvency/index.html.

———. 2020c. "Net Compensation: Wage Statistics for 2019." Office of the Chief Actuary. https://www.ssa.gov/cgi-bin/netcomp.cgi?year=2019.

———. 2020d. "Single-Year Tables Consistent with 2020 OASDI Trustees Report." Baltimore: Office of the Chief Actuary. https://www.ssa.gov/oact/TR/2020/lrIndex.html.

———. 2021a. *Annual Statistical Supplement to the Social Security Bulletin, 2020*. Washington, DC: Office of Retirement and Disability Policy.

———. 2021b. "Monthly Statistical Snapshot, June 2021." Washington, DC: Office of Retirement and Disability Policy.

Social Security Board, Bureau of Research and Statistics. 1940. *Trends in Public Assistance, 1933–1939*. Washington, DC: Government Printing Office. http://babel.hathitrust.org/cgi/pt?id=umn.31951d030003091;view=1up;seq=1.

Social Security Information Center. 2005. "60 Stops in 60 Days: Accomplishments." Department of the Treasury. https://web.archive.org/web/20060923065712/http:/strengtheningsocialsecurity.gov/60stops/.

Solender, Andrew. 2020. "Sanders, Hawley Mount Rare Bipartisan Push for $1,200 Stimulus Checks." *Forbes*, December 10, 2020.

Stevenson, Richard W. 2005. "For Bush, a Long Embrace of Social Security." *New York Times*, February 27, 2005.

Stevenson, Richard W., and Robin Toner. 2005. "Two Top G.O.P. Lawmakers Buck Bush on Social Security." *New York Times*, February 18, 2005.

Stimson, James A. 1998. *Public Opinion in America: Moods, Cycles, and Swings*. 2nd ed. Boulder, CO: Westview.

———. 2015. *Tides of Consent: How Public Opinion Shapes American Politics*. 2nd ed. New York: Cambridge University Press.

———. 2019. "Public Policy Mood, Annual 1952–2018." Electronic data set. James Stimson's website. Downloaded November 8, 2019. http://stimson.web.unc.edu/data/.

Stolberg, Sheryl Gay, and Carl Hulse. 2005. "Cool Reception on Capitol Hill to Social Security Plan." *New York Times*, February 4, 2005.

Stolberg, Sheryl Gay, and Robin Toner. 2005. "Republicans Are Chastened about Social Security Plan." *New York Times*, February 27, 2005.

Svahn, John, and Mary Ross. 1983. "Social Security Amendments of 1983: Legislative History and Summary of Provisions." *Social Security Bulletin* 46 (7): 3–48.

Tang, Ning, Olivia S. Mitchell, Gary R. Mottola, and Stephen P. Utkus. 2010. "The Efficiency of Sponsor and Participation Portfolio Choices in 401(k) Plans." *Journal of Public Economics* 94 (11): 1073–85.

Tanner, Michael D., ed. 2004. *Social Security and Its Discontents*. Washington, DC: Cato Institute.

Tax Policy Center. 2018. "Repeal $10,000 Limit on Deductible State and Local Taxes." Washington, DC: Urban Institute and Brookings Institution.

Technical Panel on Assumptions and Methods. 2015. *Report to the Social Security Advisory Board*. Washington, DC: Social Security Advisory Board.

Teles, Steven M., and Martha Derthick. 2009. "Social Security from 1980 to the Present." In *Conservatism and American Political Development*, edited by Brian J. Glenn and Steven M. Teles, 261–90. Oxford: Oxford University Press.

Tesler, Michael. 2015. "Priming Predispositions and Changing Policy Positions." *American Journal of Political Science* 59 (4): 806–24.

Trump, Donald J. 2020. "Remarks by President Trump in Press Briefing on August 13, 2020." Washington, DC. White House Press Office.

Tucker, Jasmine V., Virginia P. Reno, and Thomas N. Bethell. 2012. *Strengthening Social Security: What Do Americans Want?* Washington, DC: National Academy of Social Insurance.

US President. 2001. "President's Commission to Strengthen Social Security, Executive Order 13210 of May 2, 2001." *Federal Register* 66 (May 4): 22895.

VandeHei, Jim, and Peter Baker. 2005. "Social Security: On with the Show." *Washington Post*, March 12, 2005.

VandeHei, Jim, and Michael A. Fletcher. 2005 "Bush Social Security Plan Would Cut Future Benefits." *Washington Post*, April 29, 2005.

Vanguard. 2019. *How America Saves 2019: A Report on Vanguard 2018 Defined Contribution Plan Data*. Valley Forge, PA: Vanguard Institutional Investor Group.

Walker, Elisa A., Virginia P. Reno, and Thomas N. Bethell. 2014. *Americans Make Hard Choices on Social Security: A Survey with Trade-Off Analysis*. Washington, DC: National Academy of Social Insurance.

Wallach, Philip. 2019. "How Social Security Was Saved—and Might Be Again." *American Interest*, November 2019.

———. 2020. "Crisis Government." *National Affairs*, Summer 2019.

Wayne, Alex. 2005. "Unions Hit the Field in Social Security Overhaul Battle." *CQ Weekly*, March 28, 2005.

Weaver, Carolyn L. 1982. *The Crisis in Social Security: Economic and Political Origins*. Durham, NC: Duke University Press.

Wendt, Laura. 1938. "Census Classifications and Social Security Categories." *Social Security Bulletin* 1 (4): 3–12.

Whittaker, Julie M. 2015. *Alternative Inflation Measures for the Social Security Cost-of-Living Adjustment*. Washington, DC: Library of Congress, Congressional Research Service.

Wildavsky, Aaron. 1964. *The Politics of the Budgetary Process*. Boston: Little, Brown.

Williamson, Vanessa S. 2017. *Read My Lips: Why Americans Are Proud to Pay Taxes*. Princeton, NJ: Princeton University Press.

Witte, Edwin E. 1955. *Reflections on the Beginnings of Social Security*. Washington, DC: Department of Health, Education, and Welfare.

———. 1963. *The Development of the Social Security Act*. Madison: University of Wisconsin Press.

Wolfinger, Raymond E., and Steven J. Rosenstone. 1980. *Who Votes?* New Haven, CT: Yale University Press.

Woolley, John, and Gerhard Peters. 2020a. "Party Platforms, 1840–2020." In *The American Presidency Project*, edited by Woolley and Peters. Santa Barbara: University of California. https://www.presidency.ucsb.edu/documents/app-categories/elections-and-transitions/party-platforms.

———. 2020b. "State of the Union Addresses, 1790–2020." In *The American Presidency Project*, edited by Woolley and Peters. Santa Barbara: University of California. https://www.presidency.ucsb.edu/documents/app-categories/spoken-addresses-and-remarks/presidential/state-the-union-addresses.

WRFA. 2018. "Reed Calls for Reform of Medicare, Social Security to Prevent Insolvency." WRFA website. June 27, 2018. https://www.wrfalp.com/reed-calls-for-reform-of-medicare-social-security-to-prevent-insolvency/.

Zaller, John R. 1992. *The Nature and Origins of Mass Opinion*. New York: Cambridge University Press.

Zelizer, Julian E. 1997. "Where Is the Money Coming From? The Reconstruction of Social Security Finance, 1939–1950." *Journal of Policy History* 9 (4): 399–424.

INDEX

AARP: as an advocacy group, 105–7; credibility of, effort to undermine, 203; effectiveness of targeting voters by, 131; Medicare Prescription Drug Act, support for, 131, 204, 253; party identification of membership of, 131; policy statements by legislators prior to the 2014 elections, collection of, 102; privatization, opposition to, 204, 217, 253; public opinion of, 130–31; Republican legislators and, 163; Republican solvency bills, need for pressure on, 249, 253; survey indicating respondents were willing to contribute more, 178; as vigilant watchdog, 42

access rate, 65–66

actuarial balance, 83, 91, 279n19

actuaries: assumptions used by, criticism for, 258n17; chained price index, estimated effects of using, 243; costs of delay, need to quantify, 249; incorrect projections by, 32, 35; long-term solvency problems forecast by, 198, 247; neutral competence, reputation of the chief actuary for, 104; priorities of, 280n16; privatization plans, review of, 7; recent update by, 257n1; score keeping by, 6, 82–84, 179

advance-funded system: challenges to beginning in 1936, 27–28; instability of/political equilibrium and, 22, 27–29, 42, 72; legacy debt and transitioning to, 72, 80; national savings and, 71; original Social Security as, 21–27, 46; as a pension system, 2–3; politics of, 22–25; proposals to replace or augment pay-as-you-go with, 6–7, 13, 61, 71–72, 80, 105, 109–10, 199–200, 224; replacement of, 28–29, 72, 81, 173

Advisory Council on Social Security (1994–1996), 108–9, 198–200

advisory councils, 28, 108–9

affluent workers: Democratic districts, concentrated in, 169; Democratic presidential candidates' targeting of, 194; electoral threat from, 163, 167–68, 227, 235; increasing wage inequality and, 86; life expectancy of, 91–92; the maximum taxable wage base and, 85–87, 153, 155, 161, 168–69, 186, 246 (see also maximum taxable wage base); mobilization of, potential for, 153–54; original (1935) Social Security and, 33; Republican votes for tax increases on, 237; solvency plans and, 85–87, 146–47, 159, 169, 182, 192–95, 227, 246, 250; targeting of in 1977, 34; wage distribution for, 2019, 183. See also high-income/wealthy people/taxpayers

Affordable Care Act, 164, 226

age: awareness of Bush's privatization proposal and, 207; campaign contributions and, 151–52; knowledge of AARP's position on the Medicare prescription plan and, 131; privatization and, 214–15; retirement (see early retirement age (62); full retirement age (FRA); retirement age); senior citizens (see senior citizens); support for Social Security by, 119–21; voting participation and, 148–51 agenda setting, 15, 225–26

American Association of Retired Persons.
    See AARP

American Enterprise Institute, 104

American National Election Studies
    (ANES), 113–14

Americans for Tax Reform (ATR), 106–7, 164

attentive publics, 165–67, 174

Australia: fertility in, 239; immigration into,
    240; life expectancy in, 239; old-age to
    working-age ratio in, 238; retirement age
    in, 241; taxes as a percentage of GDP in,
    242

Baker, Howard, 191–92

Ball, Robert, 108, 198

beneficiaries, 135–38; as an electoral threat,
    162; geographic distribution of, 159–60;
    growth in the number of, 48–49; income
    taxes paid by, 5, 36, 38, 103, 144, 184 (*see
    also* payroll taxes); mobilizing, 143; popu-
    lation of, changes in, 71–72; taxpayers
    and, the politics of Social Security
    solvency and, 147–48. *See also* senior
    citizens

benefits, 5–6, 139–40; calculation of a
    retiree's initial benefits, Bush's proposal
    for, 93; cost-of-living adjustments (*see*
    cost-of-living adjustments); cuts of, the
    1983 legislation and, 37–41; disability (*see*
    disability benefits); expansionary period
    for, 29–32; incidence of costs and, 158–59;
    increasing, proposals for, 93, 180–88,
    193–95; internal rate of return, 69, 73–75,
    263n18; paid as percentage of GDP, 8–9;
    political mobilization of seniors and,
    152–53; rate of return, 68–71; reducing,
    proposals for, 92–93, 182–88; significance
    of for retirees' well-being, 140–43; value
    of, increase in, 48–50

Biden, Joe: priorities stemming from the
    Covid-19 pandemic, 191; Social Security
    reform plan drafted by, 192–95, 250–51,
    254

Bipartisan Policy Center (BPC), 191–92,
    249

bipartisanship, requirement for, 14, 228–29,
    231

Blumenthal, Richard, 179

Boehner, John, 102

Bowman, Jamaal, 169

Brady, Kevin, 276n36

Brookings Institution, 104

Bureau of Labor Statistics, 243

Bush, Barbara, 202

Bush, Cori, 169

Bush, George H. W.: the Democratic
    advantage on Social Security and, 129;
    environmental policy, discussion of, 118;
    Kuwait, invasion of, 221; taxes raised by,
    236

Bush, George W.: collaboration with AARP
    on Medicare prescription plan, 131;
    congressional action during his first
    term, cost of, 9–10; the Democratic
    advantage on Social Security and, 129–30;
    public opinion of performance on Social
    Security, 127; Social Security as a priority
    for, 195; track record with Congress,
    219–20

Bush's effort to reform Social Security:
    assessment of the failure of, 219–22;
    beginning and end of, 197; Bush's framing
    of, 205–7; calculating a retiree's initial
    benefits, proposal for, 93; campaign clash
    with Gore over, 215, 222, 229–30; campaign
    for privatization in 2005, 201–4, 230, 232;
    countercampaign against, 204–5, 217; the
    countercampaign's framing of, 206–7;
    decision to spend the surplus on tax cuts
    and, 222; Democratic legislators and,
    217–18; the individual responsibility-social
    insurance debate and, 62; polarization and,
    13, 249–50; pre-presidential advocacy
    of privatization, 199; the President's
    Commission to Strengthen Social Security,
    197, 199–201; privatization proposal, AARP
    response to, 106; public and legislative

incremental solutions (*continued*)
insolvency and, 225–29; legislators'
opinions of, 178–79; maximum taxable
wage base, proposals to raise or abolish
(*see* maximum taxable wage base, proposals to raise or abolish); as the probable
answer to avoid insolvency, 234–36;
public opinion of, 173–78, 190; realism,
need for, 196; retirement age and, 90–92,
174–75; revenue base and, 85–90; score
keeping and, 82–84; the tax rate and, 84–85
individual responsibility model, 62, 65
individual retirement accounts (IRAs),
64–65, 67, 109, 141–42, 209, 240, 263n11.
See also defined contribution plans
inflation, cost-of-living adjustments for. *See*
cost-of-living adjustments
insolvency: avoiding, past experience with
(*see* Social Security Amendments of 1977;
Social Security Amendments of 1983);
politics of the last minute, incremental
solutions and, 234–37; the problem of,
1–2; roots of, 2. *See also* solvency reform
insolvency in 2034: bipartisanship and,
228–29, 231; incremental solutions to,
225–29, 234–37; options available, 224–25;
privatization as a solution to, 229–32;
stalemate and, 233–34; stalemate and
complete policy breakdown if no solution
is found, 233–34; use of general funds to
avoid, 232–33
interest groups: attentive publics and, 166;
electoral calculations regarding, 163–64;
polarized policymakers and, 105–7. *See
also* AARP
intergenerational equity, 43
internal rate of return, 69–70, 73–75, 198,
263n18, 264n19
Italy: fertility in, 239; immigration into,
280n8; life expectancy in, 239; old-age to
working-age ratio in, 238; progressive
indexation of cost-of-living adjustments
in, 244; retirement age in, 241; taxes as a
percentage of GDP in, 242

Jacobs, Alan, 42
Japan: fertility in, 239–40; immigration into,
240; life expectancy in, 239, 240; old-age
to working-age ratio in, 238; retirement
age in, 241; taxes as a percentage of GDP
in, 242
Johnson, Sam, 180, 183–88, 249
journalists, 112, 174, 188, 253–55

Kasich, John, 199, 222
Kerrey, Bob, 199
Kingdon, John, 15
Klobuchar, Amy, 192–95
Koch, Charles, 111
Koch, David, 111
Korea: fertility in, 239; immigration into,
240; life expectancy in, 239; old-age to
working-age ratio in, 238; retirement age
in, 241; taxes as a percentage of GDP in,
242

Landon, Alf, 27, 50, 259n34
Larson, John, 179–82, 186–88, 194, 228–29,
246, 248–51
Leadership Council of Aging Organizations,
107
Lee, Frances, 190, 229
Lee, Mike, 91
legacy debt, 70–72, 80–81, 90
legislators: budgetary conflicts, prowess at
solving, 250; Bush's privatization proposal
and, 217–19; cross-pressured and the
electoral politics of Social Security (*see*
electoral consequences: legislators'
perspective); decision making by, 15–16;
dilemma faced by, 14–15; expanding
Social Security, 1950–1974, 29–32; fixing
Social Security in response to stagflation,
33–34; incremental solutions, opinions
of, 178–79; motivations of, Social Security
and, 22; polarization of, 101–4; priorities
of, Social Security and, 190; public opinion
of officeholders, positions on Social
Security and, 126–28; trade-offs required

Obama, Barack: the Democratic advantage
on Social Security and, 130; governmental shutdown confrontation and, 164;
health-care policy and party polarization,
118, 250; public opinion of, positions on
Social Security and, 127–28
Ocasio-Cortez, Alexandria, 169
old-age assistance program: to address the
immediate problem in 1935, 24–25; need
for, 15; political appeal of, 41; privatization and the revival of, proposals for, 75,
198; public support for, 51; replaced by
Supplemental Security Income (SSI)
program in 1974, 142, 261n8; seniors
collecting benefits into the 1950s, 50
old-age insurance program: to address the
long-term problem, 24; need for, 15; public
support for, 50–51. See also Social Security
old-age to working-age ratio: determinants
of, 238–40; favorable in the United
States, 238; relative severity of problems
with retirement systems around the
world and, 240
Omnibus Budget Reconciliation Act of
1990, 236
O'Neill, Thomas, 36, 103
Orszag, Peter, 249

participation rate, 66, 152
party leaders, 36, 125, 131, 169, 186, 190–91,
203–4, 219, 226, 229, 237
party platforms, 97–101, 132–33, 155, 196, 222,
266n1
Paul, Rand, 91
pay-as-you-go system: advance-funded
system replaced with a, 28–29, 42, 72, 81,
173; the debate over Social Security and,
79–80; the early years of, 32, 34, 47; immigrants and, 240; modified, move toward
in 1983, 3, 21, 42, 72, 81; national savings
and, 71; as a pension system, 3; proposals
to transform or replace, 6–7, 13, 61, 70–71,
81, 198–99; size of generations and, 71, 84;
Social Security as, 2, 21–22

payroll taxes: adjustment of in the Social
Security Amendments of 1939, 28;
dedicated tax for disability insurance,
30–31 (see also disability insurance);
dedicated tax for Medicare, 31, 88 (see also
Medicare); design of, 25–26, 55; geographic distribution of high-income
payers of, 160–62; geographic distribution of payers of, 159; increasing, impact
on workers from, 144–47; increasing
during the expansionary period, 30–31;
interest group opposition to raising,
106–7; maintenance of the original rate
through the 1940s, 28–29; maximum
taxable wage base for (see maximum
taxable wage base); mobilization against
increases, likely participants in, 153–54;
payers of, 46–47, 143–44; politics of, 24,
27, 29; public opinion of, 54–55; rate of,
47–48; rate of, raising the, 84–85; regressivity of, 54–55, 81, 84–85, 104–5, 109, 233;
taxpayer reaction to potential increases
in, 143–47; workers paying, increase in,
46–47
pension systems. See retirement/pension
systems
Pepper, Claude, 40
Perot, Ross, 127
Pew Research Center, 123–24, 190
Pickle, Jake, 40
polarization: beginning of partisan polarization on privatization, 215–16, 222,
229–30; elite, impact of, 13–14; party and
priority of fixing Social Security, 123–26;
party and public support for Social
Security, 114–19
polarized policymakers, 97–98; advisory
councils, 108–9; interest groups, 105–7;
legislators, 101–4, 229 (see also legislators); parties/party platforms, 98–99,
109–11 (see also Democrats; Republicans); policy experts, 104–5; presidents,
100–101
political equilibrium, 27–29

Social Security Amendments of 1972, 32, 243, 260n43, 260n60, 261n8

Social Security Amendments of 1977: beneficiaries protected in, 246; benefits for nondependent or divorced husbands, 73; legislators' actions to support Social Security, 33–34; lessons for future policymakers from, 225–26; relatively quick decision making for, 165; wage base indexed to average wage growth in, 87

Social Security Amendments of 1983: actuarial estimates for, 82; cost-of-living adjustments postponed by, 3, 6, 36, 38–39, 225–26; economic conditions and impending deficits leading up to, 34–35; full retirement age increased by, 90–91; the Greenspan Commission proposal and, 36–37; lessons for future policymakers from, 225–26; partisan polarization and, 118; politics of enacting, 39–42; politics of Social Security, impact on, 12–13; relatively quick decision making for, 165; as a solvency plan, 37–39; success of, 3–5

Social Security Board, 45–46, 50

Social Security trust fund: actuarial balance and, 83; balances, 1970–2035, 3–4; changes to in 1939, 28; changes to in 1983, 3, 42–43, 165; critical role of, 26; historical function of, 3; interest from, 5; as a measure of sustainability, 265n3; Medicare and disability trust funds, borrowing from, 36, 233–34; objection to the original, 27–28; as a pillar of Social Security, 14; politics and, 12–15, 41, 102–3, 165, 224, 233–34, 247; proposals for reform: investing in the stock market, 77–80, 205; proposals for reform: privatization, 230–31; proposals for reform: reform of Social Security and, 195, 198–200, 205; in the three systems of Social Security, 21–22, 28; transfer from the regular budget to, 38; upcoming depletion of, 1, 11, 43, 69, 72, 83, 92, 234

solvency plans: building blocks of comprehensive, 94; comparison of Democratic and Republican, 187–88; Democratic divisions and, 186; Democratic rhetoric and, 185–86; electoral calculations related to, 162–64; increasing payroll taxes, impact on workers from, 144–47; privatization and (see privatization, proposals for); public reaction to hypothetical, 188–90; Republican divisions and, 186–87; Republican rhetoric and, 185; scoring of, 179, 249; submitted for scoring, 2010–2020, 179–80; taxpayers and beneficiaries in the politics of, 147–48; Trump and, 185

solvency plans: Democratic: Biden, 192–95, 250–51, 254; Buttigieg, 192–95, 251; Crist, 180; Deutch, 180; Klobuchar, 192–95; Larson, 179–82, 186–88, 194, 228–29, 246, 248–51; Moore, 180; Sanders, 169, 180–82, 186–87, 192–95; Warren, 192–95, 251

solvency plans: nonpartisan: Advisory Council on Social Security, 108–9, 198–200; Ball, 198, 204–5; Bipartisan Policy Center, 191–92; Gramlich, 198–99; Greenspan Commission (see Greenspan Commission); Weaver and Schieber, 198

solvency plans: presidential: Biden, 192–95, 250–51, 254; Bush (see Bush's effort to reform Social Security); Clinton, 101, 125, 199, 247; Reagan, 35–36, 41, 56, 100–101, 118, 126, 129, 132, 250

solvency plans: Republican: Chaffetz, 180; Coburn, 180; Graham, 180, 183; Hutchison, 180, 182–83; Johnson, 180, 183–88, 249; Ribble, 180, 184–85, 187; Ryan, 180, 185, 223, 230, 246–47, 264n41

solvency reform: citizens, role of, 252–55; cost-of-living adjustments and, 242–44 (see also cost-of-living adjustments); encouraging action sooner rather than later, 247–49; presidents, role of, 249–52; principal impediment to, 247; relative severity of problems for retirement systems

A NOTE ON THE TYPE

This book has been composed in Arno, an Old-style serif typeface in the classic Venetian tradition, designed by Robert Slimbach at Adobe.